THE UNIVERSITY OF
WINCHESTER

Martial Rose Library
Tel: 01962 827306

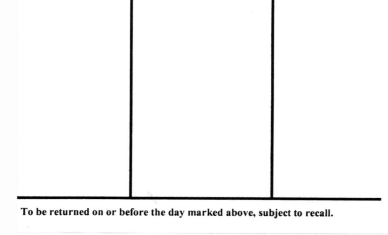

To be returned on or before the day marked above, subject to recall.

The Trail of

MARTYRDOM

Persecution and Resistance
in Sixteenth-Century England

SARAH COVINGTON

University of Notre Dame Press • *Notre Dame, Indiana*

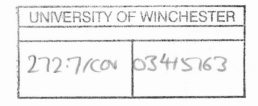
Manufactured in the United States of America

Library of Congress Cataloging-in-Publication Data
Covington, Sarah, 1965–
    The trail of martyrdom : persecution and resistance in
sixteenth-century England / Sarah Covington.
        p. cm.
    Includes bibliographical references (p.) and index.
    ISBN 0-268-04225-x (cloth : alk. paper)
    ISBN 0-268-04226-8 (pbk. : alk. paper)
    1. Martyrdom—Christianity—England.   2. Persecution—
England—History—16th century.   3. England—Church
history—16th century.   I. Title.
BX1492 .C63 2004
272'.7—dc22

                                        2003017883

∞ *This book is printed on acid-free paper.*

For my mother,

Sandra McCloud Covington, with love

CONTENTS

ACKNOWLEDGMENTS

To say that this book would not have been completed without the professional and personal guidance of the following people cannot do justice to the feelings of gratitude that I bear toward them. Above all I wish to thank Stuart Prall, Margaret L. King, and Nancy Siraisi for their contributions in critiquing and challenging the manuscript from every stage, and for their kind and supportive presence in my life, as well as their patience in enduring my preoccupation with martyrdom and its extremities. Dr. Prall was especially astute in criticizing the work and its theses, and any strengths in this book are owed in huge part to him. In addition, I wish to express my gratitude toward others who read and commented to various extents on the manuscript, most notably, Susan Wabuda, John King, and Martin Pine, as well as the NEH/John Foxe seminar participants, who helped me formulate approaches to one aspect of the manuscript, on the interrogation process.

The following institutions have also made possible my research, either through grants or through extremely supportive staff: the Huntington Library, the Emmanuel Library at Cambridge University, the British Library, and the Folger-Shakespeare Library. I also wish to thank the Renaissance Society of America, the Graduate Center of the City University of New York, and Elizabethtown College for their assistance throughout the years of my research and writing. I am greatly indebted as well to my editors at the University of Notre Dame Press, including Barbara Hanrahan, Rebecca DeBoer, and Ted Wagstaff, with whom publishing my first book has been a pleasure.

I wish to finally express gratitude to the following individuals for their support: to David Brown, for his love, as well as to Sheila Rabin, Christine Hutchins, Patricia Franz, Jennifer Cooper, Jane Wilson

Cathcart, John Reynolds, Laura Schwartz, Paul Melzer, Maryann Sluzis, Bela Vassady, and Thomas Winpenny. All have deepened my work as well as my life, and given me the confidence to push ahead, despite my very unmartyr-like proclivities to self-doubt. But above all I wish to express appreciation to my family for their support, and especially my sister, Emily Covington, the love of my life. To my father William S. Covington, who died as I was finishing this manuscript, I owe my vocation as a historian, but it is above all my mother, Sandra McCloud Covington, who has imbued my life with hope, faith, and love, and it is to her that this book is dedicated.

ABBREVIATIONS

AM (1583) John Foxe, *Acts and monuments of matters most speciall and memorable . . .* (London, 1583).

AM (1965) John Foxe, *The Acts and Monuments of John Foxe*, ed. George Townsend, 8 vols. (New York, 1965).

APC *Acts of the Privy Council of England*, ed. J. R. Dasent (London, 1890–1907).

BIHR *Bulletin of the Institute of Historical Research*

CPR *Calendar of Patent Rolls, Philip and Mary*, 4 vols. (London, 1936–39).

DNB *Dictionary of National Biography*, 63 vols. (1885–1900).

EHD *English Historical Documents*, vol. 5, 1485–1558, ed. C. H. Williams (London, 1967).

EHR *English Historical Review*

EM John Strype, *Ecclesiastical Memorials, relating chiefly to religion, and the reformation of it . . . under King Henry VIII, King Edward VI, and Queen Mary I*, 3 vols. (Oxford, 1822).

Grey Friars *Chronicle of the Grey Friars of London*, ed. J. G. Nichols, Camden Society 53 (London, 1852).

Holinshed Raphael Holinshed, *Chronicles*, ed. H. Ellis, 6 vols. (1807–8)

JEH *Journal of Ecclesiastical History*

LP *Letters and Papers, Foreign and Domestic, of the Reign of Henry VIII*, ed. J. S. Brewer, J. Gairdner, and R. S. Brodie, 21 vols. (1862–1932).

Machyn

The Diary of Henry Machyn, Citizen and Merchant Taylor of London, 1550–1563, ed. J. G. Nichols, Camden Society 42 (1848).

Narratives

Narratives of the Days of the Reformation, Chiefly from the Manuscripts of John Foxe the Martyrologist, ed. J. G. Nichols, Camden Society 77 (London, 1859).

Orig. Lett.

Original Letters relative to the English Reformation, 1531–58, ed. H. Robinson, 2 vols., Parker Society (Cambridge, 1846–47).

PP

G. R. Elton, *Policy and Police: The Enforcement of the Reformation in the Age of Thomas Cromwell* (Cambridge, 1972).

PRO

Public Record Office

Span. Cal.

Calendar of Letters, Despatches, and State Papers relating to the Negotiations between England and Spain . . ., 13 vols. (London, 1862–1954).

SP

Calendar of State Papers, Domestic series, of the reigns of Edward VI, Mary, Elizabeth and James I. 1547–[1625] preserved in the State paper department of Her Majesty's Public Record Office. 12 vols. London, 1856–72.

State Trials

State Trials, ed. William Cobbett et al., 33 vols. (London, 1809–26).

Stow

John Stow, *A Survey of London,* ed. C. L. Kingsford, 2 vols. (Oxford, 1908).

Unpub. Docs.

Acts of English Martyrs Hitherto Unpublished, ed. J. H. Pollen (London, 1891).

Wrioth. Chron.

Charles Wriothesley, *A Chronicle of England during the Reigns of the Tudors, 1485–1559,* ed. W. D. Hamilton, 2 vols., Camden Society, n.s., 11 and 20 (1875–77).

CHAPTER ONE

Contextualizing Persecution, Conceptualizing the Martyr

BETWEEN 1535 AND 1603, ENGLAND EXPERIENCED A CRISIS OF
uncertainty brought about by the Reformation, the break with Rome,
and the concomitant rise of challenging and dissenting religious groups.
The Tudor monarchs, each of whom carried different religious allegiances and policies, attempted to counter this confusion with a variety of measures that aimed to suppress the groups as well as enforce
conformity on the rest of the population. The result was that over the
course of the century hundreds if not thousands of individuals accused
others or were accused, pursued others or were pursued, or evaded the
authorities and got away—all in response to the religious and political
fluctuations of the time. From this environment came the recantation,
acquiescence, or outward obedience of most of the population, though
hundreds of others remained firm in their beliefs and in the end chose
execution or martyrdom. However, while England, by the end of the
century, settled generally into Protestantism—or a variety of Protes-
tantisms that existed alongside a still-significant Catholic community—
the settlement had by no means come as the result of any inevitable
trajectory, just as no troublesome group was ever fully expunged, but
instead lived on to elude the capacities of the government to contain it.[1]

The problem lay in part with individuals such as Thomas Benbridge, who found himself facing execution for heretical beliefs in 1558,

during the reign of Mary. At the scene of death, the chains had secured Benbridge's body to the stake and the flames were beginning to move up his legs when he suddenly called off his martyrdom. "I recant," he cried out, which was enough for the authorities to allow his friends to take him out of the fire, if only to return him, on the sheriff's orders, to prison. Only moments before, Benbridge had refused to recant his beliefs ("Away, Babylonian, away!") before an aggressive priest's exhortations. The fact that he had lasted this far, having already endured interrogations, imprisonments, and other persecutions, made his recantation all the more startling—as if a mountain climber had ended his journey just steps from a perilous and hard-won summit. Descent from that height—which represented to the martyr victory and resurrection—would not come easily, however, and over the course of his subsequent imprisonment, Benbridge recanted his recantation, "grieved" that he had signed the self-repudiating articles of faith given him at the fire. Seven days later he returned to the stake, where according to John Foxe, his "vile tormenters did rather broil him than burn him."[2]

Enforcing conformity on men such as Benbridge, while successful in some ways, was in this sense a more inconsistent and self-defeating process than has previously been claimed. The authorities had to rely upon mid- and lower-level officials who faced an opposition that manipulated its persecuted status through various strategies, thus forcing those authorities into positions of negotiation, compromise, or even inaction when it came to directing religious policy.[3] This instability is especially evident when one looks at religious persecution from the inside, and examines the entire stage-by-stage process by which a religiously suspect individual first came to the attention of the authorities and was apprehended, incarcerated, tried, convicted, and executed. Although most individuals, it should be said, did give up at some point and conform to the government's demands, success was heavily qualified by others who used imprisonment, flight, or even execution to their own advantage. Analyzing the persecution process by its stages thus leads one to a more complicated picture concerning the nature of obedience and dissent, authority and enforcement in Tudor England. Indeed, the fits and starts and individual circumstances that dominated this process become even clearer when one descends from the elevated spheres of privy councilors and lord chancellors and instead examines the process as one involving a constant tension between authorities, martyrs, and the wider population, all of whom contributed to shaping the drama of persecution laid out before them.

To understand what it meant for an individual to be brought into the persecution process, however, is to enter a complicated and frustratingly evasive world, neither clear nor heroic, but one involving people recanting before their interrogators, prison betrayers exposing the victim out of self-interest, defendants and prosecutors sparring with each other at trial, and crowds cheering on the executioner or converting at the sight of a victim's self-sacrificial torments. Those martyrs who ended up going all the way in the process, and dying at the end, ranged from weavers and fishermen to bishops, an archbishop, court ladies, sixteen-year-old apprentices, Anabaptists, Protestant divines, widows, monks, and Jesuit priests. If one factor could be said to have been shared by all—apart from a common embrace of martyrdom—it would be their persecution for beliefs that existed in a world where standards of orthodoxy were never entirely firm, and where religious correctness (as well as heresy) meant different things at different times. From Henry's Erastian "Catholicism without the pope" through the increasingly radical Protestantism of Edward's reign, and from Mary's singular Catholicism to Elizabeth's ambiguous irenicism, efforts to define, contain, and persecute an already religiously inscrutable population were in fact probably doomed, in the end, to fail.

The task of initiating an effective policy of religious enforcement was not helped by the fact that England in the sixteenth century was not yet a modern state with a professionalized police force or standing army, and structures of authority were themselves unstable. As will be seen, offices were more often than not held by individuals with varying and not always reliable personalities and motivations, which weakened any kind of united front of enforcement. Moreover, the resentment sometimes felt at the expansion in duties, combined with an occasional sympathy for the religious dissenters and their cause, made the task of these officials problematic indeed.

As for the sentiment of the population itself, the fact that persecutory policies were often either resisted, subverted, or ignored does not necessarily indicate an attachment to traditional or reformationist beliefs and practices, or a failure on the part of Tudor governments to impose religious change. Opposition or resistance to the central authorities by mid-level functionaries or average men and women could emerge from a number of reasons, with religion playing at times only a small role next to more banal factors such as indifference, overwork, or the desire to maintain community cohesion in the face of potentially disruptive measures from the center. When responses to persecutory measures did relate directly to religious sentiment—for example, in the reaction of crowds at heresy burnings—they reflected not a dichotomous opposition between "Catholic" and "Protestant," but rather an ever-shifting range of beliefs which existed within a fluid and often confusing theological spectrum.[4] In this sense, religious affiliation rested on unstable and contingent ground, as persecution could backfire on the authorities and become a force for creating sympathy if placed, for example, in the hands of a martyr able to exploit his torment for higher spiritual purposes.

One must be careful, however, not to claim that the Tudors, for all their differences and relative ineffectualities, were entirely unsuccessful in keeping the peace, asserting the royal supremacy, and maintaining the basic loyalties of their subjects. For the most part, respect for the crown would remain, even among the most apparently dangerous of the dissident groups, just as England in the sixteenth century would not descend into the kind of religious warring experienced overseas, in France and the German states. But any dream the monarchs may have harbored of religious uniformity—of a people united in a common and uncontested belief and institution under the crown's guiding hand—came to be seen as elusive and unattainable, as every Thomas Benbridge gave expression not to persecution's effectiveness, or its power, but to its ultimately impotent futility.

Persecution in England: The Theoretical Context

Any study relating to themes of early modern persecution must contend at least briefly with a number of existing theoretical and philosophical positions concerning the nature of tolerance, intolerance, power and resistance, authority and dissent. In the past, persecution, which I define here as the pursuit by authorities of groups that dissented from the crown in religious practice and belief, has been explained as the expression of collective mentalities or dominating discourses concerning the "other," reflecting characteristics of an all-powerful and inquisitional "persecuting society." This view has been discounted in recent years, however, by historians who have sought to uncover the actual practices, negotiations, and ambiguities at work as medieval and early modern authorities—as well as dissenting groups—attempted to act and react to one other.[5] Rather than a unilateral, autocratic display of power, persecution, as these historians have demonstrated, instead constituted a point of contention, varied according to specific local circumstances and contingencies, and was not always pursued consistently or even very effectively.

A parallel (and somewhat contradictory) line of thought has centered around an emphasis not on intolerance, but on tolerance and its development or "rise," and while the subject has primarily been examined through the lens of the seventeenth century, some of the debate bears attention here. The standard work that shaped much of the issue in the twentieth century was W. K. Jordan's *The Development of Religious Toleration in England,* which postulated the linear emergence of notions of toleration concomitant with the development of proto-Enlightenment "secularism" and "modernity," which are reflected in the writings, for example, of John Locke (whose vaunted toleration made a firm exception for Catholics and atheists). This view has come under assault in recent years, being criticized for its Whiggish "darkness-to-light" triumphalism, along with its underlying assumption that "religion" and "toleration" are incompatible, when in fact toleration was first formulated in a firmly religious context.[6] At the same time, other historians have taken a more balanced view by maintaining their critique of Jordan while also acknowledging that distinct developments in the notion of tolerance occurred, at least in the later seventeenth century.

The sixteenth century, however, remained—in theory at least—what we today would term firmly intolerant and persecutory in the maintenance of religious uniformity. But there were and are varieties of intolerance (and tolerance), as John Coffey has pointed out in a recent study:[7] while the development of civil tolerance—that is, the freedom of religious dissidents to worship apart from government coercion and persecution—was decidedly not in place, religious dissidents could nevertheless sometimes find themselves tolerated, albeit warily, on a local level, including by neighborhood or village functionaries. Indeed, despite the continued adherence to an unbending religious uniformity in the polemical treatises, the idea of tolerance as synonymous with

God's love and compassion was also prevalent, though such a concept could mean different things to different people. For example, the much-vilified Marian bishop, Edmund Bonner, even claimed that he was displaying boundless tolerance and charity by giving as much attention as he did to heretics who would have been treated with less patience by others in his situation.

Tolerance in this context did not mean generous-hearted and fuzzy acceptance of another's heretical views, but rather the ability or willingness to speak with and debate a lost member of the true church in order to bring him or her home again. This was important, since according to the dominant view, men and women who chose to follow heretical or divergent religious paths were not only obstinate heretics but schismatic rebels against the crown's will, and as such should be sought out and punished to the full extent of the law, even if it meant death. Justification for this resided in Paul, who enjoined his readers in Titus 3:10–11 to avoid "[the] factious man after the first and second correction," since "he is perverted and sinful and condemned by our judgment." The problem was not simply the heretic's persistence in his own error, but the threat he posed to others and to the unity of the true believers; as Tertullian had warned in the third century, heretics were "ravening wolves . . . come in sheep's clothing," whose "thoughts and treacherous spirits . . . hide within to infest the flock of Christ."[8] Augustine advanced this idea further and gave it potency when he defended the use of punishment—fines, imposed exile, and imprisonment, though not, it should be said, the death penalty—when it came to schismatics, such as the Donatists.[9] Heresy thus represented for Tertullian and Augustine—as well as sixteenth-century secular and church authorities—the threat of division working against church unity, which Paul upheld in Corinthians as of the utmost importance. Moreover, theological unity, as Edward Peters has written, also came to be seen over time as "synonymous with social cohesion in societies that regarded themselves as bound together at their most fundamental levels by religion." This placed the heretic not only in opposition to "holy Scripture, openly taught, and pertinaciously defended"—in Robert Grosseteste's words—but also in "opposition to a whole culture in all of its manifestations."[10]

It is a peculiar irony of Reformation England that many martyrs had themselves once been persecutors who held power, and that they continued to believe in the necessity of persecution even as they were themselves being targeted. As the author of the *Dialogue Concerning Heresy,* Thomas More, for example, may have implicitly advocated a kind of moderation in the way authorities or clerics should convince the heretic of his errors; yet he also gave no inch in his belief that heretics such as Thomas Hilton—"the devil's stinking martyr"—should be thrown into the flames forthwith.[11] More's fellow Catholic martyr, Bishop John Fisher, may have prided himself on the fact that no heretics were burned in the diocese of Rochester during his episcopate there from 1504 through 1534—instead, all heresy cases before him turned into abjurations—but he also minced no words when he preached in a sermon that heresy "is a perilous weed, it is the seed of the devil, the inspiration of the wicked spirits, the corruption of our hearts, the blinding of our sight, the quenching of our faith, the destruction of all good fruit, and finally the murder of our souls."[12]

Under Edward's Protestant reign from 1547 to 1553, few were burned, heresy legislation was repealed early on by the parliament, and the tolerationist work of the continental theologian Sebastian Castellio was at least given some attention.[13] Castellio, who addressed his Latin version of the Bible to the young king, advocated in his *De hereticis* for a kind of toleration by arguing, among other things, that scripture was by its nature obscure and could thus account for a diversity of views, just as centuries-long debates over the Trinity or free will and predestination proved that such issues were by their nature unresolvable by dint of their being undemonstrable. Thus, while individuals, Castellio continued, should abide by the commandments and by Jesus' injunctions, persecution of those who take an opposing stand regarding a biblical text whose meanings cannot be fully discerned is absurd.[14] Castellio, however, made an exception by allowing severe persecution for atheism and blasphemy—whose definitions were in the eyes of the beholder, of course—and while heresy executions were rare under Edward, this did not prevent the king's lieutenants from pursuing uniformity through compulsory measures, and even, in the case of iconoclasm, a kind of officially sanctioned violence.[15] Above all, the leading light of the Edwardian Reformation, Archbishop Thomas Cranmer, was no advocate of religious pluralism or toleration, especially when it came to the radical Evangelicals and Anabaptists in particular, who represented a break with the Erastian traditionalism that he retained.[16] "What wolde you have me do with [the radicals]?" he asked in a letter to William Morice, an

Evangelical, "beare with them and wyncke at their faultes, and so will-inglie suffer the gospell (by their outragious doinges) to be troden under our feete?"[17]

Persecution of Protestants under Catholic Mary reached a height-ened pitch in the 1550s, though figures such as Bonner, as mentioned, spent more time than authorities in other reigns in trying to actually debate with heretics. If this attempt at charity and tolerance failed, then it was incumbent upon the good of the realm, Bonner wrote, that "great offenders of God . . . be cut off, from the body of the commonweal, lest they corrupt other good and honest persons: like as a good surgeon cut-teth away a putrefied and a festered member, for the love he hath to the whole body, lest it infect other members adjoining to it."[18] While the extent of the cutting may have been more violent under Mary's watch, the basic premise of the statement would not have been disputed by most authorities in the sixteenth century, no matter what religious pro-gram they were pursuing.

In recent years, the nature and extent of the Marian persecutions have been reconsidered, most notably by Muriel McClendon, who argues that not only was religious uniformity unevenly enforced in a region such as that around Norwich, but that "the queen and her church-men hoped for reconciliation much more than they desired execution and martyrdom."[19] While the desire for uniformity was still evident—thus, the attempts to "reconciliate"—even a figure such as Reginald Pole seems to have exercised a practical toleration, despite the fact that he was at least partially behind many of the heresy commissions and was castigated, not without cause, by contemporaries such as Matthew Parker. While death, Pole believed, was the final necessity for the "putrid member" who willfully cast himself out of the true church, reason had to be deployed to its fullest extent beforehand to convince the "rebel son" to return home again. As one (admittedly biased) biographer put it, "[N]othing sharper could befall [Pole], than to be forced to punish more harshly those whose salvation he was seeking . . . as he thought, as he also often used to say, that he and the rest of the bishops were estab-lished not only as judges against them but as fathers." Whether the account is accurate or not, it contained the image that Pole—no stranger to image-cultivation—wished to project.[20]

During the later years of the sixteenth century, some notable voices would give expression to a sense of doubt concerning the efficacy of religious singularity backed by persecutory measures. In many respects, John Foxe's *Acts and Monuments,* and particularly its fourth edition of 1583, can be viewed as an indictment of persecution through the ages—including, somewhat uncomfortably, the persecutions which occurred under Henry, Edward, and, contemporaneously, Elizabeth. Indeed, a mark of the papists and their false church, as Foxe presents it, is violence—the violence of persecuting authorities, the violence foretold by the book of Revelation. While others of Foxe's generation did not have much of a problem in maintaining double standards when it came to issues of tolerence and intolerence, Foxe himself held to a consistency when it came to the issue of authorities wielding power through violence, even if that power was now on the side of God (and of Foxe).

Richard Hooker, writing in the reign of Elizabeth, also heralded a kind of intellectual opening when he claimed, among other things, that "No religion can wholly and only consist of untruths." However, Hooker also displayed a dislike for the potential instability of religious pluralism when he wrote that "pure and unstained religion ought to be the highest of all cares appertaining to public regiment," since "[t]he very worldly peace and prosperity, the secular happiness, the temporal and natural good estate both of all men and of all dominions, hangeth chiefly upon religion."[21] It was Hooker's contemporary Edwin Sandys who went further than the others when he stated that Catholics and Protestants could reasonably agree to disagree in a shared, ongoing communication. While unity and compromise, Sandys wrote, was probably impossible, discussion was still to be encouraged, "[f]or factions, as by disparity they are raised, so by a strangeness they are continued and grow immortal, whereas, contrariwise, they are slaked and made calmer by intercourse, by parley they are reconciled, by familiarity they are extinguished."[22] Sandys was encouraging discussion, however, and not any sort of proto-ecumenism; while religious unity might be unattainable, it was also true, according to Sandys in a different treatise, that to God, "open and public maintainers of errors and heresy . . . are thought unworthy to live."[23]

Certainly, no patience was shown for the Catholic priests under Elizabeth, at least in periods of danger or insecurity. William Cecil, in his *Execution of Justice in England,* may have stated that the problem was not with religious difference, but rather with the threat that priests, in their traitorous allegiance to Rome, posed to the crown.[24] Still, the

difference between politics and religion could be blurred, especially
to the less yielding Catholics, for whom the royal supremacy was, in
William Allen's words, "a thing most monstrous and unnatural, the very
gap to bring any realm to the thraldom of sects."[25] The Jesuits, as an
especially targeted group, wrote extensively on issues of persecution,
resistance, and nonresistance, especially after the mid-1580s when efforts
against them intensified. On the one hand, they did plead for acceptance of their presence in England, as when Robert Persons slyly encouraged Elizabeth to allow a kind of religious diversity by granting
Catholics "more favour . . . or at least toleration," especially since she
allowed "three religions"—Protestantism, Puritanism, and the Family
of Love—to exist.[26] But Persons, along with his coreligionists, was a
firm and unbending believer in the one true church, and refused to
accept the idea of toleration or freedom of conscience for anyone else.

Patterns of Persecution: An Overview

As vehement as these ideas could be in theory, the reality of persecution, with the assumption of intolerance which undergirded it, was
contingent on the specific social, cultural, political, and religious realities
of the world with which it was engaged. The times and places, and the
individuals who specifically directed and enforced policy, determined the
nature and intended scope of persecutory measures, which waxed and
waned in accordance with such developments as the eruption of internal
rebellions, national security threats (especially in Elizabeth's reign), or a
concerted change in religious policy on the part of a monarch (or his
regents) newly installed in power. The pursuit of religious dissenters was
thus never constant in the century, but erupted episodically at certain
moments of change or tension; while based to some degree on realistic
threat assessments, persecutory measures nevertheless served a symbolic
function above all, by projecting the monarch's power far and wide, and
warning the population of the consequences that could result in devi-
ating from that power's will.

Persecution of problematic religious groups was not new, of course,
in sixteenth-century England. Lollards, for example, had been sought
out and persecuted at varying times for over a century, and continued to

be subject to occasional crackdowns, as was the case in 1511 and 1512.[27] For the most part, however, such efforts still functioned in the context of the one Roman church, under the rubric of ecclesiastical courts and in accordance, more or less, with the English monarch. Everything changed, however, in the late 1520s, when Henry, the once proud "defender of the faith," began to contend with the more intense challenges brought on by the Reformation. For the first time, the church in England—not yet the Church of England—had to contend with danger in the form of Lutheran ideas, translations of the Bible into the vernacular, and the importation of various printed books and pamphlets. To counter this threat, the lord chancellor, Thomas More, as well as Bishop Longland, began to make concerted efforts to combat the encroachment of Protestantism, primarily by burning books and eventually people, including notable Evangelicals such as Thomas Bilney.

The late 1520s thus constituted what could be considered the first wave of overtly religious persecution, while the next came in 1534, when Henry finally severed all connections with Rome over the issue of his marriage. The result, over the next three or four years, was the execution of approximately forty-five individuals, including More, along with continuous, low-level harassment of nuns, monks, and others who still abided by the old faith. While not a large number, the symbolism was extremely important and did have a strong impact overseas—as intended—within the imperial, French, and papal courts.[28]

After a few years, however, a conservative reaction was instigated in part by Stephen Gardiner and Cuthbert Tunstall, who brought forward a new program that reasserted elements of Catholic doctrine, including the sacrament of the mass and clerical celibacy. As a result, in the fall of 1538 a proclamation was issued, ordering all foreign Anabaptists—who had never been much tolerated anyway—to either leave the realm, or bear the faggots of penance at Paul's Cross in London, while a small number were put to death. Following this came the passage of the Act of Six Articles, which formalized these more conservative doctrines and resulted in the creation of persecutory commissions and the execution, over the course of the next eight years, of more Anabaptists as well as notable Protestants such as Thomas Garret, Robert Barnes, and Anne Askew. This was hardly a terror, nor was it consistent, though the measures brought about by the Six Articles did result in stopping, or at least greatly slowing, the development of the Reformation under Henry.

After Henry's death and the accession to the throne of Edward, persecution slowed considerably under the regency of the Duke of Somerset. The Act of Six Articles was annulled, Catholics such as Gardiner and Edmund Bonner were committed to prison, and Protestants ascended to power. The emergence of a more radical strain of Protestantism[29] began to concern authorities over time, however, which led to an increased persecution in the last three years of the reign under the new regency of the Duke of Northumberland. This took the form of Anabaptist trials and the execution of the radicals Joan Bocher and George Van Parris, but in the end, persecution under Edward was comparatively slight—a fact which nevertheless seems to have done little to make the realm any more Protestant in 1553 than it had been in 1547. What really helped the godly cause was Mary, whose policies bolstered Protestants through martyrdom. One must not overplay the Marian persecution, however; while most of its victims tended to be arbitrarily chosen, executions did slacken somewhat by 1558 upon the regime's realization of their ineffectuality, and it is not entirely clear in what direction her reign would have gone had she lived longer.

The early years of Elizabeth's rule witnessed a low-level persecution of Catholics, since the queen's method was to proceed with caution in carrying through Protestant changes in the churches and in the reestablishment of the supremacy. Over the course of the 1560s, recusancy became an ever-increasing option among Catholics, but the laws governing them were unevenly enforced until 1570, when Pius V issued his excommunication of the queen. Soon after, John Felton was executed for posting the bull of excommunication on a church door, while the same year witnessed the death of John Story, a notorious figure who had played a leading role in the Marian persecutions, fifteen years previously. Ultimately, however, the most intense persecuting period during Elizabeth's reign occurred in the late 1580s, when various plots against the queen as well as the crisis of the Spanish Armada produced a wave of activity against the Jesuits, which only lessened somewhat in the last years of her reign.

For Elizabeth and her predecessors, an upsurge in persecutory measures, reflected in directives and proclamations, could above all represent a symbolic expression of monarchical self-assertion in an age where power was based in large part on perceptions (rather than, for example, a permanent standing army). Indeed, the necessity of projections of royal power took on more importance than ever, especially if rulers now viewed themselves as the new David or Josiah, presiding over a reborn Israel.[30] After 1534, for example, the problem was not that Henry faced any real danger from a united or incendiary opposition. Although Thomas More, John Fisher, the Carthusian monks, and others were problematic in their own way, they were executed not for the threat they represented, but for their crime of being representative figures whose deaths could send a signal of Henry's power to the imperial, papal, and French courts abroad, as well as to domestic constituents, justices, or lower-level officials who were placed in charge of enforcing the king's power at home.[31]

This becomes evident in the unfortunate case of John Lambert, whose trial or disputation in 1538 stands as a particularly acute episode in the annals of humiliation.[32] Brought before a tribunal which consisted of Cranmer, Cromwell, Stephen Gardiner, and above all King Henry himself, Lambert was made to answer for his fringe-Evangelical beliefs during a period that was witnessing a movement back toward conservatism. Forced to stand during the ordeal from noon until after dark, Lambert quivered before taunting authority and made occasional attempts to defend his theological positions by holding up Augustine like a battered flag. In the end, however, and unsurprisingly, Lambert was (in Foxe's description) "devoured" by the proceedings, and sent on to his death six days later. For all its injustice, Lambert's disputation was neither a great council (as some have claimed) nor an empty show trial, but rather a forum that displayed the workings of power and self-interest in a religiously and politically unstable age. Its veneer of legalism—or the claims it made in following in the tradition of past disputations— was a sham; yet the fact that it served as a piece of theater, a public-relations spectacle with an all-star cast, should not diminish its role in displaying the terrifying (if not quite fully realized) power of the king to the realm and in advancing the policies which would culminate in the religious correction embodied in the Act of Six Articles.

Absent a standing army or other centralized (and modern) mechanisms of force, Elizabeth also needed such crownly projections of power, which were dependent in part on the isolation and stigmatization of religiously, and by extension politically, dissenting groups. Recusants, as well as church papists, were a targeted or at least suspicious community in her reign, though enforcement against them was unevenly carried out; the fact that most of them avoided the kind of punishments meted out to their priests or more extreme coreligionists did not prevent them from having to face fines, property seizure, or impoverishment. Certainly the threat from Spain (and Rome) was real, but Elizabeth's ability to mobilize the country and even forge a nascent sense of patriotism depended in part on her containing these groups within the bounds of suspicion, where they remained from then on, strong yet underground. More ambiguous were the Puritans, who constituted another persecuted group, though not to the same extent as Catholics, given their profession to belong to the true (albeit purer) church, as well as their connections to the high seats of power. Nevertheless, the "diversity, variety [and] contention" which they embodied repelled the queen, who used on them, as well as on the very different Separatists, a number of intimidating tactics that resulted in imprisonment or even flight from the realm.[33]

Persecuting Individuals, Persecuting Structures of Authority

As brilliant as Henry or Elizabeth could be in exploiting the power of public forums or utilizing dissent to strengthen their own calls for uniformity, few of their directives would be obeyed without the acquiescence of those officials or local religious leaders who ostensibly worked in their name. The identity of these figures and the nature of their duties thus also deserves a brief overview, for they constituted not simply an essential link in the chain of persecution, but also an autonomous, sometimes wayward, and frequently overlooked group of individuals who play recurring roles in this study, as well as in the drama of persecution and martyrdom as a whole. For centuries, England had benefited (and sometimes suffered) from these individuals, who constituted layers of formal and informal authority, from privy council members and bishops at the top down to the lowliest petty constable or parish churchwarden. Beginning with the religious upheavels and the assertion of the royal supremacy in the sixteenth century, however, it became more important than ever that these layers be coordinated, and that the ecclesiastical realm—even during the reign of Mary—subsume itself under the directives of the secular.[34]

At the very top, members of the privy council could be particularly eager to direct, formulate, and oversee persecutory policies, joining special commissions and sometimes even involving themselves in direct apprehensions, but their motives were not entirely clear, and may have had less to do with religious idealism than with opportunism and professional advancement at court. Among the privy councilors in Mary's reign, for example, was Sir Anthony Browne, who had held Protestant beliefs in Edward's time, only to change over to Catholicism in Mary's, and end his life sufficiently acceptable to Elizabeth to be knighted by her before parliament in 1566.[35] Joining him was Richard Rich, whose only constancy lay in his changeability in every reign from Henry's through Elizabeth's, from the time he betrayed Thomas More in the 1530s, through his torture of Anne Askew in the 1540s and his role in expediting Joan Bocher's death, under Edward. Rich only rarely attended meetings of the privy council, though with Browne he eagerly apprehended and sent down to London heretics from Essex. Despite these actions, he had enough of Elizabeth's trust to accompany her to London in 1558 and gain a place on other commissions, though he somehow managed to hold firm in his dissent against the Act of Uniformity.[36]

The most powerful official on the local level was the justice of the peace, who often hung on jealously to his prestigious position over the course of the century, regardless of the monarch in power. As one who had been chosen by the crown or the lord chancellor, the justice was always a notable of landed wealth whose primary function was to maintain order whenever it was threatened. Beginning in Henry's reign, however, an increasing number of statutes, proclamations, oaths, or royal circulars began to place added responsibilities of enforcement and oversight onto his office, increasing his presence not only in secular matters but in the ecclesiastical sphere as well. This was not always to the justice's liking, since preserving order meant that he now had to enter into religious disputes and delinquency cases, and even serve at times as the secular arm of a persecuting clergy. If a religious suspect needed to be apprehended, it was the justice who had to summon men to carry through the task, bear the costs of moving the offender to jail, and often provide food and lodging expenses as well.[37] Logistical problems only increased when the prisoner was coming over from a distant place such as Calais, as was the case in the 1530s, when Lord Lisle frequently bemoaned the expense and difficulty of sending religious nonconformists over the Channel for persecution. At one point, Cromwell frostily replied to these complaints that "in such matters as touch the King's highness every subject is bound to bear his expenses . . . as I myself must bear his charges to the court from where I abide."[38]

Despite these attempts to control justices, resistance to the highest authorities persisted throughout the century, especially when justices held different economic and religious interests from those operating from the center. During Mary's reign, for example, justices from the southeast became known for their Protestant sympathies, while in the 1570s, the laxity of local justices in pursuing Catholics was blamed on the fact that an inordinate number of them were recusants.[39] In the latter case, letters were subsequently issued from the privy council to figures such as Bishop John Aylmer of London[40] to put pressure on uncooperative officials, while justices were compelled more forcefully to take the oath of supremacy—which many of them avoided, citing illness or other excuses. A few were even ejected from their magistracies, while others were punished in lesser ways. In 1578, for instance, six justices from Norfolk—among them Humphrey Bedington, Robert de Grey, John Downes, Robert Downes, and John Drury—appeared before the privy council, where they were questioned for their recusancy and subsequently fined or jailed upon their refusal to conform.[41]

The justice of the peace was not the only officer to find his responsibilities restructured, or his traditional powers attenuated or increased over the course of the period. The sheriff, most notably, had once been an indispensable part of enforcement, but in the sixteenth century he underwent something of a demotion, as new offices were created to usurp functions which had previously been his alone. In many ways, however, and at least as far as religious persecutions were concerned, the sheriff did remain a vitally important presence; as a bridge between secular and religious worlds, he was given the responsibility by oath to assist the ecclesiastical courts and, if a sentence of heresy had been rendered, to bring the accused men and women to the next and final stages of punishment. In addition to impaneling juries and issuing writs for the quarter sessions, the sheriff was also expected to oversee the county jail and the conduct of its keeper—a matter which greatly affected the fate of the heretic-prisoner. The requirement that he preside at executions—that he leap into the fray of religious persecution at its most incendiary moments—gave him added visibility, which extended to his frequent mention in the martyrological accounts that followed. Despite this questionable prominence, however, the sheriff by the sixteenth century was

a much-diminished figure, appearing in the records as a faceless functionary, not powerful in his own right, but rather a visible but silent
expediter of someone else's directives.

The sheriff was assisted by his bailiffs, who tended to be equated
with the lower end of law enforcement alongside their cousins, the petty
constables. Although their generally thankless work made bailiffs the
targets of disdain and satire, they were indispensable in keeping the peace,
enforcing the law, undertaking responsibilities often at great danger to
themselves, and fulfilling jobs effectively enough to be reelected over a
period of years. In the lives of religious dissidents, petty constables and
bailiffs tended to represent the muscular arm of persecution, serving as
physical apprehenders or general overseers of inflammatory situations.
In their secular duties, too, bailiffs and petty constables were often bear-
ers of bad news and thus unwelcome surprise visitors, and as such, frequently unwilling to bring on retaliation or stir up more trouble than
was necessary. Almost more than the sheriffs or high constables, bailiffs
and petty constables, as J. A. Sharpe has written, could often find the
laws they were expected to enforce at odds with local ideas and the best
interests of their fellow villagers, whose ranks and sentiments they shared.

It is difficult to fully gauge the nature of these officials' religious allegiances, especially when many of them remain anonymous. Only rarely
will one encounter the beliefs of an official such as the sheriff Richard
Hopkins, who, according to Foxe, embraced Protestantism in Mary's
reign and was imprisoned in the Fleet "for the faithful and constant confessing of God's holy gospel."[42] Lacking such clear accounts, one may
ask, for example, if failure to enforce directives resulted from an official's
own dissenting religious views, or if he believed, despite sympathy with
the monarch, that enforcement would simply be futile and unnecessarily
disruptive. Apart from religion, one might also question the extent to
which class played a role, especially when some officials were of a distinctly lower social standing than those they were meant to target. This
was often the case with law enforcers and recusants in Elizabeth's reign,
or more generally among the aforementioned bailiffs and petty constables who shared more in common with average men and women in
the community than they did with the prominent individuals who in-
habited the higher tiers of enforcement.

Religious authorities were also enjoined to keep the peace and strive
for uniformity in the name of the crown; in this, bishops—many of

whom were newly invested because the previous regime's bishops were imprisoned or deprived of their sees—were expected to serve their monarch and to ensure conformity in their dioceses. On one level, traditional powers of enforcement once available to bishops, such as excommunication or penance, were weakened or rendered moot over the course of the century. The bishop, however, whether Catholic or Protestant, could utilize his ability to call for a visitation, which served as a fruitful means by which he could receive information about heretics, measure the conformity of his community, or initiate further persecutory activities. Though he took his cues from the government throughout the century, a bishop could also be enthusiastic—sometimes over-enthusiastic—in his own right. Bishop John Stokesley of London personally went after gospellers throughout the 1530s, with his initiatives eventually leading to conflicts with Thomas Cromwell.[43] While More, Cranmer, and others played a larger part in the trial of the Lutheran John Frith, for example, it was Stokesley who read the final condemnation of heresy and who personally oversaw the delivery of Frith to the executioner.[44]

The reign of Edward also witnessed the apprehension and trial of Anabaptist radicals, made on the order of bishops such as John Hooper, whose archbishop superior, Cranmer, took an active part in interrogating the radicals himself.[45] The most infamous persecuting bishop in the century, however, was Edmund Bonner, whose demonization at the hands of his Protestant enemies should not lead one to overlook the fact that he was the most visible and probably most active such figure in Mary's reign.[46] Bonner's tactics will be examined in later chapters, but his orders to apprehend suspects in his diocese of London certainly bordered on the zealous, especially when victims of his wrath were locked away in his own personal coalhouse.[47]

Elsewhere (and much lower) in the ecclesiastical sphere of enforcement were churchwardens, who dealt with all matters pertaining to parish life, from crowd control to poor relief to the destruction of vermin. While churchwardens did not function significantly on the level of apprehending and pursuing religious dissidents, they were charged with lesser or more mundane persecutory duties, sometimes to the point of confusion. In 1548, for example, the privy council in Edward's reign ordered that churchwardens oversee the destruction of all images, and in 1550 the removal of every Latin service book, all of which would be replaced again, seven years later, during Mary's reign. This could become an expensive business indeed for the parish, which was expected at least in part to pay the cost of the replaced rood-screens, vestments, stone altars, plates, service books, censers, and other equipment, most of which would again be destroyed under Elizabeth.[48]

There is not enough surviving evidence to ascertain the extent to which churchwardens and bishops carried out visitational and other duties; certainly corruption or a reluctance to fulfill their statutory duties was a complaint often lodged against them. Further problems arose when the churchwardens themselves joined with the laity to resist the directives or religious orientation of the bishops. Failure to comply on the churchwardens' part could lead to punishing measures such as fines, but even in the relatively more efficient time of Elizabeth, and especially after the disciplining Canons of 1571 were released, a substantial number of churchwardens could present problems to the authorities. Like other local officials, churchwardens could therefore be caught between royal policy and the opinions they shared with their own communities, or between their own enforcement duties and the inhibiting factor of class difference. They also risked, like bailiffs and petty constables, unwittingly provoking religious contention by their presence, or by entering the homes of people to check on church absenteeism, when they were busy enough preventing youths from enjoying sports on the churchgrounds.

Despite the layers of local authority in place, communities were able to claim quasi-autonomous spaces such as alehouses and woods, thereby eluding the official eye. As far as religious dissidents or secret conventicles were concerned, such places not only provided protection from apprehension, but also constituted sites where heterodox or treasonous beliefs could be expressed. Adding to the difficulties for the authorities was the fact that religious dissidents existed alongside adolescent apprentices, prostitutes, thieves, vagrants, highway robbers, and a rising class of the newly poor. While heretics or traitors were thus perceived as belonging to an entirely different and more serious category of offense, their transgressions nevertheless existed in a realm of larger deviance, characterized by disruptions emanating from the enclosure movement, greater urbanization, demographic expansions, economic fluctuations, and periodic political revolts. The more intensified accusations and pursuits that constituted the witch-hunt under Elizabeth only increased the strain experienced by officials, who in the case of southeast England even found themselves pursuing witches where heretical enclaves had once been prevalent, thus expanding the confusing context of which religious heterodoxy was simply a part. [49]

Sources and the Scope of Exposition

Apart from official documents contained in state papers, the best sources for understanding the nuances of sixteenth-century persecution are later sixteenth-century martyrological accounts such as John Foxe's *Acts and Monuments,* William Roper's *Life of Thomas More,* and the works of Richard Verstegan and William Allen. In addition are the sources written by the victims themselves in the form of letters from prison and accounts of trials. These range from the lengthy treatises composed in the Tower by Thomas More, to the (later-amended) account by Anne Askew of her torture and interrogation, and to the prolix writings issued out of prison by the Protestant martyrs in Mary's reign. The problems with relying too heavily on these sources, however, are obvious: written from the perspective of the victim with the intent of elevating him or her to the ranks of martyrdom, the accounts portray the officials, authorities, and interrogators in the worst possible light—indeed, often as ogres modeled more on a Nero than on reality. Historical veracity is thus often shunted aside in favor of self-conscious scriptural evocations, which further prevent the reader from gaining full access to the individuals involved and the way in which events might have transpired.

Problems with such sources have only increased with the recent scholarship of Susan Wabuda, Thomas Freeman, and others, who have contributed greatly toward an understanding of the ways in which Foxe—as well as his colleagues and fellow editors, Henry Bull and Miles Coverdale—tended to omit inappropriate or even embarrassing details and invent others as their documents were edited and shaped into a grand narrative of providential dimensions.[50] While Foxe and other chroniclers were certainly careful to uphold a level of historicism in their endeavors, their purposes often collided with an equally strong tendency to shift the harmonic or dissonant elements of their narratives in order to reach the best possible martyrological arrangement. Still, martyrologies must be taken seriously as historical sources, for one thing because a great many of them are corroborated by official documents or by comments and writings from even antagonistic figures such as Edmund Bonner, who defended himself for the record and wrote equally biased treatises and letters to the privy council detailing the difficulties he faced in pursuing heretics. Equally important, however, are the supplemental papers such as the letters from Marian martyrs, located in the British Library or Cambridge University's Emmanual Library collection, which can also provide an added and necessary, if limited, perspective.

While martyrologies contribute considerably toward providing accounts of prison life and trials, other areas of the persecution process are by their nature shrouded in secrecy, if they are not absent altogether. Records of or by spies or informers, for example, provided authorities with useful information, but the information was primarily transmitted verbally, or, if in writing, through the wisp of a letter or behind indecipherable initials. This secrecy was of course intended by figures such as Francis Walsingham, who proved himself capable of cultivating these contacts, but who also knew the value of discretion and the art of leaving few traces. On the other hand, records of secular trials or church courts—those that survive—while also fragmentary and one-sided, or transcribed long after the fact, can provide a rich store of material in uncovering the dynamics of interrogations as well as formal trial procedures. As often in the case of early modern records, however, the evidence that covers the lower end of the population is lacking, though interrogations of the humble do appear, albeit sparsely and selectively, in Foxe. The nature of those individuals' beliefs is more difficult to ascertain, as Foxe had a tendency to list all of his martyrs as orthodox Protestants, when in fact they—and especially the more humble among them—could have been Anabaptists, Sacramentarians, or others of more radical inclination. Still, for all their problems, trial transcripts of more notable figures can perhaps shed a dim light on the nature of the law as it worked for all levels of society, humble and eminent alike, and should therefore be utilized by historians to a greater extent than they have so far.

Historians of Tudor England have long been familiar with sources such as martyrologies or trial records, but to approach them with a different set of questions reveals lesser-known or even obscure figures whose roles in the drama of persecution and martyrdom were as essential in their own way as that of the more renowned heroes (and villains). Little attention has been given, for example, to the backgrounds and identities of the numerous informers, interrogators, or jailers who shuffled across the stage, supporting the leading actors while adding their own peculiar presences to the drama at hand. Similarly over-looked—indeed, the subject of this book—have been the processes and rituals which led up to martyrdom's final denouement at the stake or on the gallows. Peter Lake and Michael Questier, among others, have contributed in recent years to an understanding of imprisonment and execution, and of the strategies by which religious dissidents exploited such settings. I seek to further their investigations and to explore more overlooked aspects of the martyr's ordeal, as he or she was physically pursued or examined, faced with the choice to flee the realm or to stay behind, and forced to choose to answer questions with meekness or defiance.

A study that extends across decades, regions, and historical sources cannot of course be entirely comprehensive or in-depth about the par-ticularities, for example, of a locality. However, to limit an essentially thematic topic to a few years or a single reign is to diminish a larger picture of persecution and the manner in which it could shift over time in intensity and character. Broader patterns of continuity and change must therefore be examined at the same time that specific events are placed within their own particular social and historical contexts. While the motivations to persecute in 1538 were not the same as they were in 1588—and the set of events and circumstances which determined those motiva-tions were also at variance—other developments, in the area of personnel and methods of enforcement, bear striking testimony to a shared and connective, if unwieldy, experience of persecution. Prisons and the state of being imprisoned, for instance, changed very little between the early and late century, while the development of an information and appre-hension system remained problematic throughout. The use of torture, on the other hand, increased markedly under Elizabeth, as did the sub-ordination of the charge (and perception) of heresy under treason, with a concomitant judicial shift from ecclesiastical to secular courts, from the punishment of burning to that of drawing and quartering. The ini-tiative to persecute, however, remained firmly in the hands of secular officials throughout the century, even in the reign of Mary, as bishops took their cues from the privy council, and justices of the peace were charged with overseeing the enforcement of new religious policy. In this sense, one can discern a movement toward a secularizing break with the past, since the Tudor monarchs—again, including Mary—utilized the new powers available to them, especially those that were contained within the idea of the supremacy.

In spite of these new powers wielded by authorities over religious groups, Tudor governments were nevertheless dependent on the willingness of common individuals to come forward and aid in the process of locating dissident religious heretics or enclaves. Chapter 2 describes the process by which such suspects were brought to the attention of authorities in the first place, which was frequently by way of the accusations and denunciations of others. To their credit, Tudor governments were careful to parse true from false accusations and to be wary of the character of certain informers; moreover, figures such as Cromwell or Walsingham often succeeded in cultivating networks of spies whom they installed—or who had voluntarily installed themselves—in monasteries or prisons. Still, the system was never efficient; not only were many accusations arbitrary and prejudiced, but many were also brought forward too often by independent agents and dominated above all by personal factors, without any rational, bureaucratized foundation to contain and control them.

The weakness of the Tudor enforcement system is especially evident when it came to the actual apprehension of religious suspects, which is also the subject of chapter 2. It was here, in fact, that individuals first exercised their resistance to the state by evading capture with the help of accomplices and "underground" networks, and by fleeing to refuges overseas. While authorities such as Stephen Gardiner initially encouraged departures and Elizabeth employed banishment as a tool, such measures tended to backfire when Protestants or Catholics began to form coherent communities overseas and strengthen their movement by issuing, and illegally exporting to England, propagandistic tracts. To counter this, governments sometimes resorted to extradition attempts, though the law, which was still developing, was unavailing; even kidnapping was occasionally used, though ultimately authorities were forced to acknowledge that communities which had fled abroad were only strengthened, not weakened, in the end.

For those who were captured, prison—which is the subject of chapter 3—was the next stage of persecution and the first step on the road to martyrdom. Conditions of Tudor jails were notorious, and in many ways their reputation for stench, filth, and corrupt wardens served

as a deterrent for those who might otherwise have broken the law or joined a heretical enclave. If one did find oneself in prison, languishing alongside hardened murderers, this could also constitute an ongoing pressure to recant, conform, or inform as an ever-tempting strategy for release. Many—perhaps most—in fact did recant and gain their freedom, while others used the opportunity to write letters, recount their interrogations, pray, and prepare themselves for what lay ahead. In this sense, the jail experience, it will be argued, also contained within itself built-in, subversive opportunities which the prisoner could exploit, allowing him to evangelize felons, use the prison's laxity to forge communities of coreligionists, and write letters, in coal or blood if need be, to a rapt audience of fellow believers on the outside.

Chapter 4 focuses on interrogations and trials, which were arguably the most important forum where persecutor and persecuted met. Relatively few studies have been done on this most essential aspect of the process, which not only allowed both sides to plead and argue their case before the court and the country, but also revealed the fundamental and ultimately unresolvable issues that dominated the realm in the wake of the Reformation. Again, the process was undertaken not by faceless entities of the law, but rather by individuals who, as will be seen, brought to the interrogation sessions or trial particular traits, an often complicated past, and even an intimate familiarity with the defendant. For their part, defendants faced these interrogators with particular traits of their own, and resorted to a number of tactics, including defiance, holy passivity, rational argumentation, or silence in order to express agency in yet another forum that opened up areas not only for resistance but for outright assertion.

The last chapter, on executions, takes the persecution process to its final stage and indicates, once again, that the display was an opportunity for a multiplicity of discourses to circulate, rather than a simple monologic "theater of state power." The argument here will echo that of Lake and Questier, who have recently used Elizabethan executions of Catholics to argue against Foucauldian notions of the "state" and of traditionally rigid categorizations of "Catholicism," "Protestantism," and "ideology." [51] Executions, not only in Elizabethan times but earlier, were fluid affairs that involved a complicated and delicate exchange among authorities, those about to be executed, and the crowd. By examining all the elements involved, and the particular role they played, one may gain a clearer sense of the execution—and the persecution process as a whole—as one that played out against an unstable background, and conveyed messages that lay well beyond anything which had been intended by the authorities.

It should be pointed out, finally, that a common characteristic of all the Tudors, to their credit perhaps, was a respect for the law and for the parliamentary process, both of which served as a brake on persecution and prevented England in some ways from lapsing into the kind of bloody violence experienced in France at the time. All the monarchs, including Mary, proceeded with some amount of caution to enact or repeal laws, and took care generally to apply the law when dealing with even the humblest subjects. At the same time, what John Scarisbrick has said about Henry applied to all the Tudors in varying degrees: while they were mindful of the law, they also "could be less inhibited when [they were] bent on blood and the victims were important figures." Those victims, however, were not entirely powerless against the monarchs even in bloodthirsty times, and could evade or manipulate their persecution if need be by utilizing the administrative weakness of the state along with the opportunities found in the experience of prison or execution. While the Tudor governments did have a very real and powerful impact upon the lives of English people, they were nevertheless still weak and driven by individuals—indeed, in some ways, rising and falling by those individuals.

In this sense, the government's case in persecuting dissenters was inevitably a losing one, since it led in the end to the creation of martyrs;[52] no government can counter individuals willing to die in the name of their cause, who know that the glory of their death will cast all the more infamy onto their foes. Martyrs in fact depend upon persecutors to oppress all the harder, since the truth for which they will die is then all the more hard-won and victorious. It is not to diminish the heightened level of a martyr's religiosity to thus state once again that such elements of calculation often coursed through the choice of death. This was especially so in sixteenth-century England, where religious proclivities could be fluid. It became important that persecution and martyrdom be presented as a public event, a drama of tyranny and cruelty overcome by the spiritually superior individual for the edification and, it was to be hoped, conversion of others. By publicizing one's own persecution through prison letters, transcripts of interrogation sessions, and self-displays at executions, the martyr or his followers could thereby resist the intentions of the authorities, as those authorities well knew. While the government could convey its actions through the prism of legality and even a professed claim of patience and toleration, its attempts to instill uniformity amounted to little as long as martyrs continued to slip through its futile grasp.

CHAPTER TWO

"For the bird of the air shall betray thy voice"

Informing and Apprehending

THE INTENTIONS OF TUDOR AUTHORITIES IN PERSECUTING DISSENT may have been expressed in projections of royal omnipotence backed by legalistic proclamations, but in reality, most religious troublemakers came to the attention of officials and were subsequently apprehended in an arbitrary and luckless manner. There were some notable exceptions, of course, especially among individuals who had enjoyed prominence in one reign, only to find their views in disfavor in the next; for them, their capture and incarceration—if they did not flee to the Continent first—was only a matter of time. Others, however, were targeted and apprehended as the result of betrayal by neighbors, a rash outburst of blasphemous words spoken from the midst of a crowd, or even by simply being the wrong person in the wrong place at the wrong time, which was the case in 1555, for example, when searchers came to apprehend John Glover but found his brother Robert, sick and lying in bed, who was taken instead. The sheriff, according to John Foxe, was inclined to dismiss Robert, "saying that he was not the man for whom they were sent"; but "being feared with the stout words of the officer, contending with him to have him stayed till the bishop's coming, he was constrained to carry him away against his will, and so laid him fast while the bishop came."

The chance element behind these captures reflects, more than anything else, the contingent and inconsistent nature of persecutory measures throughout the century, and above all, the frequent lack of coordination between governmental initiatives and local willingness to carry out those initiatives. At various times, directives were issued from the government enjoining justices, constables, newly empowered commissioners, bishops, and other officials or local authorities to search out heretics, seize them, incarcerate them, and thus control the spread of their dangerously divisive ideas. In 1538, for example, Thomas Cromwell put his signature to a document which ordered a royal commission to "search for and examine Anabaptists, receive back into the Church such as renounce their error, [and] hand over those who persist in it to the secular arm for punishment."[1] As local officials with presumed knowledge of their communities—or as royal agents empowered to embed themselves in the life of the counties—it was the locals' duty to investigate and specifically name and target those heretics or religious troublemakers and summon support for their capture. This was not an easy task, however, and compliance with the directive never would be a guarantee.

Since resources available to a more impersonal, efficient, and modern judicial system or policing force were absent, everything depended instead on the initiative of individuals, who were in turn affected by such considerations as the social status of the suspect, the nature of community sentiment, the geographical (and religious) layout of a region, and the presence or influence of sympathetic friends or neighbors. Perhaps in light of these complications, the middlemen were sometimes dispensed with altogether, with high authorities themselves taking matters into their own hands, at least by example. The Evangelical John Petite, for instance, was praying in a private room in his "owne poore howse" one night when he was startled to look up and see Thomas More hovering over him; when asked why he was there, More answered, "Ye say ye have none of these newe bookes?" "Your lordship [sees] . . . my bookes and my closett," Petite said in an admission of guilt that led him to Newgate, where he languished and eventually died in "a doungeone upon a padd of strawe."

Despite the occasional crackdown by men such as More, the frequent inefficiency of local officials resulted from the general confusion and policy changes wrought by the Reformation, when the enemy at various times could take on an Anabaptist, Sacramentarian, Lutheran,

Evangelical, and Catholic coloration. It was not even always clear, for that matter—to the authorities, or anyone else—what an Anabaptist, for example, exactly *was,* much less where he or she dwelled or traveled. Officials were thus being asked to stretch their capacities to hunt down a shifting enemy of indeterminate number—a number which could also be inflated by fear and misperception, as was the case during the 1580s, when an increasingly prevalent Protestant sentiment (or paranoia) led to the belief by many that every cupboard in every suspicious house held within it a papal fifth column. As a result, and perhaps unsurprisingly, many officials, apart from royal commissioners who owed their fealty and position to the crown, resisted such duties.

The physical layout of sixteenth-century England was also double-edged when it came to the targeting and pursuit of religious trouble-makers. On the one hand, the world on both an urban and village level tended to be small and watchful, making noticeable the appearance of anyone different, such as the "strange woman" who came to Beacons-field, in Buckinghamshire, around 1530 and was noted to be "a wretched madwoman [who] lives in William Edmond's house." While London, especially, could grant vagrants or wanderers a degree of anonymity, even then its tangled and congested life ensured that one's personal business would become a public matter, for always there were people lurking, overhearing, standing around, encroaching on another's space, or casting suspicious eyes on anything transient and odd. This proximity made for many sudden detections, especially during religiously significant cere-monies. For example, in 1555 a woman, seeing a hearse and other prepa-rations being made for a procession, asked another onlooker what all of it meant; told that it was to honor the pope, to whom she must pray, the woman replied "that I will not, for he needeth not my prayers." Over-heard "by certain who stood by," the woman was "carried into the cage at London-bridge to cool herself." Other instances of sudden appre-hension occurred within crowds at sermons or during executions: after witnessing the burning of John Noyes in Mary's time, the young servant John Jarvis remarked, "Good Lord, how the sinews of his arms shrink up!" Behind him, however, stood two bailiffs, who misheard the boy's words as blasphemous and then proceeded to haul him before the justice.[2]

But while Tudor society was watchful, it was not all-seeing, and nor was the central government able to exercise broad surveillance powers over every secret conventicle or wayward religious group.[3] The fact that the world was socially compact helped in matters of self-monitoring and control, yet what was tightly knit could also be protective, as sympathizers in the community rallied to the side of their local "dissident," hiding him in woods, fields, neighbors' homes, or even haystacks and hollowed-out walls.[4] Even the more presumably impersonal environs of London did not prevent neighborhood or conventicle familiarity from allowing religious troublemakers to elude authorities. Since Tudor methods of enforcement were dependent on the cooperation of everyone, and not simply local enforcement officials, this could be a problem; at the same time, even the most sympathetic and self-protecting groups could not prevent the capture of dissidents when all it took was one informer in their midst, one betrayer—a Judas figure rattling at the fringes with his bag of gold and mixed motivations, ready at the first offer to give up the cause.[5]

Keeping Watch: The Mid-Level Officials

Lacking the mechanisms to exert top-down control over the realm or ensure the unanimous compliance of local officials, Tudor governments were forced to rely on public self-surveillance and informing to keep watch not only among individuals but also between officials themselves.[6] Proclamations and letters were thus sent out to sheriffs and justices of the peace, compelling them to scrutinize bishops and other clerical men; according to one circular released by Cromwell in 1534, officials were to make "diligent search, wait and espial in any place in your sheriffwick whether the said bishop do truly, sincerely, and without all manner cloak, colour, and [dissimulate], or execute, and accomplish our will and commandment," and to immediately report any bishop acting "coldly" or using "any manner sinister addition, wrong interpretation or painted colours."[7] This was indicative of the increasing control that was exercised over the ecclesiastical sphere in the wake of the Reformation, but bishops were hardly powerless, especially when they were charged themselves with watching over lesser lay officials and ensuring that ecclesiastical policies were being carried out. Whether those bishops were able to succeed in enforcing their orders on those officials was a different matter, however.[8]

Some officials were more direct reporters of information, working on the front lines to search out, detect, and notify their superiors of suspicious activity. The summoner was an especially unpopular figure who served as a kind of detection-official, watchfully roaming the local churches, alehouses, and other public places. It was an Essex summoner named Atwell who, in the 1550s, would uncover the apprentice William Hunter reading a Bible in Brentwood Chapel, which led to a heated argument followed by Atwell's notifying the local vicar, who took the matter from there.[9] In addition to these thankless tasks, the summoner was further burdened with the duty of dispensing citations, at some risk to himself. During the same period, for example, a local summoner appeared with a citation at the home of Joyce Lewes's husband, who then "compelled the said sumner [summoner] to eat the citation indeed, by setting a dagger to his heart; and when he had eaten it, he caused him to drink to it, and so sent him away."[10]

Over the course of the sixteenth century, however, the summoner would be increasingly supplanted by bailiffs, petty constables, and other officials, who entered homes at churchtime to check on absenteeism, offered reports at visitation times, or planted themselves in alehouses or in front of church entrances, listening for any subversive utterance.[11] Beginning with Henry, royal commissions were also created to inquire after, hunt down, and examine religious deviants.[12] Commisioners, who were expected to aid the local bishop along with parsons, curates, church-wardens, and all lay officials, acted as individual informers at the same time that they worked together in checking not only who was absent from church, but how effectively the diocesan administration was functioning.[13] One of the more famous commissions, for example, was established by Mary in the 1550s and directed toward London;[14] while no records of its proceedings have survived, at least fifteen individuals are known to have been sent on to Bishop Bonner as a result of its efforts.[15]

In purely religious matters it was really the churchwarden who best fulfilled the role of low-level official informer, as he was charged with the duty of reporting abuses in his parish by roaming the aisles, checking on parishioners' homes during church service, taking note of who was receiving communion and how often, and watching for any strangers in the pews.[16] The fact that the parish was small and compact made the churchwarden's task easier, just as it was incumbent upon every parishioner to provide information to him. And no matter was too trivial: church singers who refused to perform in the new regime had to be reported, as did those who rejected the liturgy as it was defined by the new monarch. Typical was a case from 1520, in Oxfordshire, where "A certain girl of full years does not come to church as other Christians do, and this year she has not received the sacrament of the altar: she lives with Joan Grene."[17] When not conducting informing rounds of their own, churchwardens were also burdened with the responsibility of taking cases that came before them and filtering the true from the false or the serious from the trivial. In this, their knowledge of local affairs served them well, allowing them to expedite only those cases backed by strong evidence and "public fame," or solid community consensus. In this sense, the falsely accused were thus often protected by churchwardens, whose detection of malice or other motives stopped the information before it could proceed further to church courts.[18]

The functions required of officials and laid out in directives and circulars, while not constituting a system per se, ensured that information flowed up a channel, not through one person, but through many. A churchwarden, for example, would report a questionable activity to a vicar, who would then transmit the information to a constable, after which it would be sent up to a high authority such as a bishop or privy councilor. This means of conveyance could constitute a strength as well as a weakness: while officials were available to receive the information and transmit it to higher authorities, the nature and extent of that information could often be arbitrary or distorted by the indirectness of the path by which it had traveled. Rather than moving from one layer of bureaucratic officialdom to another, information was really transmitted from one individual to another, from high constable to justice to king's secretary, and was thus dependent on that individual's willingness to pass the news on further, or to have it end, for whatever reason, with him.

The targeting and capture of religious troublemakers was not always preceded by the tangled transmission of information, however; instead, officials could be faced with sudden detections requiring quick action, as was the case in 1575, when a constable literally stumbled upon a gathering of Anabaptists in a house in Aldersgate Street in London, where he proceeded to take names and then hastily send for reinforcements.[19] Recognizing this, authorities directed officials not only to be on the lookout in general, but also to station themselves in places that attracted concentrated groups of people, where information could be quickly gathered. The pulpit at Paul's Cross in London was one such place, where officials could measure the degree of orthodoxy not only on the ground but also in the pulpit. Execution sites could also be seen as instrumental places of monitoring and apprehension, as Mary and her council recognized when they stated in a circular letter that a number of officers and others should be appointed to sites of execution, where they "may be charged to apprehend and commit to ward, all such as shall comfort, aid or praise" those who are put to death. Later, however, the plan backfired when the burnings began to turn into good propaganda for the other side, compelling Mary to rescind her order and to limit the public's attendance by scheduling executions early in the morning.[20]

Informers and Their Patrons

Working in the spaces between public and private, or between high and low, were individuals who offered themselves up either on a freelance or a quasi-officially sponsored level as informers, or conduits of information useful to the authorities in targeting religious as well as political or economic troublemakers. England's legal history had for some time accommodated or encouraged such individuals to come forward: in legislation, the word "informer" first appeared briefly and imprecisely in the *Articuli super Cartus* during the reigns of Edward I and Edward II, with information in the form of querelae—or written complaints about local administrations—becoming something of a fixture beginning in the late thirteenth century.[21] In a parallel development, the rise of the grand jury also came into effect around the same time, when witnesses (including informers) could come anonymously forward to state their knowledge of violations of the law, after which they and the jurors were sworn to secrecy on the testimony and deliberations presented.

Ideally, the grand jury functioned as the sieve through which private gossip or false and malicious charges were determined to be worthy of a summary judgment or public trial. This was no small matter, for slanderous accusations—that a certain person was a heretic or an Anabaptist, for example—prevailed across the century, and were part of a much larger context where cases of defamation overwhelmed and spilled over from the church courts and constituted an ever-present tension in society and social relations.[22] Grand jurors were also expected to supplement neighbors' complaints by doing some informing of their own, to act as "the eyes of [the] country to spy out and bring [offenders] to their deserved punishment."[23] Like other local officials, however, grand jurors could often be torn between local loyalties and loyalty to the overarching law, which led to their frequent lapses into unreliability or passivity; the fact that the social standing of grand jurors was often lower than those they had to charge made their responsibilities all the more difficult to fulfill.[24]

It was the sixteenth century with its numerous enactment of penal laws, however, that gave an injection of life into the role of the informer. The years from 1550 to the first decades of the next century, from Edward's through Elizabeth's reigns, would become the most active period for professional informers, who worked primarily in the economic realm and through the Court of the Exchequer.[25] Marketing, customs, and foreign trade offenses constituted the vast majority of cases, with religious offenses adding up to less than 5 percent of the total—a figure which is unsurprising, since economic matters were more lucrative for informers whose income was not always very good or consistent.[26] The revenue they received derived from the fines paid by the offenders who were reported, with part of the money reverting to the crown. Eventually, however, Henry and later Elizabeth would give up their share and direct it instead to worthy local causes or charities, while part of the spoils also extended to mayors, local justices, or in Elizabeth's time, churchwardens, perhaps to ensure the penal laws' passage through an often reluctant parliament.[27]

Despite protections theoretically guaranteed by the grand jury and other judicial mechanisms, it had become almost a given by the late Middle Ages, even though potential abuses were acknowledged, that an individual could be brought to trial without benefit of a formal jury presentment or indictment. By the fifteenth century, political troubles compelled the crown to push through statutes that bypassed the usual indicting grand jury altogether and allowed police to arrest and proceed to trial solely on the information of private persons.[28] This would resound most famously in the 1534 trial of Thomas More, whose chief objection to the charges against him was that they were based solely on the information, or testimony, of one man, Sir Richard Rich.[29]

But at least More had the benefit of knowing his accuser, which was more than many religious dissidents experienced. Not surprisingly, the secrecy and anonymity inherent in the act of informing led to abuses, such as blackmail or false information, which the criminal code had sought to take into further consideration by making accusers answer for their charges in public. One of the more important pieces of legislation, Statute 25, Henry VIII, c. 14, enacted in 1534,[30] thus ordered that no individual was to be arraigned for heresy except on the presentment of twelve men before commissioners of oyer and terminer and justices of the peace.[31] The statute was a revision of the seminal fifteenth-century anti-heresy law known as *De haeretico comburendo,* which had empowered bishops to arrest heretical suspects on the basis of fame alone, even if it was, as mentioned, based on one person's testimony or suspicion.[32] Still, even after the law's passage, abuses existed and questions arose, such as whether priests had a duty to inform on those who confessed to them (the answer was yes),[33] or the extent to which problematic informers with questionable or criminal backgrounds should be given credibility at all.

While legal mechanisms encouraged individuals to come forward, the chief means by which to cultivate such men was through patronage— a fact which was recognized by nearly all who held positions of power at some point in the sixteenth century. The cultivators of information often belonged to the upper ranks of the government and the church: Thomas Cromwell, for example, was a particularly effective recipient, and patron, of information gathered from individuals who personally reported to him on the effects of Henry's religious and political policies. There even seems to have been some amount of competition among informers to distinguish themselves before Cromwell as the conveyers of the best and most well-intended reports. For example, according to the correspondent William Marshall in a letter to Cromwell, "now some dare not tell [you] the truth, and others use deceitful flattery, and indeed many things go amiss." But Marshall assured Cromwell that he himself spoke with "good intent" when he reported on the "rabblement of seditious preachers" at Paul's Cross.[34]

During the same period of Henry's reign, Thomas Cranmer was also the recipient of information through his connection to Henry Tourney, a member of the Calais garrison and a committed Evangelical who found himself in conflict with the more conservative Lord Lisle, who dominated the province. When Lisle—who imposed on the region what Cranmer referred to as "hypocrisy, false faith, and blindness of God and his Word"—proceeded to dismiss Tourney, Cranmer (and Cromwell) came to his rescue, demanding that Tourney be reinstated, which Lisle reluctantly agreed to do. While Cranmer was thus concerned with preserving some kind of Evangelical presence in a place of "such ignorance and blindness," it certainly helped that Tourney was and continued to be an informer of good standing.[35]

The most effective and sophisticated cultivator or recipient of informants in the entire century, however, was Francis Walsingham. Himself a Protestant in his private convictions, Walsingham had an appetite for information that was voracious, and which only increased later in Elizabeth's reign, when priests began arriving more frequently from the Continent and Catholics were generally growing bolder toward the state.[36] To counter this threat, Walsingham decided to change tactics from the relatively lax policy that had been in place and increase the amount of the information he received from a variety of sources. Since much of the problem originated with English Catholics from the Continent, Walsingham used his overseas connections to extract information out of everyone, from ambassadors to semi-secret agents to members of the exile community, who chose to turn on others. In addition, Walsingham was known to install his agents, disguised as students or servants, in overseas seminaries, which allowed him to gather information on the priests before they embarked to England.[37] If those priests did manage to reach the shores of England, Walsingham then posted informers and spies at ports and key coastal localities to uncover their comings and goings, in addition to charging those informers with reporting on any suspicious economic activity.[38]

The better sort of informer for Walsingham—and one who was put to increasing use within England after 1581—was the infiltrator who was able to gain access to groups of Catholics and report in with a steady stream of damaging information. One figure, Robert Bernard, had already been in touch with Walsingham when he drafted the following letter, offering up his services once more while also emphasizing his need for money:

> I must humbly beseech you consider of me . . . I owe my host in
> London above 4 pounds who threatens to have me in prison for the

same . . . I beseech you to give me order whereby I may, with less trouble to your Honour, receive monthly that which it may seem good to you to bestow upon me. I was never in better credit with the papists, nor of so great acquaintance among them, for I have attained the means to have access to all the prisons in London, the Tower only excepted, whereby there is nothing that shall come over or go over, nor anything be done here within the country but I am assured to hear thereof.[39]

Bernard's information was valuable, as he went on to report the activities of the Earl of Westmoreland in Rome, or the departure from the Continent to England of yet more seminary priests.[40] In general, however, Bernard only held a short-term correspondence with Walsingham and vanished, after a year's worth of reports, from the records. This seems to have been typical, since men who carried out tasks of infiltration always fell into the danger of being suspected sooner or later by others; moreover, Walsingham's inherent lack of trust in men also compelled him to keep these individuals, already questionable by their nature, at a distance. An exception was the notorious Nicholas Berden (whose real name was Thomas Rogers), who served Walsingham for five years and proceeded to cause more damage to the Catholic recusant community than any other informer. Originally employed by the prominent Catholic George Gilbert, Berden at some point was enlisted into Walsingham's service while in Rome, where he was eventually imprisoned for a time (when Catholics discovered his real loyalty). Upon release in 1584, Berden returned to England and presented a letter to one of Walsingham's secretaries. "I profess myself a spy," he wrote, "but am not one for gain but to serve my country." Walsingham re-enlisted him immediately.

Berden proceeded over the following years to use his access to Catholic contacts and report, primarily from London, who was associating with whom, which priest was hiding where, and by what channel Catholic books were being brought into England. He was able to do this by insinuating himself into the recusant community, and gaining the trust of priests by, among other things, convincing them that he knew Walsingham well, and could thus ensure the release of Catholic prisoners from time to time.[41] In one case, Berden wrote Walsingham,

I thank you for sparing [the prisoner] Christopher Dryland's life at the last sessions at my request. It has much increased my credit among the papists that by my endeavor his life was saved, for they suppose that some friend at my request moved your Honour therein. I protest I abhor the man in regard to his profession, but he has a great opinion of me, thinking me very apt to serve the papists' turns, and, moreover, [he is] a man of great credit among them of all factions, and so a meet man to be sent over, thereby to avow and maintain my credit to all practitioners.[42]

Berden's years of productivity in serving Walsingham and betraying Catholics seem to have come to a happy conclusion, when he finally expressed his wish to stop informing—he was always falling under suspicion anyway—and "enter a more public course of life." Walsingham assented, and Berden was granted his request, which was an appointment in the household of the Earl of Leicester as "Purveyor of the Poultry."[43]

An especially fertile location to install spies was an enclosed environment such as a monastery, conventicle, or a household, where informers like Berden could blend in with the community and gain the trust of others.[44] In the early 1530s, before their dissolution, virtually all monasteries had at least one individual overseeing various situations, reporting to Cromwell of any mutterings against the king or of continued, active loyalties to Rome. Sometimes these informers simply came forward and offered their services, as was the case with the monk William Fordam, who wrote in 1535 that he had heard that "Cromwell has spoken good words of him," and thus offered "to be wholly at his service."[45] Other informers, such as Jasper Fyloll, were specifically appointed by Cromwell, in this case to the London Charterhouse, residence of the Carthusians, to report on activities and sentiments within.[46] The Carthusians were also reported on by Cromwell's man Thomas Bedyll, who wrote in 1535 of his distributing reform-oriented books which, among other things, argued "against the primacy of the bishop of Rome, and also of [Saint] Peter, declaring evidently the equalitie of the apostelles by the law of God." Rather than convert to the reformed cause, however, the monks remained unmoved, and three weeks later, partly as a result of Bedyll's information, three were committed to the Marshalsea, a prison in the borough of Southwark.[47]

Obviously, no informers in a monastery, or any other closed community, wanted their identity as informers disclosed, which led many correspondents to express their trust that Cromwell would keep their names anonymous. For those others whose identity was revealed, their fate was, unsurprisingly, not a happy one. In a 1536 letter to Cromwell, Roger Neckham, a Worcester monk, complained that his master, Richard Chylde, "bated" him, "the worse because I was your minister." Moreover, Neckham continued,

> I have endured great displeasure. I have ridden to courts to quiet our tenants. I have declared to them the preeminence of our Prince, and how he studies the quietness of his subjects, so that they all exclaim, "God save our Prince! We will be faithful to him in word and deed, body and goods." I intend henceforward to leave Martha's part, and to follow Mary's, relying on you alone. My prosperity rests upon you, for I know the severity of our master.[48]

Prisons were also good places to cultivate informers, especially among inmates who wished to escape their fate and secure their release. There was nothing new about this, but it was especially beneficial that sixteenth-century prisons were permeable spaces, with much interaction, and thus information to glean, among the population. In one case from 1537, a desperate monk from Lentune Abbey named Hamlyt Penkeryche found himself imprisoned in the Fleet, where he expressed a desire "to come before Cromwell to show of slanderous words spoken" about the king, queen, and Cromwell; the brief note ended with the words, "Begs to be examined." Informers could also volunteer to enter prison in return for compensation, as one anonymous person did late in the century, posing as a fellow sufferer among the Catholic prisoners in the jail at Exeter.[49] Another informer who had prearranged his incarceration was the Walsingham spy Walter Williams, who in 1582 entered prison under the pretense of being a Catholic. Williams was candid in writing to Walsingham that "I shall want money to bring me up, for my prison fellow wants money and I pay as well for him as myself." Moreover, while it could not have been easy to languish in such a place—"I have been a long time upon bare ground in my clothes and at night lodged among thieves and [rogues] in a place not fit for men but dogs," he wrote—apparently he did not make much effort in his duties and was not a wholehearted success. According to a later letter, written sarcastically by the fellow prison "papist" on whom he was supposed to spy, Williams "prayeth little, unless it be somewhat before dinner that God may give him a good appetite to the same."[50]

In the previous reign, of Mary, a particularly well-known prison spy who showed up the advantages as well as the weaknesses of the system was Nicholas Grimbald, who was incarcerated in Oxford's Bocardo Prison for his Protestant leanings before he eventually recanted under interrogation and revealed everything he knew, especially about the Protestant bishop and fellow prisoner, Nicholas Ridley. Grimbald's betrayals and new embrace of popery were kept secret, however, from the others, who nevertheless suspected that some spy was in their midst.[51] Still, Ridley continued to side with Grimbald,[52] not knowing that Grimbald was turning his prison writings over to the authorities all the while. Eventually, the intended recipient of those writings, Ridley's brother-in-law, George Shipside, was arrested as well and imprisoned in solitary confinement, but still Ridley refused to believe that any treachery had taken place. "It will not sink into my head," he continued, "to think that Grimbald would ever play me such a Judas's part." In May of 1555, Grimbald, however, was removed from Bocardo, sent to Marshalsea prison in London, and then released. "I have heard that Master Grimbald hath gotten his liberty," Ridley wrote John Bradford, and later added, in another letter, that "[Grimbald] escaped not without some becking and bowing (alas) of his knee unto Baal." [53]

Though he was praised by the Protestant polemicist John Bale, whose absence from England at this time probably made him ignorant of the situation, Grimbald apparently had long enjoyed a reputation for being something of a self-server. According to one anonymously penned poem:

> You have praised few, but many have you branded with infamy,
> That you may gain brief praise, O Grimald.
> Those whom you have just blamed you now praise, O deceiver!
> That you may gain brief praise, O Grimald.[54]

Certainly Grimbald had a past. In 1549, as a thirty-year-old lecturer at Christ Church College at Oxford and an ardent Protestant, he had written a letter to William Cecil, then serving as Master of the Court of Requests under the Duke of Somerset, asking him for better living accommodations. Cecil seems to have answered the young man's peti-tion, with some benefits attached, because Grimbald's next letter ex-claimed with gratitude that "you brought it about that when quiet for my studies was not to be had, I could be placed in a situation not only most desirable, but most advantageous for my literary progress—a thing on which I congratulate myself exceedingly!" Therefore, Grimbald added, "I shall not only show that I am mindful of this great kindness of yours . . . and grateful to such a patron as you, in short devoted to you, but I pledge and promise besides that I will be most eager for learning, most studious of holy things, most bitter against the Papacy, most un-wearied in displaying my talent, most ready to extend and adorn the Christian state." Grimbald then wrote, almost as an afterthought, that "As you asked on my departure, I have collected the names of those who have not yet rejected the evil conceptions acquired on religious matters, and I have made them into a list, which I am sending you along with this letter." Apparently no love was lost for those he informed on, who he described as the "drones," the "idle, the negligent, the pastors in name only"; indeed, Grimbald spent more time attacking their characters than he did specifying any kind of religious views they actually held.[55]

During Edward's reign, Grimbald had faced the bishops in St. Paul's with the words: "Much better it is to be deprived of life for God's sake than to be deprived of God himself for the sake of life." Yet only a few years later, Grimbald, after his betrayals, paid Laurence Saunders a visit, the night before Saunders was to be burned in Coventry. During their time together, Saunders took a drinking vessel and asked if Grimbald would pledge to take a drink from the cup of martyrdom, but Grimbald equivocated—"shrugging and shrinking," in Foxe's words—claiming that he would drink to Saunders's health. "But of that other which you mean," he said, "I will not promise you." "Well," a resigned Saunders replied, "my dear Lord Jesus hath [partaken] of a more bitter cup than mine shall be."[56]

Informers such as Grimbald resided in the nether regions of decent social convention, propelled as they were by treachery and mercenary desires; not surprisingly, they earned a reputation, in one contemporary's words, as working "partleye for theire owne singular gayne, parteleye for malice, corrupcion, and other devilisshe affection."[57] The individuals who belonged to the world of more serious informing were not nec-essarily common ruffians, however, but were members of the court, servants of the privy council, bishops' officers, monks, provincial notables, or, in William Holt's case, a foreman to the king's tailor and an informer of good standing who betrayed the Lutheran Andrew Hewet in the 1530s and handed over John Frith's writings directly to Thomas More.[58] Of course, "singular gayne" and "corrupcion" functioned at these levels too, as those in the highest reaches of government could turn to a kind of casual informing when it suited them. Thomas Cranmer, for example, knew the value of good and reputation-boosting information when, in the 1530s, he provided Henry with news of sensitive matters wherever they arose, thereby ensuring that he remained in the king's good graces; in one case from 1534, the archbishop reported to the king that Richard Benger of Kent, a member of the clergy and also, as it happened, a longstanding enemy of Cranmer's, was speaking seditious words—a charge that led Benger down a path toward condemnation (in a trial presided over by Cranmer).[59]

In this case, informing was motivated at least partially by opportunism or vindictiveness, but in other instances a genuine religiosity could play a role, transforming the act of informing into a heartfelt gesture of atonement, as if turning in those who continued in sin constituted nothing less than a step toward one's own redemption. What to one person constituted sheer skulduggery could thus, by the same token, be seen by another as a good and public-spirited act of turning over those who deserved punishment. In Elizabeth's reign, for example, Henry Lok was considered, by the Catholics he informed upon, a disreputable scoundrel, and one who had no compunction in appealing to Robert Cecil for "employment, however mean"; at the same time, however, Lok was known by others as a godly subject and even earned some fame as a writer of Puritan hymns.[60]

Whether they were impelled by religion or not, some of the more dangerous informers were those who had once been members of troublesome groups and intimate with their workings, but who now turned away from their cohorts, out of disgruntlement or pressure. It is important to point out that many individuals who were members of dissident groups were probably not willing to name names or betray their coreligionists. A somewhat typical case was that of the Catholic Anthony Brown, who in 1538 was asked by local Norfolk worthies to name his friends and associates; Brown, however, held to his own council, even under the threat of torture, though he did agree to personally deny the papal supremacy without affirming the king's supremacy, before finally retreating to his hermitage.[61] The government, acknowledging this resistance, thus sought to use legal force in compelling ordinary individuals to name others, especially when they themselves had abjured. Such was the case in the Coventry and Lichfield heresy trials in 1511, when abjurers were expected, by a clause in their confessions, to identify heretical associates; according to the generic statement that was to be read:

> ... I utterly forsake, renounce and abjure and swear upon this book that after this hour I shall never openly nor privately hold, declare or teach heresy errors, nor any manner of the doctrine against the faith ... Furthermore, I swear that if I may know any person or persons, men or women, suspect[ed] of errors or heresies ... or any private conventicles contrary to the common doctrine of the holy church I shall denounce them to you the aforesaid reverend father, your successors or officers or to their ordinaries as soon as I goodly, so help me God.[62]

For those more willing to betray their coreligionists, personal grudge could play a role, as when in the 1530s Thomas Salter caused trouble for the Carthusian leader John Houghton after he had been punished by the monks for rebelling and running away. In revenge, Salter sent a series of letters to Cromwell naming the monks in his midst who proved especially obstinate.[63] At Greenwich in 1532, one of the more notorious of Cromwell's monastery-informers was Richard Lyst, who began to target his superior, Friar Forest, and charge him with a variety of misdeeds, including murder. Eventually Forest—who above all secretly refused to declare the king supreme head of the Church of England—was in fact transferred and placed under supervision, which eventually led to more problems that ended, finally, in his burning at Smithfield.[64]

When legal tactics failed to bring coreligionists to betray their fellows, a less subtle pressure was applied. Toward the end of the century, Anne Bellamy proceeded while in prison, as a result of pressure from Richard Topcliffe, "to accuse her own father, mother, and other friends and relatives, twenty-six persons in all"—including Robert Southwell.[65] Probably the most damaging case of naming names, however, occurred with the London preacher and evangelist Edward Crome, who in the 1540s turned in friends and colleagues who had shared the same

Evangelical temperament as he.[66] After running into trouble with the authorities for preaching in 1546 at Mercers' Chapel in London, Crome was brought before the council for a first and then a second time, before finally agreeing to recant.[67] "I do . . . now most humbly submit myself to the king's majesty's merciful clemency being most sorry for my said offence," he declared, and then added that he would proceed to help the authorities "in the disclosing and opening of all things."[68]

Crome proceeded to name all his coreligionists, which set in motion one of the century's most dramatic episodes of religious persecution. Over the following weeks, more than twenty individuals were directly brought before the authorities and interrogated and imprisoned, while sixty fled to the Continent—all casualties of Crome's actions. Most of them he had considered good friends and allies: Hugh Latimer, who once occupied the bishopric at Worcester but resigned in the face of the conservative Act of Six Articles, had once advised Crome not to recant, but now—thanks to Crome—faced his interrogators as they attempted to glean information and "fish out the bottom of his stomach";[69] John Lascalles, who was described as a gentleman at court and would eventually die at the stake, was also named by his friend Crome, as was the physician William Hewisk, the St. Bride's vicar John Taylor (or Cardmaker), and the former Bishop of Salisbury, Nicholas Shaxton. Perhaps the most damaging of Crome's disclosures resulted in the arrest of the Lincolnshire gentleman John Kyme and his wife Anne—better known by her maiden name, Askew. Although Askew had been under suspicion for a while, the naming of her by Crome represented a real treasure catch for officials, associated as she had been with various noblewomen and Catherine Parr herself; her capture would precipitate events that would lead to her brutal torture and death.[70]

Aside from the ambiguities of the Crome case—many of his coreligionists would forgive and justify his actions—perceptions of the informer ultimately depended on the cause for which he was working. Hugh Latimer, for example, had no problem with informers when they worked in tandem with Edward's Protestant government, which he loyally served as bishop. "For God's sake make new promoters [informers]!" he declared in a 1550 sermon. "There lack promoters such as were in King Henry the Seventh's days . . . to promote transgressors, as rent-raisers, oppressors of the poor, extortioners, bribers, usurers."[71] In 1552 the privy council, partly as a result, even took steps—though the plan ultimately went nowhere—to create a so-called "Committee of Ten," which would sponsor the work of informers and then report its progress at the end of every law term.[72]

Despite the informers prevalent at court, in monasteries or prisons, or in port towns, it is an overstatement to imply that spies and disgruntled coreligionists roamed the land—though Walsingham and others would have liked to project that impression. Many informers were not even very helpful, and could in fact be hindrances or nuisances. In Mary's time, for example, Stephen Gardiner was approached by Edward Alabaster, who brought with him the fugitive married priest Thomas Whittle in hopes of a reward; but Alabaster, in Foxe's words, was "highly checked and rated of the bishop, [who asked] if there were no man unto whom he might bring such rascals but to him: 'Hence,' quoth he, 'out of my sight, thou varlet! What dost thou trouble me with such matters.'"[73]

Naming Names: Neighbors and Families

For all the attempts to exert control through mid-level officials or informers, the government relied above all on ordinary men and women to come forward and reveal the heretic or secret agitator in their midst—even if the individual in question was a close neighbor or family member. As Cynthia Herrup has written, it was the "private individual [who] was the most important law-enforcing officer in the community," as "[p]ublic obligation intruded on private life repeatedly."[74] This was not new to the sixteenth century: in both religious and political matters, the responsibility of individuals to report offenses, or to take part in the collective law-enforcement action known as the hue and cry,[75] had for centuries been deeply embedded into the law and English consciousness; indeed, in the case of treason it was considered equally traitorous not to report comments, no matter how casually overheard.[76]

The government's encouragement to the community that it accuse and turn over one of its own was met, however, by a public willingness that waxed and waned in accordance with social conditions at any particular time.[77] Sometimes the impulse to point fingers overreached even that of the government, especially when political or economic tensions coincided with the stigmatization and suspicion of particular groups. While the subject of the witch-hunts is outside the scope of this book,[78] the increasing prevalence of such accusations (and trials) during the reign of Elizabeth can be considered in this context. Similarly, the threat of Spain and specifically the Armada of 1588 brought about an increasing suspicion in the land and an anti-Spanish nationalism that associated Catholics, especially Catholic priests and Jesuits, with treason and made them particular targets for a public more willing to volunteer their suspicions to authorities.[79]

Perhaps the strongest motivation in coming forward was not religious fervor or proto-patriotism but rather a desire on the part of the community to maintain cohesion by reporting on problematic and threatening elements in its midst.[80] One must keep in mind that the majority of English men and women probably resided either neutrally or confusedly between the extreme poles of Protestant and Catholic, and thus were less concerned with the specifics of another's religion than with the problem of keeping the peace in a disordered world. In 1558, for example, the widow Alice Warner of Ratliffe testified that a suspicious group of "Frenchmen" and "Dutchmen" had entered her King's Head tavern, where they ordered a roasted pig, beer, and a fire, referred to each other as "brother," and then requested that they have access to the room "at their pleasure," presumably to share in Bible-reading. Warner came forward to inform of her own accord, though she may have been compelled to do so by another informer, a tailor named William Ellerby, who testified earlier that he knew as a fact that thirty or so men and women, including the Protestant John Rough, assembled at her tavern.[81] Religion in this case certainly played a part, in the sense that no one wanted to be known as a host to illegal conventicles, but it was not conventicles so much as their illegality and their potential to attract disorder (and a bad reputation) that perhaps most concerned proprietors such as Warner.

Neighbors also had little hesitation in coming forward as a stern collective to hinder a difficult presence in their midst, especially if the individual seemed to court trouble with provocative behavior. When, in his own words, Edward Underhill attempted to remove a pyx from the altar, "women conspired against me," to the point where murder of the hot gospeller was on many of their minds.[82] In many if not most cases, to be known as a heretic was to almost invite ill-treatment, not only because of the perception of difference, but also because one was marked as a potential disrupter of community norms. When a husband and wife from Kington, in Herefordshire, both reported to be "earneste and zeal-ous embraser[s] of Goddes worde"—or Evangelicals—lost most of their cattle in 1535, for example, their neighbors "seemed to rejoyse at their losse and decaye," since the heretics who had "forsaken . . . their cath-lick fayth" had asked for it.[83] In 1531, Richard Hilles was also shunned by his neighbors and churchwardens when he refused to contribute candles before the images; eventually, he became so beleaguered that he finally left the country altogether.[84] Apparently, the mistake Hilles made in refusing to make contributions, such as candles, could be a point of contention among the community: in 1531, for example, Grace Palmer also would not contribute candles—a refusal which was only inflamed by her statement to others not to make pilgrimages to images, "for there you shall find but a piece of timber painted." Eventually, the neighbors turned her in.[85]

Enclosed communities, particularly colleges or clerical milieus, could be subject to pressure from the collective to expel difficult individuals and maintain conformity, as was the case in 1543, when Robert Testwood entered Windsor College and almost immediately began to alienate the dean and canons with his loud and assertive Lutheranism. After offend-ing a priest over dinner by challenging the pope's authority, Testwood was rendered an outcast by other clerics, who shunned and spat at him in passing. Testwood, however, only worsened his case when he began to confront pilgrims who had come to "kiss [the] spur and have an old hat set upon their heads" at the shrine of "Henry of Windsor." Admon-ishing them "for running a whoring to such stocks and stones," he then moved on to confront others who were "licking and kissing a white lady made of alabaster" located behind the high altar. Watching how they stroked the image and then their faces—"as if there had been great virtue in touching the picture"—he proceeded to take a key in his pos-session and with it cut off the statue's nose, declaring, "Lo! good people, you see what it is; nothing but earth and dust." This action especially offended the canons and others in the community, one of whom drew his dagger at Testwood, which forced Testwood to eventually enlist a kind of armed guard to protect himself as he went about the school. Soon after, however, he was at it again when he joked that a fellow min-ister could take various relics, including Henry of Windsor's spurs and hat, and ride off on a horse, "Whereat the others changed colour, and wist not what to say." Eventually Testwood was turned over.[86]

Acts of betrayal and informing could also arise within households, though sometimes family members were given no choice and were forced into informing upon or assisting in the apprehension of their own. Thus, in Essex during the reign of Mary, the father of nineteen-year-old William Hunter was told by the authorities that he had to find his fugitive heretic son or never show his face again; the father complied and two days later turned over his son.[87] Religious difference, however, could also divide families, leading to rejection and expulsion, if not always informing or betrayal. When the Protestant Julius Palmer found himself on the run and needing support during Mary's reign, for example, he returned to his mother, who called him a heretic and exclaimed that "Thou shalt have Christ's curse and mine, wheresoever thou go," and then ordered him "to depart from my house, and out of my sight, and never take me more for thy mother hereafter."[88]

Other family members were compelled by more fiscal desires to deliver their relatives over to the authorities. One Alice Johnson, the unrelated aunt by marriage of twelve-year-old John Davis, had, by 1546, developed a "deadly hate" toward the child, based on the inheritance he would one day receive from his father. Knowing that the boy's secret inclination of reading the New Testament was now forbidden in the conservative aftermath of the Six Articles' passage, Alice entrapped Davis with a complicated stratagem that resulted in his leaving behind written evidence of his beliefs, which led in turn to his being turned over to the bailiffs for questioning.[89]

Despite the anecdotal evidence of family tensions and informing, the cases of husbands turning in wives or parents handing over children are rare. The more common reaction on the part of a family, if a member had strayed from the family's religion, would have been to talk to and even threaten the individual with the implications of what his actions would mean not only for himself, but for the family, while the most extreme response would have been that of Julius Palmer's mother, with her curses and ultimately her banishment of Julius from the family home. Concerns for maintaining peace or adhering to the crown's policies were strong, but not so strong as to override loyalty to family by turning relatives over; to do so would only bring more trouble down on the family and taint it in the eyes of the community. While sixteenth-century England thus remained a country where people defined themselves as subjects of the crown, such allegiance did not necessarily extinguish connections to one's own family, parish, and community, all of which could conflict with the crown in deep ways.

Seizure and Arrest

This community reluctance was especially clear when it came to the actual apprehension or capture of dissidents—many of whom enjoyed a large following in the community and continued as a result to circulate and elude capture. Part of the problem was that the seizure and arrest of such individuals was a haphazard and often dreaded task, involving large numbers of men, lay and official, who needed to be organized to chase down an elusive prey, confront the suspect—who could be a neighbor—and generally summon up an actively persecutory state of mind when the will may not have been there.[90] But community reluctance to get out in force in support of the authorities was not limited to religious matters alone, as not all members of a community, or neighboring communities, were willing to cooperate when they had nothing personally to gain by capturing an offender, no matter what his crime had been. In order to address this reluctance, governments held those communities responsible by making them pay for damages from an unresolved crime, as in 1584, when a statute made neighboring hundreds liable for half the damages from a crime, with money to be given over to the constables, who would in turn pay the justice of the peace. Despite the measure, the public willingness to cooperate was not necessarily ensured, and would in fact remain a problem for the authorities throughout the period.[91]

Legalities in general shrouded the process of capture, as all apprehensions were theoretically to be reinforced by a warrant, which could grant the holder unlimited powers of search and seizure. Such documentation required the authorization of justices of the peace, though the initiative to apprehend individuals, no matter how common or lowly they were, almost always came from those even higher up, primarily from the chancellor or members of the privy council. The basis for warrants, as well as measures relating to apprehensions, rested on long-held common-law theories—for example, the Anglo-Saxon notion of hamscon—that protected individuals from being subject to arbitrary searches and seizures. Edward Coke in the next century would pick up on this idea when he asserted, in a statement that would come to be accepted as sacrosanct, that the right against unnecessary invasion of the home had been unequivocally expressed in article thirty-nine of the Magna Carta.[92] Coke's argument, however, essentially resulted from a misreading of the document, which claimed no such thing.[93] Moreover, the idea of such protections, while good enough in theory, did not prevent warrants of the most generalized nature from being issued in ever-proliferating numbers from the fourteenth through the seventeenth centuries, as the power to enter homes would be extended not only to justices but to leaders of craft guilds, apprentice-masters, innkeepers, mayors, wardens, and any others who were chosen as deputies.[94]

Authorities, for that matter, did not necessarily need a warrant in the first place to make an arrest or conduct a search, especially when they assumed that as officers of the crown they possessed inherent rights and discretionary powers based on their commissions.[95] During the time of Mary, for example, Richard Woodman's own experience in Edmund Bonner's coalhouse had come as a result of his acquiescing to a warrantless justice—an act he was determined would not happen again, when he demanded the next time to see a document from the bailiffs. This sense of their own overriding privileges also led officials to engage in deceptive practices when it came time for capture. In one episode involving William Paget, a high member of Mary's council and the lord privy seal, a visit to Europe for ostensible health reasons really masked an attempt to look out for and capture the Duchess of Suffolk and her husband. The attempt failed, though Paget may have been responsible instead for the overseas apprehension of John Checke. In another case indirectly involving Paget, a man appeared at the London house of cook (and Protestant) George Tankerfield and claimed that as Paget's personal messenger, he wished for Tankerfield to prepare a banquet for the great man. Tankerfield was out walking in the fields, so his wife, eager to bring in some money, ran to tell him, though he immediately spotted the ruse and said, "A banquet, woman! Indeed it is such a banquet as will not be very pleasant to the flesh; but God's will be done." Returning home, Tankerfield recognized the messenger as the yeoman of the guard, who then took him in custody, leaving the wife behind with her spits and her brickbats. [96]

The options for a man such as Tankerfield to take flight became in some ways more limited over the course of the sixteenth century. One of Henry's first acts upon his break with Rome, for example, was the exemption of traitors from seeking sanctuary in churches; later, from 1534 through 1540, an increasing though carefully limited number of felonious acts would also be taken off the list of protections, as monasteries—which also had served as sanctuaries—were abolished altogether.[97] Though the issue of sanctuary was not entirely resolved until the next century, the idea of a church—whatever that "church" now was—offering sanctuary to its own religious rebels, even if those rebels were clothed in the nomenclature of "traitor," made no sense anyway, and was rendered moot by the instabilities of the age. Equally significant for the fugitive was the increasing proliferation of inns and taverns over the course of the century, though these possible refuges also carried their dangers, as an itinerant Julius Palmer found out in 1556, when he arrived at the Cardinal's Hat in Reading, only to provoke suspicion among other patrons and eventually the attention of officers bearing lanterns and warrants, who stormed in and committed him to ward.[98]

The increasing control over the land represented by the enclosure movement also limited the options of religious fugitives, though advantage could be taken of the inaccessible and desolate north, or—in the case of hedge preachers—the woods. Toward the end of the century, the rise of vagrancy and migrations to London compelled more people to take to the roads, which could be advantageous to the heretic who wished to hide himself in a crowd, even though the unpaved roads could become difficult to traverse; highwaymen, too, could appear at any time, to take advantage of the heretic's naïveté. A better means of escape existed by way of rivers, and the open shore with its many ports held obvious advantages, as was the case in 1537, when one worthy managed to get through customs on an elaborate pretense, and then sail away, yelling traitorous words about the king back to shore.[99]

On the Run

Stories of individuals eluding capture abound over the course of the century. The Protestant George Eagles was one of the more famous fugitives, and the target of proclamations that were issued across Essex, Suffolk, Norfolk, and Kent calling for his capture; after much hiding "in privy closets and barns, in holes and thickets, in fields and woods,"

Eagles was finally discovered by a reward-hungry pursuer and taken to prison in Colchester.[100] Equally notorious were Edmund Campion and Robert Persons, who were startled to find posters seeking their apprehension when they surreptitiously arrived in England in 1581; though capture did eventually come, the period of elusiveness beforehand would constitute a great frustration for the authorities.[101]

A more enduring and illuminating (if extreme) example of elusiveness occurred in the case of the Protestant preacher Thomas Rose, whose following grew over the course of the 1520s and 1530s to the point that when his apprehension was sought for encouraging iconoclasm and rood-burning, officials had difficulty summoning enough men to help in the job. When Rose finally was taken into custody, his coreligionists then attempted to free him from the commissary by force, until they were persuaded not to take such drastic measures. Rose then received something of a reprieve upon the consecration of Cranmer as archbishop and was free to preach again for a time, but the passage of the Act of Six Articles in 1539 ensured that he would fall into trouble once more. Tracked by injunctions from the Duke of Norfolk that whoever captured him should "hang him on the next tree," Rose proceeded to escape for a time overseas, having benefited from the aid of yet more accomplices. The death of Henry and the accession of Edward then allowed Rose to be pardoned and his preaching license restored, but six years later, Mary's accession forced him underground, where he led a secret London congregation and was helped by the great Protestant supporter, Lady Elizabeth Vane. Only a betrayal from within the congregation's ranks would lead to Rose's apprehension, along with thirty-five others, at a shearman's house in Bow-church-yard.[102]

Incompetence on the part of constables was one reason for these levels of evasion, as was the case on a summer night in 1556, when the Protestant widow Agnes Wardall outwitted a large group of men who had converged on her house, first by hiding in a cupboard and then running out into the dark fields, crawling through nettles, and hiding in a ditch. Throughout the ordeal, her pursuers continued to search, often coming close to where she hid, only to move on, inexplicably; in the end, she was saved by a sympathetic passerby, who sent her a secret signal to lay quiet and wait until the men moved on, thus delivering her, in Foxe's words, "by the might and power of God," from their cruelties and "malignant devices."[103]

Wardall was aided by the cover of darkness, yet many searches and seizures continued to be conducted at night because of the element of surprise they carried. In one of Thomas Garret's apprehensions during the reign of Mary, the catch did not take place until after midnight, when authorities seized the fugitive from his own bed.[104] Thirty years later, in 1594, the hunted priest John Gerard was also subject to a midnight raid. "I had just fallen asleep," he wrote, "when John [his companion] and I were woken up together by the sudden uproar outside." Gerard continues:

> . . . There were sharp raps on the door—it was clear the men intended to break it down if we did not open quickly. There was no escape. That door was the only way out of the room and the men were barring it, so I told John to get up and open to them. The next moment men 'armed with swords and staves' burst in and filled the room, while many more stood outside, unable to get in. . . . They ordered me to get up and dress, which I did. Everything I possessed was examined but they found nothing that could compromise my friends. Then they took me off in custody with my companion: but God blessed us, for neither of us was addressed or showed any fear.[105]

Night ostensibly allowed authorities to work with a minimum of interference from potentially volatile or protesting crowds. In the case of Robert Samuel, during Mary's reign, officials "came immediately flocking about his house, and beset it with a great company, and so took him in the night season, because they durst not do it in the daytime, for fear of trouble and turmoil." Part of this may have pointed to the increasing unpopularity of Mary's policies, as well as the potential of a community to protect its own; as with directives that enjoined officials to burn heretics only early in the morning, before crowds had gathered, night apprehensions suggest the same concern on the part of authorities to seize their targets with the least amount of trouble from sympathetic followers. [106]

The problem of neighbors harboring fugitives, however, continued long after Mary's rule had ended, even when the enemy was now Catholic, and plots against the queen compelled Elizabeth and her parliament to step up persecutory efforts. According to a statute from 1585, all Jesuits and seminary priests were to leave the realm within forty days or face death as traitors; individuals who received and comforted them were to be adjudged felons "without benefit of clergy, and suffer death, lose and forfeit as in case of one attainted of felony." Those who failed to report such fugitives to the justices would be fined and imprisoned, while justices who neglected to pass on the information they received would have to "forfeit the sum of two hundred marks."[107] The measure had some deterrent effect on individuals such as Lady Arundel, though others, such as Lord Vaux, simply decided to transfer priests to "inns or suchlike places." Indeed, enough families continued to sponsor the activities of live-in chaplains, for example, that commentators such as Robert Southwell would write, in 1588, that "people up to now who would not even speak to a priest, much less admit one to the house, do not only receive us but press us to come and stay with them."[108]

Despite strict injunctions against aiding or harboring fugitives, the interior of homes also contained secret hiding places where the pursued, with the help of others, could elude their captors. Sixteenth-century houses varied across region and from city to country, ranging from a peasant's two-room, one-floor cottage to increasingly elaborate manor houses with their separate family and servant wings and their multitude of private chambers.[109] To expand on limited spaces in more modest homes, lofts would be constructed which also doubled, if need be, as hiding places, just as closets could serve as both storage areas and surreptitious prayer rooms.[110] In the reign of Elizabeth, wealthier recusant families would benefit from the relative spaciousness of their houses, which could shelter a priest in a room sufficiently distant that he would only see his patrons when dispensing mass. In other cases, individuals could find shelter in one of the contraptions built by the Jesuit lay brother Nicholas Owen, who became renowned for his woodworking skills and his construction of at least four hundred secret alcoves within walls of thick masonry, underneath staircases, or even in converted sewage tunnels. This was not easy, since it was especially difficult for a priest to find concealment, as he carried with him the extra weight of vestments, chalices, and other sacramental accessories. New hiding places also had to be constructed when pursuers, for example, learned that many priests hid behind chimneys and thus could be smoked out, or that a sliding panel could be uncovered by knocking on the walls for signs of hollowness.[111]

The most extreme way in which to elude the authorities, however, was to escape to the Continent, where sympathetic foreign governments offered a conditional asylum. Officially, this was not always easy, unless, like the Jesuit William Bishop, one were simple banished from England by the authorities. The only way to legally depart the realm was to apply for a royal license, but such a document was difficult to obtain, and was closed, anyway, to religious offenders.[112] An exception was the Protestant John Checke, who was able to acquire a temporary license in 1553, probably out of family connections and a stated desire to study in Italy,[113] while another successful applicant from the same period was Richard Bertie, who was given a release when he argued before Gardiner that he had to travel overseas to collect a large sum of money owed by Charles V, the Holy Roman Emperor, to his wife, the Duchess of Suffolk.[114]

Individuals who willingly chose to flee, legally or not, risked being punished under the fourteenth-century statute of 5 Richard II, st. 1, c.2, which stated that all moveable goods would be forfeited upon their departure. To enforce these laws, commissioners were appointed to investigate the possessions of exiles, noting their findings through the visitation and presentment process. The instructions to one commission in 1556 stated:

> . . . [W]here we understande that dyverse of our subjects despisinge the catholique faithe & religion by us restored & set forth within thys our Realme have in contempt thereof & of our lawes withdrawn themselves from their severall habytacions & dwellinges and remayne abrode in places secret and unknowen where they have neither iust occasion or commandment to abyde . . . Our pleasure & commandement is . . . to make lyke inquisicion serche & examynacon . . . what gooddes & cattalls they & every of them had and were possessed of at theyre severall departures or at eny tyme sence . . . And after such Inquery serche and examenacyon so dult had & made Oure pleasure & commandement ys that all the goodes cattalls & leases of them and every of them shallbe or may come to your knowledge as aforesayde ye shall cause to be put under your sure & safe custody . . . And to make substantyall bokes & Inventoryes of all the same & every parte & parcell thereof in suche manner & forme as before is expressed & declared . . .[115]

By this proclamation, for example, the "landes, goodes and catalles" belonging to the Duchess of Suffolk were to be searched out and inventoried, according to a letter from the privy council to Sir Edward Montague and other Lincolnshire commissioners.[116] But in this case and others, land was to only be held temporarily or leased out by the trustee-government—much to the consternation of Mary, who unsuccessfully attempted to convince parliament to pass a statute permanently confiscating all such property. It was not until Elizabeth that the House of Commons would approve such a measure, which resulted in the permanent distraint of the Catholic exiles' lands.[117] Serious losses thus ensued for those who fled, especially when the chief prosecutor in the matter was the hated pursuivant Thomas Felton, who traveled with his agents up and down the realm, taking inventory, enforcing often haphazard laws, and lining his pockets along the way.[118]

Despite warnings against leaving the realm, however, some departures were quietly encouraged, at least initially.[119] Upon the accession of Mary, Protestants were considered a relatively small group of stubborn nuisances, with England better off for their absence. In one encounter from 1553, for example, Stephen Gardiner summoned the Protestant Thomas Mowntayne to his private chambers, only to find himself on the receiving end of a lecture concerning the achievements of Henry and Edward; to his credit, Gardiner continued to listen, but when Mowntayne then got down on his knees to pray aloud "that God would shortly cast down forever that shameful idol the Mass," Gardiner lost his patience and yelled, "Away with him! It is the stubbornest knave that ever I talked with."[120] It was surprising that Mowntayne had even appeared before Gardiner, since the invitation may have been a ruse to scare him out of the country before any consultation could take place. According to the Spanish ambassador Simon Renard, Gardiner once bragged of his dispatching abilities, claiming that "When he hears of any preacher or leader of the sect, he summons him to appear at his house, and the preacher, fearing he may be put in the Tower, does not appear, but on the contrary absents himself." Gardiner would then send off a warrant, timed with calculation to arrive after the offender had fled.[121]

Gardiner soon realized, however, that contrary to dissipating the heretical community, exile only strengthened it. Over the course of Mary's reign, nearly eight hundred individuals would leave for the Continent, most of them consisting of gentry and clergy who had the means to "flie the infection of the antichristian doctrine by departure out of the realm."[122] The policy of flight was in fact encouraged by leaders of the Protestant community, such as Nicholas Ridley, who quoted Christ— "When they persecute you in one city, flee unto another"—and used examples such as Paul, who "was conveyed by night [from Damascus], let down in a basket out at a window over the wall," and Helias, the prophet, who "fled the persecution of wicked Jezebel."[123] Ridley perhaps sensed that the restoration of Catholicism would tempt weaker-willed Protestants back into the fold, but he was also inherently recognizing the fragility of English Protestantism as a whole, which at that point had not yet gained a hold over the land, and which, in fact, would emerge a different, stronger entity after the trials of exile that he was encouraging.

Despite the support that an exiled community could offer, the journey was not an easy one, as the account of the aforementioned Richard Bertie and his wife, Katherine, the Duchess of Suffolk, illustrate. After obtaining his license to leave, Bertie made plans to have Katherine surreptitiously follow him in a barge, accompanied by her year-old daughter and four servants. Leaving home at dawn and dressed "like a mean merchant's wife," Katherine was almost detected by her torch-bearing herald, whom she managed to elude before launching out on her boat during a thick mist. Soon, the privy council and others in the land learned of her departure, but she eventually rendezvoused with her ship and proceeded to sail away, eventually landing in Brabant. Reunited with her husband, Katherine disguised herself "like the women of the Netherlands with hukes," and began the journey to safety. But she and her entourage suffered on foot through rain, frost, and ice; the baby wailed; inns refused to take in the group, and mistook Bertie for a lance-knight and the Duchess "his woman." Compounding matters was the fact that Bertie spoke little Dutch, and encountered no one who could speak English, Latin, French, or Italian. Eventually, however, he managed to reunite with François Perucel, a shoemaker and former leader of a French refugee church in London, who obtained permission from the magistrates for the family to settle in town. Safe for a time, the Berties found themselves having to flee again when they learned of new pursuits after them, but they were saved by a letter of invitation from sympathetic emissaries in Wessel, where they settled and proceeded to wait out the rest of Mary's days living "in great quietness and honour."[124]

The education and status of exiled Protestants were complemented by the financial assistance of sympathetic English merchants, resulting in forceful printing efforts which exploited the state of exile for propagandistic ends. In Geneva, Strasbourg, Emden, and Basel, English Protestants were especially fruitful in their efforts, under the aegis of printers such as Rowland Hall, to publish treatises, polemical pamphlets, English versions of the New Testament, and a book of Psalms; more important for the cause, however, was the publication of letters by incarcerated coreligionists back home, which were smuggled out of prison, and the efforts of exiles Edmund Grindal, John Foxe, and others to compile documents into a larger, martyrologically oriented compilation—a project that would lead to the publication of the martyr letters edited by Miles Coverdale and Henry Bull, and more essentially, Foxe's great work, the *Acts and Monuments*.[125]

Over twenty years later, the same abilities to withstand and even exploit hardship would be exhibited by the exiled Catholic community led by Robert Persons, Edmund Campion, and William Allen, who traveled to Rome, Louvain, or, more traitorously, Madrid, releasing highly influential writings and organizing missionary enterprises and seminaries, much to the consternation of the government back home.[126] Persons and his associates represented the new wave of English Catholicism after the aging of the Marian bishops and the stagnation of the traditional seignorial families; theirs was a movement that was largely shaped by foreign elements, from funding through influence in doctrinal changes, which combined with the solidarity created by exile to produce a coherent and well-connected community with its own manifestos, books of encouragement, and martyrologies.[127] While the subsequent mission to England in the 1570s and 1580s could lapse into discord, the overall skill displayed by the English exiles was not only remarkable by sixteenth-century standards, but also led to the kind of self-creation and mobilization of purpose that only a state of displacement could bring.[128]

Once the danger of more prominent exiles became clear, Tudor governments attempted to move against them in a number of ways, with extradition constituting a particular obsession. Despite the fact that England became one of the first countries to contemplate ideas of modern international law, no formal law of extradition emerged until the nineteenth century. Instead, issues involving extradition were contained in individual treaties that mentioned an obligation on the part of foreign governments to apprehend and send back an enemy who had committed political crimes against the state.[129] None of this, however, was a guarantee, as treaties could be bent if not broken by the the monarch; indeed, England was no model in this sense, harboring as it did religious (if not treasonous) fugitives from the Continent at various times, or refusing, as Elizabeth did, to grant Mary Queen of Scots' request to extradite the murderers of her confidante David Riccio, in 1567.

Those regions overseas such as Geneva or the German cities in Mary's time, or Rome, France, or Spain in Edward's and Elizabeth's, did not grant refuge for any other reason than the fact that the asylum-seekers were of like-minded religious persuasion or were useful to exploit against a common enemy. While the exiled English were thus able to enjoy a measure of jurisdictional immunity, the governments which allowed them in were just as strict and intolerant when it came to laws about treason, and therefore concerned when the English crown, knowing that governments such as Strasbourg had protocols against the harboring of traitors from another realm, attempted to emphasize the political or seditious aspects of the refugees. In 1528, for example, John Hacket reported to Wolsey that while one Harmon was the "root of great mischief" as the leader of overseas Lutherans, he could best be returned home "if the King has any action of treason against him"; moreover, all overseas Lutherans could be better punished if they were "included with traitors" and thus carried the weight of an unpardonable offense.[130]

To avoid bearing the possible weight of treason and thereby jeopardizing their stay abroad, refugees had to assert in religiously sympathetic countries that they were being victimized for their beliefs, and not any politically oriented crime.[131] In 1556, for example, John Hales protested what he suspected was an extradition warrant secretly delivered by one of Mary's commissioners to the authorities of Frankfurt; appearing before "the Consul," Hales successfully argued that the warrant had been issued for no other reason than "to vexe hym and others that for theyr refuge and concyens sake were [they] commed thyther to flye persecucion in Englande."[132] Less fortunate was John Knox, one of the more famous victims of banishment, who alarmed the authorities in his refuge city of Frankfurt by an alleged speech claiming that Charles V was worse than Nero; furthermore, his pamphlet entitled *Admonition to England* contained enough treasonous statements—including the Nero remark—to compel the German city to take action, or face the wrath of the emperor. It helped that a few of Knox's exiled coreligionists not only wanted Knox expelled, but encouraged the Frankfurt council to banish him, their ire based on disputes concerning doctrine; the result was that Knox was told to depart immediately, which he proceeded to do, accompanied for the first four miles out of the city by his saddened friends and supporters.[133]

Despite attempts to compel their fugitives' extradition through charges of treason, Tudor governments were, for the most part, unsuccessful in gaining foreign governments' acquiescence. Still, they tried, and when treason did not work, lesser charges were attempted—as in the case of the traitor Richard "Blancherose" Hosier, who sought refuge in France and was charged with murder and thievery by the English when treason alone failed. Even the intervention of Henry, who went so far as to threaten war over the issue, failed to move Francis I to release the man to English custody, and nothing came of the matter. [134] One of the few successful extraditions in the century, however, would also become one of the most notorious, when in 1535 Henry and Cromwell appealed to the authorities in Antwerp to send the exile and Bible-translator William Tyndale home, so he could stand trial on grounds of heresy and of spreading sedition. Charles V was contacted, though he refused to grant the request on the grounds that Henry had no proof or evidence to support his demand.[135] "When the Emperor . . . knows that Tyndale has committed anything by word or writing to justify doing what the King asks," Charles wrote in a letter to Henry, "he will take steps to comply with his request and the treaty"; for now, "the general opinion is that Tyndale is only persecuted for his attachment to the Queen's [Anne Boleyn's] cause, which it is thought all the best men in England favor."[136]

A breakthrough in the matter of Tyndale's extradition would only occur when Henry Phillips, a mysterious character, disgraced and impoverished back home, traveled to Antwerp under the pay of an unclear source and soon made his way into Tyndale's confidence. One night, Phillips lured Tyndale into a trap by notifying local officers and having him ultimately arrested on charges of disobeying the laws of the Low Countries. Although Antwerp itself had quietly condoned Lutheranism from the beginning, Henry Phillips's machinations at the court of Charles V—to whom he professed loyalty over his own king—ensured Tyndale's doom as Charles's mind concerning the matter of Tyndale soon changed. Over the course of the next year, Tyndale's fellow community of English merchants frantically attempted to secure their leader's freedom, for reasons having less to do with religion than with outrage over the violation of traditional diplomatic privileges granted to them over the years; in the end, however, the pleas of his friends failed to prevent the case from being bounced back and forth between the governments, until Tyndale was eventually returned to England and burned.[137]

The questionable legalities behind Tyndale's forcible return to England were moderate in comparison to tactics that could include, albeit rarely, the barely official practice of outright kidnapping. In Mary's reign, the Protestant John Checke, as mentioned, began his sojourn overseas legally enough, when he obtained a license to leave the realm and was subsequently able to travel freely through Strasbourg, Emden, and other parts, directing an anti-Marian propaganda campaign along the way—all of which marked him as a particular target back home. The moment of his capture came in 1555, when Checke, falling for a ruse of Privy Councilor William Paget's, was suddenly seized on the highway by an official of Phillips's and, in Strype's words, "blindfolded, bound, and thrown into a waggon, and so conveyed on shipboard, and brought over sea unto the Tower of London." Shortly after, he was interrogated and proceeded to recant, leading to the pathetic spectacle of his being paraded about as the most famous betrayer of his fellow heretics.[138]

The kidnapping of John Story in the time of Elizabeth was also somewhat exceptional in terms of the notoriety of its victim and the perseverance of the pursuers, yet it cannot be seen as completely outside the realm of apprehending practices in the sixteenth century. A former member of parliament and chancellor to Bishop Bonner, Story, as will be seen, was one of the most diligent persecutors in Mary's arsenal, which would make him a good catch for Elizabethans who wished to settle old scores.[139] After a series of imprisonments and releases, Story by 1565 was living in Antwerp, where he took up inquisitional activities against Protestants and served as a confidant to the Duke of Alva. It would be his subsequent employment in the Spanish Customs House—and the machinations of one William Parker—that would spell his downfall, however. Charged with preventing English books from coming into the Continent, Story was lured by three merchants, hired by Parker, to examine a ship that had docked at Bergen-op-Zoom; as Story was examining the cargo, Parker suddenly lowered the hatches and, with his catch trapped inside, proceeded to sail the ship to Yarmouth.[140] Alva would subsequently make two formal pleas for the imprisoned Story's release, on the grounds that Story was now a Spanish subject, but the duke's petitions went unheeded, as Story was tried for treason and afterwards drawn and quartered in a particularly brutal execution.

Quo Vadis?

In their attempts to seek out and capture religious troublemakers, the best that the Tudors could hope for, ultimately, was an atmosphere of vigilance conducive to acts of informing and apprehending. This was fine when the religious affiliations of the local community matched the crown's, thus ensuring a coordination between the center and the counties or regions. Religious policy, however, changed so much over the course of the century that disjunctures in loyalty were bound to occur, and the idea of coming forward seemed more problematic—and destabilizing to the community—than it was worth. Contemporaries did speak of betrayals and treacheries, as was the case in a dispatch during Elizabeth's reign from the Spanish ambassador, who wrote in 1564 that "the evil lies in universal distrust, for a father dares not trust his own son."[141] But this was something of an exaggeration, for the cases of sons actually coming forward to turn in their fathers for the crime of Catholicism were rare, even though religious tensions and divisions pervaded the sixteenth-century English family and could lead to accusations that resulted in imprisonment and even tragedy.

As a way of projecting their power beyond its actual capabilities, Tudor governments also could encourage the tactic of displaying prized catches before the public: Robert Glover, for example, was "cruelly" paraded about the streets after his apprehension,[142] while in 1553, Edward Underhill, who was initially seized by the sheriff and high constable at night, was conspicuously accompanied by two guards through London the next day.[143] The humiliating act of being captured thus served the authorities well as a public deterrent, and though some suspects may have held their heads high, especially when they viewed the spectacle as a crown-of-thorn-wearing *imitatio christi*, others viewed the prospect of being hauled before the authorities and public with dread, thus underlining the sense of danger that associating with (or becoming) religious outlaws could bring.

Such spectacles were necessary, above all, in the authorities' attempt to ensure religious conformity and unanimity, since initiatives from above would come to nothing if acquiescence was lacking on the part of local functionaries and the larger population. And in many ways, these attempts succeeded, as the heretic or dissident was now separated from the community, stripped of his sheep's clothing and displayed as the wolf he really was. At the same time, enough resistance existed, even in the cases of the worst or most stigmatized offenders, to cause authorities trouble: for one thing, too many—or simply enough—accomplices were present to lend their aid, compelled by a variety of motives that ranged from religious sympathy to confusion or indifference over the government's changing policies. Moreover, while the zeal that existed at the top may have been taken up by the justices and commissioners and even trickled down to some of the populace, general obedience—at least to the king's or queen's representatives—was not a guarantee, even among sheriffs and constables who were required to hold up their end of the system.

Ideally, a partial solution for every Tudor government faced with religious deviants would have been to somehow sever the lines that connected networks of support within and outside the realm. While individuals such as Cromwell or Walsingham made efforts to do so, the continued administrative weakness of sixteenth-century governments combined with a genuinely divided public sentiment to make any attempt along those lines impossible. In addition, members of various religious persuasions also knew how to scatter themselves when necessary in order to escape capture, as a concentrated group, from the government's net. What Origen had once observed in regard to the early church could in this sense apply to England: persecution, he wrote, may have indeed been effective in its occasional hammer blows, but the very diffusion of the church, and the government's inability to coordinate its officials from top to bottom, ensured that the besieged would go on, like Israelites in Joshua's day.[144]

In the search-and-apprehension stage of persecution, one thus begins to witness for the first time the suspects themselves actively resisting authority, either on their own or with the help of others, thereby adding another element to the ambiguous relations existing between the crown, the mid-level functionaries, and the larger population. This ability to actively seize control over their own fates allowed religious dissidents to begin shaping their own martyrological narratives and to influence public opinion in doing so. Righteous individuals running from the authorities, harassed and besieged and having to hide in dark corners or rely on others who could betray or aid them, was a common trope in the Acts of the Apostles and in the early martyrologies, as they well knew. Constantly on the move as hunted fugitives, they likened themselves to Jesus, Paul, and the apostles, and found themselves living out Augustine's notion of the wandering pilgrim, eternally exiled. Above all, stories of escape constituted a testament to fortitude, cleverness, desperation, and victorious evasion, as what became a test of strength for individuals, such as the Duchess of Suffolk, soon evolved into a mythology that elevated not only her but—even more important—her Protestantism.

Still, not everyone, even when offered the chance, chose, in the end, to flee. In 1555 during Mary's reign, for example, the Protestant bishop John Hooper, who earlier in his career had opted for flight out of the country, now decided that while "he was not ignorant of the evils that should happen towards him (for he was admonished by certain of his friends to get him away, and shift for himself), yet he would not prevent [officials from taking him], but tarried still, saying: 'Once I did flee, and take me to my feet; but now, because I am called to this place and vocation, I am thoroughly persuaded to tarry, and to live and die with my sheep.'"[145] His coreligionist Hugh Latimer would similarly yield himself up to the officials: when a pursuivant was sent out by Stephen Gardiner, Latimer received warning in sufficient time to escape; instead, he prepared himself for the journey to London, and told the official when he finally appeared, "My friend, you be a welcome messenger to me. And be it known unto you, and to all the world, that I go as willingly to London at this present, being called by my prince to render a reckoning of my doctrine, as ever I was at any place in the world." Though many authorities secretly hoped that Latimer would in fact flee—knowing that "his constancy should deface them in their popery"—he made the trip to the Tower and the privy council, joking as he passed Smithfield that the fiery place "had long groaned for him."[146]

The actions of Hooper and Latimer were consistent with their later embrace of the suffering that accompanied imprisonment and eventually execution; by passively yielding themselves to the authorities, they were evoking another aspect of Jesus, for example, who stood in Gethsemene knowing of the coming betrayal, or who upon capture told one of his apostles to put away his sword, saying, that "these things must be."[147] In this sense, they were self-consciously playing out a part in the first act of the nascent drama of martyrdom, just as those who informed on them—their Judases, or Nicholas Grimbalds—were themselves recognized as embodying their own roles in the providential production. For those who chose to face their capture, the beginning outlines of a new self-creation was taking place, as was the case with Richard Woodman: after having been apprehended, and taking leave of his father, brother, wife, children, and friends, he was brought to prison, where he would later be examined and condemned to death as a Protestant heretic in Mary's reign. In spite of this, he wrote in a letter to a Mistress Roberts of Hawkhurst, "I praise my Lord God that hath separated me from my mother's womb, all this that hath happened unto me hath been easy, light, and most delectable and joyful of any treasure that ever I possessed." With these words he foretold the martyrdom that lay ahead.[148]

CHAPTER THREE

"To pray, to curse, and to write letters"

The Martyrdom of Prison

THE PRIMARY MEANS BY WHICH THE TUDORS ATTEMPTED TO control the more threatening elements of religious instability was through imprisonment, which confined dissidents to their own separate and brutalized sphere. This was understandable, if such individuals were to be seen as challenging the very basis of the crown's religious identity, along with its concomitant policies, laws, and institutions. The problem, however, was that the policy of imprisonment did not work, not because of the often overly harsh, day-to-day punishments it meted out, but because of the success dissidents had in manipulating the state of incarceration to their own advantage. Like the drama of being informed upon and apprehended, imprisonment, as dissidents well knew, resonated with scriptural precedent and could be exploited as a theatricalized, biblical stage set of suffering. In the attempt to publicize their conditions toward these ends, prisoners were aided by the porousness of sixteenth-century jails, which abounded with messengers, smugglers, helpers (including many prominent women), and even, in the case of Catholics in Elizabeth's reign, receivers of mass and young catechumens. The fact that prisoners were often placed together in the same confined spaces only further strengthened their support networks and rendered encroaching martyrdom a public and collective, as well as private, struggle; in this sense, not only did prison constitute an entire world unto itself, but so did it also provide the crucible by which religious identities and communities were forged.

For all its larger resonances, sixteenth-century imprisonment was nevertheless a rough experience—a life-threatening battle against rapacious wardens, oppressive irons, bare floors, dank walls, stench, pestilence, and water so putrid that, it was joked, even "the rats drown themselves."[1] Ranging from temporary lock-ups at sheriffs' residences to notorious institutions such as London's Newgate, prisons did not noticeably improve over the course of the century, despite periodic attempts at reform; for religious dissidents, this meant dwelling among common criminals to wait out their trials or sentencings for indefinite periods of squalor. Many of them, as a result, chose to recant if they were given the option, in order to escape such a fate; thus, prison became a kind of martyr-processing center, a filtering zone that drained away the stalwart from the weak, or—to use a constant phrase from prison writings—the wheat from the chaff. As for individuals who chose to stay behind, authorities expressed concern at the ability of many of them to transcend their own constraints and even continue to cause havoc. As Maliverny Catlyn wrote in a letter to Walsingham during Elizabeth's reign, "if you mean to stop the stream, choke the spring, for believe me, the prisons of England are very nourishers of papists. Banish them, for God's sake, or let them remain close prisoners, that they may not daily poison others."[2]

Imprisonment in the Sixteenth Century

The modern notion of institutional and permanent incarceration was not yet present in sixteenth-century England, though certainly more than a few inmates unwittingly served permanent life sentences by dying in jail. Prisons were intended simply to keep dangerous suspects in custody, holding them for an indeterminate period until trial and the subsequent ordering of punishment.[3] A long history lay behind this practice, as jails had existed in England since before the Norman Conquest; over the course of the centuries, however, an increasing number of imprisonable offenses—by 1520 there would be 180 such laws, covering moral transgressions and vagrancy—created an expansion in detention cells and the number of inmates contained within.[4] Not surprisingly, administration and control of prisons became increasingly strained by the burden, and the sixteenth century witnessed an uneven attempt on the part of the Tudors to deal with the problem of escapees, prison maintenance, and various disorders arising from the conditions of incarceration. Adding to the complications were the changes in prison administration caused by the break with Rome: on one level, ecclesiastical or monastic prisons were abolished or radically circumscribed, as was the policy known as benefit of clergy, which had enabled clerics to transfer from temporal to ecclesiastical or bishops' prisons, where many proceeded either to escape or receive lighter sentences.[5] In addition, the dissolution of the monasteries, which no longer existed as places of shelter,[6] may have increased the number of vagrants who roamed the country or led to the establishment of institutions such as Bridewell. The identity of religious dissidents in prison also changed; whereas in previous centuries imprisoned nonconformists consisted largely of Lollards—whose frequent imprisonment in the jail at St. Paul's gave it the name Lollards' Tower[7]—the sixteenth century witnessed prisoners of varied confessional persuasions, from extreme Evangelicals to Jesuits.

Many types of prisons continued to exist in England throughout the century, the most basic of which were makeshift county jails, such as gatehouses, manors, and castles, which functioned initially as temporary holding-pens upon immediate apprehension, but later became more permanent residences.[8] In Essex during Mary's time, for example, Colchester Castle contained a jail that served as a frequent destination point for a large number of Protestants, among them William Mount, his wife Alice, and their daughter Rose Allin, all of whom were then transferred to the town jail at Mote Hall before their execution.[9] During the same period, a significant congregation of twenty-two Protestant prisoners at the castle became such a cause célèbre that when it came time to transfer down to London, a crowd of one thousand came out to support them.[10] Castles also became a frequent destination for Catholic recusants in Elizabeth's time: in the north, where Catholicism remained strong, the county castles of York or Hull hosted a wide range of recusants, including gentlemen, blacksmiths, hatters, and a significant number of women.[11] Another prison was located at the barely controlled Wisbech Castle in Cambridgeshire, where the mostly clerical prison population managed to elude the Puritan keeper by breaking the locks of doors that divided them, mingling freely, and harassing him by interrupting his Genevan prayers with their whistles and bangs from the floorboards above.[12] Religious practices also took place at Wisbech: according to one prisoner-priest who found himself incarcerated at the castle, "Sometimes I had an opportunity of celebrating the Holy Mysteries, for from the lower room . . . in the dead of night we were enabled to obtain vestments by a rope which was let down from our window, and in the early morning, before the wardens and other prisoners were awake, we returned them in the same manner."[13]

It was the sheriff's duty, as the king's officer, to not only deliver prisoners but also maintain the jails and appoint wardens or keepers to oversee them; with the growth of the prison population, however, sheriffs began to house the newly apprehended in their own residences, many of which consisted of separate buildings known as counters or compters. In London the compters in Poultry Street and Wood Street were especially notorious places of incarceration, with both open all night to receive individuals who had offended against the city laws, namely in disturbing the peace.[14] Like county jails, while such enclosures had only been intended as temporary quarters, by the sixteenth century many felons and religious dissidents were known to languish for longer periods of time. One of the more disreputable compters in the sixteenth century was located at Bread Street and run by Richard Husband, described by John Stow as "a headstrong man who dealt hard with the prisoners for his own advantage." So abusive was Husband, with his irons and his sideline business of charging "thieves and strumpets" for lodgings, that he himself was committed for a time to Newgate and then released, only to be committed again.[15] Along with sheriffs' jails, another notorious "residential" prison that should be noted, albeit one on the wane in the sixteenth century, was controlled by the bishop, who incarcerated individuals on his property for purposes of questioning. Once used to incarcerate secular clerks—who were granted their own sphere of containment by the aforementioned benefit of clergy—the bishop's prison was now a frequent though by no means exclusive stop for religious offenders, the most famous of which resided on Edmund Bonner's property, in his coalhouse.

Within towns, prisons were also maintained as part of a larger municipal responsibility. The mayor of Oxford, Alderman Irish, kept a jail in his official residence, which in 1555 witnessed the presence of Nicholas

Ridley, who often complained, as will be seen, of his conditions and treatment.[16] It was London, however, that contained the most infamous municipal prisons, where offenders were sent from the farthest reaches of the land. Each of these penal houses tended to carry their own reputation, based in part on the types of prisoners residing within: Newgate, the most notorious, was primarily a criminal prison controlled by the City of London, though this did not prevent it from receiving a significant number of religious dissidents, including Anne Askew. Less brutal was Ludgate, which existed—though again, not exclusively—as a holding-pen for debtors, who, it should be noted, constituted the majority of all inmates in sixteenth-century England.

London's prisons could also fall under the jurisdiction of the crown and its courts. Along with Ludgate, another prison known for its debtors was the Fleet, which was controlled by the courts of Common Pleas, Chancery, Exchequer, and Star Chamber; as a debtors' prison, the Fleet would become, in Elizabeth's time, a frequent destination for unpaying recusants, who were contained within its ancient stone walls and surrounded by a moat.[17] Marshalsea prison was also located in London, though it was controlled by the court of the King's Bench, which had previously enjoyed a long-standing association with ecclesiastical courts, thus accounting for the continued presence of a large number of religious dissidents. The most notable of the royal prisons, however, was the Tower, originally built by William I, and known then as the White Tower, with the intention of incarcerating his enemies; in the sixteenth century, the more noteworthy or treasonous of the king's close enemies tended to be housed there, including Thomas More, Thomas Cranmer, Robert Southwell, Edmund Campion, and others.

Despite the increase in penal laws and inmates over the course of the century, it should be borne in mind that prisons generally remained small, at least by modern standards. In 1532 London's Ludgate contained on its list fifty-nine names, while Poultry Counter in the same year held all of eight individuals. Coalhouses and residences could not carry more than ten individuals; other prisons, however, experienced noticeable growth, including the Fleet, which held two hundred prisoners by 1600. It is not clear how many of these were religious dissidents, especially when, by the time of Elizabeth, the status of a religious prisoner had dramatically changed and involved other charges, such as treason or, in recusants' cases, debt. Certainly, contemporaries tended to inflate the numbers:

according to a report by the Spanish ambassador to Philip II in 1582, eleven thousand Catholics languished in prison, while Robert Persons claimed fifty thousand. In reality, surviving keepers' certificates from nine prisons between 1583 and 1588 classify anywhere from approximately seventy to one hundred individuals, including priests, "committed for matters of religion."[18]

As for the choice of where to send a recently apprehended individual, the decision rested in the hands of courts such as the King's Bench or Exchequer, as well as privy councilors, sheriffs, and bishops. Many of the orders to imprison—and where to imprison—could be capriciously decided and even illegal, though accountability was negligible: one of the charges against Wolsey in 1534 held him responsible for wrongfully imprisoning Sir John Stanley, but it was one charge meant to cushion many, and it certainly did not prevent Thomas More, for example, from illegally imprisoning suspects, or even Thomas Cranmer, in 1539, for bearing primary responsibility in the long detention of the friar William Watts.[19] For many prisoners, it was simply accepted that many incarcerations were initiated without formal legal charges or evidential procedures, and that except for periodic jail deliveries—when justices would travel the circuits overseeing cases and clearing prisons of their inmates—the stay would be a long one that consisted of waiting for hearings which never came, or for a crime long forgotten.[20]

Among apprehended individuals of higher note, sometimes the place of imprisonment could be negotiated before a body such as the privy council, though the effort produced mixed results. When John Philpot was threatened by John Story with imprisonment at Lollards' Tower in 1555, for example, he replied, "Sir, I am a poor gentleman; therefore I trust of your gentleness you will not commit me to so vile [a place], being found no heinous trespasser." But Story was unmoved, and even suggested a crueler destination: Bishop Bonner's coalhouse. "Sir," Philpot again replied, "if I were a dog you could not appoint me a worse and more vile place . . . God give you a more merciful heart." Even this failed to persuade Story or the rest of the council, and Philpot proceeded to the coalhouse to face "a great pair of stocks" (though "thanks be to God, we have not played on those organs yet"). Edward Underhill was similarly unlucky, even though he too tried to cite his status as a gentleman as mitigation: after his apprehension in 1553, Underhill, like Philpot, also faced members of the privy council—with whom he conducted an acidic exchange—and was met with debate over the appropriate prison for him. "Have this gentleman unto the Fleet until we may talk further with him," ordered the Earl of Sussex. "To the Fleet!" scoffed Robert Southwell; "have him to the Marshalsea!" John Gage then injected, "Have this gentleman to Newgate!", which particularly panicked Underhill, who begged Lord Arundel that "I trust you will not see me thus used, to be sent to Newgate," since, as he later put it, "I am a Gentleman, as you know, and one of your fellows." But Underhill was unsuccessful, and proceeded to Newgate, thus unable to prevent the particularly nasty spell that he knew, even then, lay ahead for him.[21]

Life in Prison

The sixteenth century witnessed a proliferation of reports detailing life in prison, with the more graphic accounts emerging from the pens of religious dissidents themselves. The chronicles of pain and hardship that make up these writings cannot be taken as representative of imprisonment as it was experienced by everyone; though they often coexisted with common criminals, debtors, or others, religious dissidents were still a distinct and often elite minority whose exceptional status could set them apart for special treatment as well as targeted victimization. Testimonies of prison life which emerge directly or indirectly from the pens of these literate individuals should thus be treated with some caution, or at least considered within their own literary and religious context. Moreover, while there is no reason to disbelieve the accounts of suffering and torture that prisoners experienced, secondhand reports by biased observers, such as John Foxe, may have carried elements of exaggeration, especially when it came to portraying an oppressor such as Edmund Bonner and his notorious coalhouse. While the experiences recorded by religious dissidents cannot therefore be judged as entirely comprehensive accounts of prison life in general, the fact that many dissidents were of a higher social standing and frequently set apart from others did not prevent them from experiencing the hardship common to all, and capturing their experiences in a representative, albeit fragmented, way.

Though religious dissidents could be thrown into a variety of prisons and treated like other criminals, certain aspects of their situation, however, were unique to them. For one thing, the changeability of religious policies over the course of the century ensured that a certain amount of mobility in and out of prison would exist as many religious offenders— or at least those who managed to survive an execution sentence—were released upon the accession of a new monarch more in line with their doctrine. Among the more notable cases were John Hooper, who was imprisoned upon Henry's passage of the conservative Acts of Six Articles in 1539, only to be released and raised to a central position under Edward, and returned to jail again under Mary; similarly, Bonner spent his years under Edward languishing in prison, only to be released by Mary, and returned again by Elizabeth. The only individuals, in fact, whose imprisonment remained constant were Anabaptists and other nonorthodox sects, until Elizabeth added Catholics to their number at the end of the century.

Incarceration also tended to differ for religious troublemakers in that it served as a vehicle of psychological and physical harassment in its own right. Release in many cases could come fairly swiftly and at any time, if only the prisoner chose to recant and agree to make penance; even in the time of Mary, when persecution of religious dissidents reached its zenith, evidence points to a considerable effort on the part of authorities to give problematic individuals the chance to turn away from their heretical beliefs. Sometimes the effort to bring on a recantation could even turn into a full, formal exhortation, as was the case at York Cathedral in 1580, when Catholic prisoners were urged to "forsake their vayne and erronious opinions of popery, and conforme them selves with all Dutifull obedience to true religion now established." Instead, the congregation of prisoners coughed, made noises, held their hands to their ears, and refused to recite the Lord's Prayer, all of which sent them back to prison."[22]

Most individuals, however, were not so stalwart, especially in the case of average men and women who were released from imprisonment after only one night's stay, upon "clarification" of previously suspect opinions. Due to the fragmented evidence of prison rolls, it is difficult to estimate the number of prisoners who expedited their release by recanting and returning to the government's favor, though it is probably the case, judging by the available records, that a good majority ended up doing whatever was necessary to get out. In Mary's reign, for example, the Protestant John Checke made his famous recantation while in prison, and Bishop Robert Ferrar was on the brink of doing the same, before he was persuaded otherwise by John Bradford.[23] Others who broke under the strain of prison never recovered from their retreat. During Edward's reign, Sir James Hales of Kent had served as a judge and notable partisan for the reformed cause, with one of his duties that of overseeing the deprivation of Stephen Gardiner; as a result of his associations, he was incarcerated at the Queen's Bench upon Mary's—and now Lord Chancellor Gardiner's—accession to power. After his transfer to the Fleet, Hales was approached by one Foster, who attempted to convince him of his error in remaining in a heretic faith; when Hales showed himself, in Strype's words, "inclinable to relent," the bishop of Chichester, George Day, finished the process, and gained Hales's recantation. The act so tormented Hales, however, that he sent his servant away from his cell and attempted to commit suicide by stabbing himself repeatedly with a penknife; thwarted and still in despair, Hales finally did succeed upon release from prison, when he died after throwing himself in a shallow pond.[24]

Prisoners of a stronger constitution tended to stay clear of vacillators, however, especially if they sensed a possible recanter-turned-informer in their midst. Certainly, informers, as discussed in chapter 2, were a frequent menace among communities of religious prisoners, whether they volunteered to enter the prison for the job—as was the case with Nicholas Berden, who caused damage not only to Hooper but also to the entire community—or wished to secure their release through informing, as did Benjamin Beard, who seems to have been imprisoned in the Fleet for debt but who reported the activities of imprisoned Catholics. The priest John Gerard himself made the mistake of befriending a fellow priest who subsequently joined him in the Poultry Counter. "However," he wrote, "I noticed that he was a little unsteady and seemed rather too anxious to be free again, so I was careful not to confide in him." Later, Gerard continued, "possibly he wanted to ingratiate himself with the authorities and so secure his liberty or something of the kind. I cannot say; but whatever it was, he informed on me."[25]

Religious dissidents often did not dwell in one jail, but frequently found themselves moved about from one place to another: the Congregationalist leader Robert Browne, for example, claimed to have been incarcerated in thirty-two prisons, until he finally perished in the jail at Northampton.[26] Somewhat more typical was John Bradford, who, in Mary's reign, began his prison life in the Tower, only to be transferred to the King's Bench and the compter in the Poultry, and finally, before his burning, Newgate. Immediately after the Lady Jane episode, Hugh Latimer, Nicholas Ridley, and Thomas Cranmer were, like Bradford, sent on to the Tower, where they "together read over the New Testament with great deliberation and painful study"; soon after, these three were transferred to the Bocardo town prison at Oxford, where their trial would be conducted, and then scattered, with Cranmer remaining in Bocardo, Latimer taken to the bailiff's house, and Ridley to the mayor's residence.[27]

Entering one prison after another in this manner was a last-minute business, leaving the suspect with little time to prepare clothes or necessities for the hardship ahead. On the one hand, when Thomas Cranmer first entered the Tower after Mary had come to the throne, he was allowed in an almost leisurely way to bring in a range of clothing—including his episcopal vestments—along with carpets, beddings, hangings, and cushions; but over time his possessions were auctioned off, his great library at home sold and eventually dispersed, and when he was transferred to Oxford for trial, authorities ordered him only to bring with him what he could carry.[28] The first encounter with prison itself came as a shock, especially for suspects whose offenses were never felonious and whose personalities were not hardened to the criminal mold. In 1555, for example, the Protestant Robert Glover entered the prison at Lichfield and was relegated to the dungeon, which was "very cold, with small light"; given a pile of straw on which to sleep, Glover languished for months, though he had brought with him "my New Testament in Latin, and a Prayer-book, which I privily stole in."[29] Edward Underhill went to Newgate with only his Bible and his lute, the latter proving useful when it came to earning the good graces of the keeper, as will be seen.[30] During Elizabeth's reign, Robert Southwell, upon his Tower imprisonment in 1592, was also denied any belongings, until his mother successfully petitioned the queen that since he was a gentleman, he be sent "what he needed to sustain his life," which turned out to be "meat, and a Bible, and the works of St. Bernard, which he himself wanted for his solace."[31]

Though many prisoners were allowed to walk freely through the premises once they had settled in, irons in the form of manacles, chains, rings, and collars were sometimes employed, not to inflict pain but rather to secure the prisoner; in many instances, however, the result was that prisoners were left to pine away, forgotten, against their damp stone walls. In 1555, the Protestant preacher Robert Samuel underwent such an ordeal as a prisoner in Bishop Hopton's custody, "where he was chained bolt-upright to a great post, in such sort, that standing only on tiptoe he was fain to stay up the whole poise or weight of his body thereby."[32] The same period witnessed Richard Woodman enduring a similar experience, involving, in his words, the "wearing onewhile bolts, otherwise shackles, otherwise lying on the bare ground; sometime sitting in the stocks; sometime bound with cords, that all my body hath been swollen; much like to be overcome for the pain that hath been in my flesh."[33] For more dangerous prisoners, or for religious or political prisoners who were singled out for especially brutal treatment, chains were supplemented by "close supervision," in what Miles Coverdale described as "dungeons, ugsome holes, dark, loathsome, and stinking corners." In the 1590s, John Gerard languished in the Poultry Counter under solitary confinement, where he was fettered with rusty chains; still, he wrote, "I made them bright and shining by wearing them every day and moving about in them . . . [and] when the prisoners below started singing lewd songs and Geneva psalms, I was able to drown out their noise with the less unpleasant sound of my clanking chains."[34]

But for all the attempts at security, sixteenth-century jails could also be an unstable link in the chain of persecution, as the number of prison escapes attests. In a sensational case from 1538, for example, Hexham, in the north of England, was the scene of the flight of numerous individuals, among them Richard More, a priest from Chichester.[35] In 1556, Robert Crowhurste, "an hereticke and a seditiouse personne," escaped from the King's Bench, though he was later apprehended and committed once more to the jail, with the felony of escape now added to his offenses.[36] Escape occurred through a number of factors: the sympathy of jailers, for example, could be enlisted, as was the case toward the end of Mary's reign, when they were taken to task by the governor of the Tower for allowing Protestant prisoners to flee. One jailer, John Bawde, was thrown into the Tower's Little Ease—a dungeon with no space to lie down or stand up—for the crime of trying to help Alice Tankerville escape.[37] Barring sympathy, the noted venality of jailers could also be employed, which the "Statute of Negligent Escapes," first enacted in 1504, attempted to address with its series of stringent fines against keepers who had allowed felons or traitors to flee.[38] Flight was also possible in light of the fact that prisoners could sometimes leave the prison for a

themselves with sharing rooms in the Tower Chambers, or hope for the best in the self-explanatory Twopenny Ward, Beggar's Ward, Bolton's Ward, and Dungeon. Not all attempts to maintain separate accommodations were successful or recognized, however; while a tower was built at Newgate to house women, for example, it was not at all surprising for women to dwell among men, or children—sometimes infants—with their elders. "I am with an evil woman," Hooper wrote at one point, while in 1556, Joan Dangerfield was incarcerated along with her weeks-old child, "placed among thieves and murderers," and kept in such a state until her child had to be sent away due to illness, and she herself perished.[41]

Necessary "fees" or garnishes not only determined one's accommodations but predominated every step of the way. A stipend was exacted from prisoners if they entered or left the facility, if they wished to purchase a blanket, a meal, the protection of an inmate, the release of iron fetters, even the privilege of having doors opened by the turnkey. Upon entering the Tower, Thomas More was told by the porter to relinquish his "upper garment" as a fee; when More jokingly attempted to hand over his hat as an upper garment, the porter dourly replied, "No, sir. I must have your gown."[42] As an essentially commercial enterprise, the prison was thus a well-oiled cash machine which could bring quick destitution to the well-off or lead others to the worst fate of all: the outstretched hands grasping through the prison gates for the charity of the outside world. "Art thou poor and in prison?" Dekker later asked; "Then thou art buried before thou art dead."[43]

Even if one was of notable standing or could pay exorbitant fees, living conditions left much to be desired, with the cold, the stench, the noise, and such lack of light that the Congregationalist leader Robert Browne wrote that "he could not see his hand at noon-day."[44] John Gerard also dwelled in a dark garret at the Poultry Counter, with a door so low that he had to crawl through on his knees; "[b]ut this proved an advantage, since it helped to keep out the smell of the privy next door, which was not slight . . . [and] often kept me awake at night."[45] Newgate, especially, seems to have emitted distinct vapors, creating a miasma which affected the surrounding locality: Underhill was so sickened by the "evil savours" of the place that he complained to the keeper, who in an act of kindness transferred the prisoner to his own parlour, "where he himself lay"; still, the room was situated near the kitchen and emitted a "savour of which I could not abide."[46] Languishing in the Fleet in Mary's reign, John Hooper described a similar experience when he wrote, "I have continued a long time, having nothing appointed to me for my bed but a little pad of straw, a rotten covering, with a tick and a few feathers therein, the chamber being vile and stinking . . . of the one side of which prison is the sink and filth of all the house, and on the other side the town-ditch; so that the stench of the house hath infected me with sundry diseases."[47]

Toward the end of Elizabeth's reign, conditions were not much improved, as a petition from prisoners slowly perishing in the Wood Compter hole attests. Numbering "fifty poor men or thereabouts," they wrote of "lying upon bare boards, still languishing in great need, cold and misery, who, by reason of this dangerous and troublesome [place] be almost famished and hunger-starved to death; others very sore sick" and desperate due to the lack of "relief and sustenance."[48] A contemporary description of the hole in another prison described a hellish scene of "the child weeping over his dying father, the mother over her sick child; one friend over another, who can no sooner rise from him, but he is ready to stumble over another in as miserable a plight as him." In the end, "if a man come thither [to this place] he at first will think himself in some churchyard that hath been fattened with some great plague, for they lie together like so many graves."[49]

"For worse then Dogs, lye we in that foule kennell," went the poem from the Elizabethan era, though the description applied to one of the lower rungs of accommodation, which did not convey the whole prison experience.[50] Like everything else, diets, for example, varied according to one's ability to pay. At the upper end—or master's side—one could enjoy a meal by oneself or perhaps sit at the keeper's table before a dinner of beef broth, roasted veal, fresh fish, fresh bread, and wine; the poor, on the other hand, constantly had to "arme themselves against that battaile of hunger," scramble past similarly hungry souls, and find a seat at the mess, all for the privilege of bearing "a platter . . . full of powder Beefe and Brewis," or perhaps the usual fare of salt fish, stale bread, and brackish water. The complete withholding of food also served as punishment: in 1555, for example, Robert Samuel, in addition to being chained upright to a wall, was allotted "two or three mouthfuls of bread and three spoonfuls of water" every day; eventually, he suffered a vision where a figure clad in white appeared before him with the words, "Samuel, Samuel, be of good cheer, and take a good heart unto thee: for after this day shalt thou never be either hungry or thirsty."[51]

The strain of prison life also led to other deteriorations: Latimer, while confined to the house of the bailiff, was described by Ridley as having become "crazed"—a description which at the time encompassed both nervous and physical collapse and could explain his bizarre behavior at his disputation. Twenty years earlier, one William Cowbridge was reported by Foxe to have become so starved and sleep-deprived in prison that "he lost his wits and reason; whereby (as it is in the manner of madmen) he uttered many unseemly and indiscreet words."[52] Edmund Bonner's own tendency to unleash his temperament at full throttle was even ascribed by Feckenham, the dean of St. Paul's, as a kind of sixteenth-century, post-traumatic, stress response. "Bear with my lord," Feckenham told the rector of Hadham, after Bonner had struck him, "for truly his long imprisonment in the Marshalsea, and the misusing of him there, hath altered him, that in these passions he is not ruler of himself."[53]

The torments of prison life could sometimes lead to suicide, though the precise numbers are unclear, and may have been small in any case, due to the stigmatization that the act held for religious dissidents. One of the more famous, albeit dubious, cases of "suicide" in the century was that of Richard Hunne, a tailor with anticlerical tendencies, who was confined to Lollards' Tower in 1515 and the next day found hanging in his cell—ostensibly a suicide, though considered by many to be a homicide, ordered by William Horsey, chancellor of the Bishop of London.[54] Certainly, authorities displayed some degree of concern over the matter, which may have been the rationale for close supervision. John Gerard, for example, had his knife, scissors, and razors taken from him after being tortured in the 1580s, while Robert Southwell from the beginning was constantly monitored, first in Richard Topcliffe's house and then the Gatehouse—though how much this had to do with worry about suicide and how much with his being considered "a most lewd and dangerous person" is not entirely clear.[55]

It is not surprising that in such an overcrowded and unsanitary environment, ailments were common: during his fifteen-month imprisonment in the Tower, Thomas More was afflicted with chest pains, along with "gravell and stone, and with the crampe that divers nightes gryped his legges."[56] When the reformer John Frith and others were accused of heresy and ordered imprisoned, they were cast down into "a deep cave" where "the salt fish was laid; so that, through the filthy stench thereof, they were all infected, and certain of them, taking their death in the same prison, shortly upon the same being taken out of the prison into their chambers, there deceased."[57] Twenty years later, John Philpot was baited by John Story, during one of his examinations, about his "fat" appearance, to which Philpot later replied that "I am . . . kept all day in a close chamber: wherefore it is no marvel that my flesh is puffed up."[58] Fevers were also a frequent occurrence; "three or four days I have been somewhat in a fervent heat," Ridley wrote his friend William Punt in 1554, "and felt in my body a disposition to an ague."[59] Worse was a common and often fatal illness known as "jail fever," probably a form of typhus, which was caused by a lack of sanitation, and could reach epidemic proportions that afflicted everyone associated with the penal world, from prisoners to judges, lawyers, jurors, and witnesses; in the sixteenth century, the most virulent such outbreak would occur at the Oxford assizes in 1577, which would claim the lives of nearly three hundred people.

Occasionally, however, illness could provide grounds for release from prison. After a month in Newgate, fever overtook Edward Underhill, brought on by "the evil savours, and great unquietness of the lodgings, as also by occasion of drinking of a draught of strong Hollock wine." When transferred to better lodgings, Underhill's condition failed to improve, which led his wife to turn to the master of requests John Throgmorton—who also happened to be a kinsman of Underhill's—and petition him to release her husband on grounds of illness. The petition was successful, and soon Underhill was carried out to a waiting horse-litter and transported to his house, though he remained ill for months after, "my face so lean and pale that I was the very Image of Death."[60] Similarly, during Elizabeth's reign, certain Catholic recusants of notable standing were also released by the privy council due to illness. In the late 1570s, for example, Rooke Greene petitioned the council that he be set free from Colchester Castle due to ill-health and a father-in-law's death; the council agreed, though with the hope that Greene would be induced to conform by the man who was to supervise the recusant's freedom.[61] Though poorer prisoners, along with those who had committed more serious crimes, were no doubt given lesser, if any, consideration, not all successful petitioners were notable individuals. A group of more obscure recusant prisoners at Bury, in Suffolk, for example, were at least transferred to temporary quarters after petitioning the council that they wished to avoid an epidemic of the plague, while during the same period, Henry Everard, a recusant of modest means, was given a reprieve from jail after having told the council that his wife was dying, leaving fourteen children in his care.[62]

In general, however, prison often portended death, which resulted from neglect or even malicious intent, whether it be consumption, respiratory disease—which took the life of the Congregationalist Richard Fitz in the late 1560s—or starvation, which claimed victims such as Martin Hunt, who pined away in the King's Bench in 1556.[63] Others, especially among more anonymous and lower-class individuals, expired under mysterious circumstances after periods of being chained against walls or in bonds. In 1555, for example, the death of the London clothmaker and Protestant William Wiseman was considered so suspicious—whether "through famine, or ill handling of some murdering papists"—that a coroner was called in with twelve men to investigate, though no final cause was ever established. Less mysterious, perhaps, was the case of John Porter, who in 1541 was sent down to the dungeon of Newgate, where his nocturnal groanings led other prisoners to believe he had been placed in an iron device called "the devil on the neck," involving "straining and wrenching the neck of a man with his legs together, in such sort as the more he stirreth in it, the straiter it presseth him; so that within three or four hours it breaketh and crusheth a man's back and body in pieces." After eight days of this, Porter was found dead.

The travels (and travails) of those prisoners' bodies after death was not much better. The jail at the Queen's Bench was the place of death of one of the most famous Protestants in Mary's reign, the weaver John Careless, who left behind a large body of letters and was placed by Foxe in the ranks of the martyrs, though "he came not to the full martyrdom of his body." The cause of his death was unclear, but afterwards, his body was "buried in the fields, in a dunghill."[64] William Wiseman, the clothmaker, shared this ultimate destination when he was cast out into the fields, with the commandment that "no man should bury him"; nevertheless, writes Foxe, "some good Tobits there were, which buried him in the evening, as was commonly they did all the rest, thrown out in like sort, whom they were wont privately by night to cover." The limbo fate of Careless and Wiseman was shared by many (though not all) dead prisoners, religious dissidents and criminals alike; buried without ceremony in the adjacent fields, they lay forgotten and unclaimed, under the presumption that this was what they deserved.

Prison Relationships

Within the prison walls, religious dissidents had to navigate a multitude of relationships with authorities as well as other prisoners, some of whom were religious dissidents, albeit of a different stripe, than they. Dominating their stay in prison—and determining the level of treatment they received—was the keeper or warden, a man who earned his office by appointment or purchase, and proceeded to live off garnishes and "fees," which he attributed to the cost of upkeep.[65] It was the responsibility of keepers and their jailer to dispatch policies from above, which with some notable exceptions was done with a certain degree of efficiency and obedience; this meant, for example, that it was up to them to tighten or loosen the levels of harassment when necessary, to show friendliness or hostility, and to serve as key expediters of directives emerging from on high.[66] But keepers, who were expected to reside in the prisons, were also self-interested individuals, so notorious in their rapacity that it was said even a dead man could not escape their grasp, since carrying a coffin outside of the prison gates required another fee, this time from the dead man's friends. Every prisoner knew this and could sometimes use it to his advantage: in the 1590s, for example, John Gerard was accused by the jailer of celebrating mass and threatened that the matter would be investigated. "You will do nothing of the kind," Gerard replied, "but if you do, you must realize that you won't get another farthing from me or from any of the Catholics here for our cells. You can put the whole lot of us with the paupers in the common gaol if you wish, but there we won't have to pay anything and it's you who'll be the loser." Thwarted, the jailer walked away.[67]

Keepers were often in close contact with higher authorities, many of whom had directly appointed them. In 1553, the warden of the Fleet was John Babington, the direct appointee of Stephen Gardiner; Babington's more notable charges included John Hooper, who in Edward's reign had played a hand in Gardiner's own imprisonment, and now found himself sent down to the Fleet from Richmond. Hooper immediately proceeded to pay the warden a standard, if inflated, fee of five pounds sterling to obtain his liberty in moving about the prison, but Babington, unhappy with this payment, submitted a complaint to Gardiner, and sent Hooper to solitary confinement in the tower-chamber for three months. After Hooper's release from close chamber, the warden and his wife, according to a letter written by Hooper, still "complained untruly of me to their great friend the bishop of Winchester" and used the pretext of another argument to obtain permission in putting him into the wards. In this state, Hooper wrote, "I have been sick; and the doors, bars, hasps, and chains being all closed and made fast upon me, I have mourned, called and cried for help. But the warden, when he hath known me many times ready to die . . . hath commanded the doors to be kept fast, and charged that none of his men should come at me, saying, 'Let him alone; it were a good riddance of him.'" Despite Hooper's continuing to pay Babington "like a baron," the warden "hath . . . used me worse and more vilely than the veriest slave that ever came to the hall-commons."[68]

As the most infamous and visible prison in the country, Newgate played host to a series of notable keepers, one of the more renowned being Andrew Alexander, in Foxe's words, a "cruel wretch" who "of all gaolers exceeded all others."[69] Periodically, Foxe writes, Alexander would "hasten poor lambs to the slaughter" by approaching Bonner, Story, and others, crying, "Rid my prison! Rid my prison! I am too old to be pestered by these heretics." While subject to bribes and able to display extreme cruelty to prisoners such as John Philpot, Alexander seemed more concerned with keeping his prison in a state of order than in persecuting heretics, whose religion he probably did not mind as much as their inclination to stir up trouble. In 1554, for example, John Rogers decided to make a case for his fellow prisoners by demanding that they be entitled to one meal a day as long as they paid, and that "other meals should be given to them that lacked on the other (or common) side of the prison. But Alexander, their keeper . . . would in no case suffer that." Alexander could also display a marked degree of kindness, which was the case with Edward Underhill, due in part to Underhill's fame, but also to his ability to play the lute. Shortly after arriving at Newgate, Underhill was taken into the confidence of a fellow prisoner well versed in the peccadillos of the keeper and his wife: "They both do love music very well," the prisoner told Underhill, knowing that Underhill was skilled at the lute; "wherefore you with your lute, and I to play with you on my rebeck [violin], will please them greatly." Indeed, the prisoner added, "[Alexander and his wife] loveth to be merry, and to drink wine . . . If you will bestow upon them every dinner and supper a quart of wine, and some music, you shall be their white son, and have all the favour that they can shew you." The strategy apparently succeeded, for Alexander seems to have shown Underhill every advantage when the need arose.[70]

Other keepers, or their assistants, were also known for their charity toward prisoners, which was not surprising in light of the deference often held toward those inmates of a superior rank. Such a case is that of the lieutenant of the Tower, who approached Thomas More in his chamber, asking if he would accept his good will "and such poor cheer as he had." Later, however, as More's imprisonment worsened with his continued refusal to take the oath, such good graces were withheld.[71] Other times, jailers would display sympathy after the prisoner had endured harsh treatment at others' hands. After being tortured in the Tower, John Gerard, for example, later wrote that "the [jailer] seemed really sorry for me," which led the man to lay a fire for him and provide him with supper; during the same period and after another torture session, "[my] warder brought me back to my room. His eyes seemed to be swollen with tears. He assured me that his wife, whom I had never seen, had wept and prayed for me all the time."[72]

It was understandable, to some extent, that jailers would also develop a bond with their prisoners after a period of daily contact. When in 1541, reformer Adam Damlip found himself imprisoned at the Marshalsea due to the more conservative climate brought on by the Act of Six Articles, he proved himself so endearing and well-behaved that the keeper, John Massy, allowed the "great treasure" to walk freely among the other "common and rascal sort of prisoners . . . rebuking vice and sin."[73] During Mary's time, in Coventry prison, John Careless was in so much good favor with his jailer that he was allowed one day to leave his lock-up and move about the city with his companions; at the end of the day, however, Careless made sure to maintain his good standing with the keeper by returning to the jail at the appointed hour. Another good relationship between keeper and prisoner occurred in the case of John Bradford, who during his stay at the Poultry Counter was allowed to preach twice daily and even "administer the sacraments"; also, while at the Queen's Bench prison, he was given permission to leave for a night and walk through London without his keeper, in order to "visit one that was sick, lying by the Still-yard."[74]

Keepers' wives played a visible role as well in determining the quality of one's prison stay. In his letters, Nicholas Ridley complained of his jailer's wife, Mrs. Irish, an "old, ill-tempered and most superstitious woman, who indeed takes it to herself as a matter of praise that she is to guard me most strictly and cautiously." Occasionally, when the mood struck her, she ordered Ridley's writing materials to be confiscated, while on other occasions she attempted to undermine Ridley by claiming that Hugh Latimer had apostatized or recanted, and that Hooper had been executed for high treason.[75] Another particularly sadistic keeper's wife— at least if John Foxe's account is to be believed—was Agnes Penicote, whose husband presided over the Salisbury jail. In 1556, Alice Coberley was detained in the keeper's house while her husband languished in another prison. Apparently seeking to provoke Alice, Agnes heated a key "fire-hot" and then asked Alice to fetch it for her; when Alice proceeded to obtain the key, which resulted in her "piteously burn[ing] her hand," Agnes cried, "Ah! Thou . . . that canst not abide the burning of the key, how wilt thou be able to abide burning thy whole body?"[76] Not all keepers' wives were so vicious, however: in 1555, the wife of the sympathetic jailer at the Poultry Street compter is reported to have said to Bradford, "O Master Bradford, I come to bring you heavy news," thereupon informing him that he would be sent on to Newgate, and shortly afterwards burned.[77]

It is difficult to estimate the extent to which men such as Babington or Alexander adhered to a particular religious allegiance over and above their normal concern with order and personal revenue. A few jailers in the King's Bench, according to Strype, did show such favor to their Protestant charges during the time of Mary, to the point where it was said they "secretly favored the gospel."[78] In 1558, another keeper, John Bowler, had started as a "very perverse papist" until he overheard the conversations of Bradford and Sandys; eventually he came to "mislike popery and to favour the gospel," and became "so persuaded in true religion, that on a Sunday, when they had mass in the chapel, he bringeth up a service-book, a manchet, and a glass of wine, and there [Dr. Sandys] ministered the communion to Bradford and Bowler. Thus Bowler was their son begotten in bonds."[79] Years later, during Elizabeth's reign, it was known that Simon Houghton, the keeper of Newgate, allowed contacts between priests in his care and the larger London populace; though his sympathy is not necessarily an indication of Catholicism, his wife was a proud and outspoken recusant.[80] In general, however, wardens and keepers were office men, functionaries or determined royal servants along the lines of Babington—Hooper's warden—who was described by Foxe as a "papist," when in fact he was probably more concerned with maintaining the favor of his patron, Stephen Gardiner.

Not all keepers wielded benign sovereignty over their enclosed realms, however, as privy council members and others came and went; keepers sometimes administered harsher measures, including torture, which was employed, for the most part, in a prison environment. Anne Askew, most famously, was crippled across the rack during her sojourn in the Tower not by her keeper—whose jurisidictional powers technically did not include torture—but by privy councillor Richard Rich, while in the 1580s, Richard Topcliffe, who tortured notoriously, conducted his business primarily out of the prisons. Robert Southwell would himself pass through stages of deterioration before encountering Topcliffe. After a spell in London's Gatehouse, Southwell appeared in court "so full of lice, that covered his clothes, that he was pitied by all who saw him." Afterwards, however, he was transferred to Newgate, where he was relegated to an area nicknamed limbo, so-called because it was the place where robbers awaited the hangman. Formal torture was finally used by Topcliffe, who wished to have Southwell incriminate others; the result was a series of sessions, where Southwell was "hanged up by the hands, put in irons, kept from sleep, and such like devices to men usual."[81]

Apart from torture, a common tactic of psychological warfare was to isolate a prisoner in solitary confinement. During Mary's reign, according to Foxe, the Protestant George Marsh was kept in a "dark dungeon," though "some of the citizens who loved him in God, for the gospel's sake . . . would sometimes in the evening, at a hole upon the wall of the city (that went into the said dark prison) call to him, and ask him how he did"; in addition, they would cast money into the hold, "about ten pence at one time, and two shillings at another time; for which he gave God thanks, and used the same to his necessity."[82] Periods of solitary confinement could vary, with one of the more extreme cases occurring once more with Southwell, who was kept in close confinement and barred visitors for three years, so that, in Garnet's words, "it was scarcely possible to know whether he was alive or dead." Only two sympathetic women seem to have even laid eyes on him in that time, when they "went on purpose to the Tower garden, pretending a wish to buy flowers, which grow there in a beautiful sort; and they saw him from afar, and received his blessing."

Keepers and higher officials could also exert their power—or extend their eyes and ears—by assigning for the care of notable prisoners servants who reported the ongoing activities of their charges, or stifled efforts at inter-prison communication and smuggling. In a letter to the also-imprisoned Thomas Cranmer, Nicholas Ridley complained that "My [own] man is trusty; but it grieveth both him and me, that when I send him with any thing to you, your man will not let him come up to see you, as he may to Master Latimer, and you to me."[83] Thomas More's servant never betrayed his master, though he had to swear before the lieutenant of the Tower that "if he should hear or see him at any time speak or write any manner of thing against the King, the council, or the state of the realm, he should open it to the Lieutenant, that the lieutenant might [immediately] reveal it to the council."[84] Servants such as Awood were, for the most part, sympathetic, however, and unwilling to carry through with the commands laid upon them; the pretext of being a servant could also allow others to slip in by disguise—as was the case with the Wisbech Castle Catholics, who received sons of gentlemen masquerading as servants for the purpose of giving them instruction in the faith.

Prisoners, in general, benefited from an influx of visitors who could convey information to and from the outside world or bring money, food, and other comforts. The number of visitors who gained access to prisoners is, in fact, one of the more remarkable aspects of Tudor imprisonment, and a testament to the weaknesses of the system as a whole. In 1593, Richard Topcliffe himself complained that Wisbech Castle allowed "access to [the prisoners] . . . from all parts . . . of England," to the point where "they have infected the greatest part of the town."[85] Similarly, Robert Persons, during the same period, would even argue, from the Catholic viewpoint, that "priests who are shut up in prisons are sometimes of more use to us there than if they were at liberty. For these men, being always definitely in the same place, make possible the visits of many people who are unable to discover the whereabouts of other priests."[86] Authorities were aware of these deficiencies and attempted to remedy them at times by relegating prisoners to close supervision or radically restricting visitors, but such efforts were difficult in times of political confusion or in the face of corrupt keepers.[87]

The very act of visiting a prisoner held religious importance, though the nature and meaning of the visits varied according to religious affiliation. Catholics at the end of the century, for example, sought out the blessings and sacraments that could only be dispensed by priests. Thus John Gerard, during a brighter and more open period of imprisonment, wrote that "so many Catholics came to visit me that there were often as many as six or eight people at a time waiting their turn to see me," many of whom wished to receive communion or his blessings. When Gerard soon after found himself shut up in close confinement in the Tower, one of them, Francis Page, nevertheless managed to walk every day below Gerard's window, where he doffed his hat and received a blessing; when Page was eventually seized on suspicion, "[he] said simply that he liked walking by the broad flowing Thames and came there merely for pleasure."[88] Protestant visitors earlier in the century were impelled, for their part, by an awareness that they were carrying on in the tradition of Epaphroditus, who had served as the messenger between the imprisoned apostle Paul and the Philippians,[89] and that what they were doing contributed to larger gestures on behalf of the entire community as it lived the gospel and the injunctions of Jesus from the book of Matthew: "Naked, and you covered me, sick and you visited me; I was in prison, and you came to me."[90]

One of the most important messengers to the Marian Protestants was Augustine Bernher, a Swiss resident of England and ardent reformer, whose friendship with Hugh Latimer—to whom he considered himself a servant and disciple—led him to long-standing ties with the reform community beginning in the 1540s. Upon Latimer's initial incarceration at Oxford, Bernher insisted on joining his "master" in prison, but was later told to leave, due to his status as a foreigner and outsider. Instead of leaving Oxford, however, he used his freedom to serve as an agent not only for Latimer, but for Ridley, Cranmer, and others, smuggling books and ensuring print runs overseas, conveying messages back and forth between prisoners, and informing them about developments from the outside world. Sometimes Bernher's eagerness to help led him into risky situations that could cause some tension between himself and the prisoners. In a letter from John Careless in 1556, Bernher was commended for his "hearty boldness" in putting himself at risk; but, Careless continued, "I would not have you thrust yourself in danger, when you can do [God's people] no good, or at leastwise when they may well enough spare that good you would do them: for if you should chance to be taken, you shall not only be no comfort unto them, but also a great discomfort, adding sorrow unto their sorrow." Indeed, Careless wrote, "I cannot allow, nor be contented, that you should rashly or negligently thrust yourself into that place where your wicked enemies did continually haunt, yea, and lay wait for you, when any other of God's people doth require your company."[91]

A significant number of supporters were also women, who provided prisoners with clothing or food. When Carthusian monks were imprisoned in the 1530s, for example, they received visits from Margaret Clement, who bribed her way into Newgate disguised as a milkmaid, and proceeded to provide the prisoners with food and clean linen.[92] In the time of Mary, Walter Marlar's wife sewed John Bradford a shirt to wear for his burning, while John Careless's sister provided a garment which Careless wrote would "harness me, and weapon me well to go fight against that bloody beast of Babylon." At Oxford, women of means, such as Ann Warcup, the Duchess of Suffolk, and especially Elizabeth Vane, would smuggle books and much-needed funds to Latimer, Cranmer, Ridley, and others, while receiving in turn epistolary advice or words of comfort if, for example, they had stumbled and attended mass.[93] Elizabeth Vane was especially close to John Philpot, with whom she shared an almost intimate correspondence, including a letter from Philpot—later heavily excised by John Foxe, due to its embarrassing implications—that ended with ardor and the small illustration of a heart.[94] Like Bernher, sometimes women, and allies in general, had to be restrained by prisoners in their eagerness to offer help. Thus John Bradford wrote to Elizabeth Brown in 1555 that "I am afraid to write unto you, because you so overcharge yourself at all times, even whensoever I do but send to you commendations. I would be more bold on you than many others, and therefore you might suspend so great tokens till I should write unto you of my need."[95] Other female sustainers, the more notable being Anne Warcup and Joan Wilkinson, also aided or corresponded with figures such as Bradford, until they were compelled to find safer refuge in exile overseas.[96]

Actually coming to the aid of a prisoner was, unsurprisingly, a risky endeavor. In 1553, John Hooper's servant, William Downton, was stripped and searched for letters as he came to visit his master at the Fleet; only "a little remembrance of good people's names, that gave their alms" to Hooper was found, but Downton was imprisoned all the same.[97] Similarly, after George Shipside, Ridley's brother-in-law, was betrayed, he was detained and harshly interrogated about possessing Ridley's writings; he was eventually released, despite the fact that he had managed to hold out and refrain from revealing information.[98] Others were impelled, after a time, to cloak their comings and goings in secrecy. In a letter to Augustine Bernher, John Bradford wrote that "if you come late at night, I shall speak with you; but come as secretly as you can," since, as he later put it, "[the] keeper telleth me that it is death to speak with me, but yet, I trust, that I shall speak with you."[99]

Even family members were not spared from pressures or threats. In 1543 the Protestant John Marbeck was apprehended for possessing spurious writings and taken to the Marshalsea, where he was placed in isolation, put in irons, and prevented from receiving visits from his wife, who wished to "help him with such things as he lacked." Stephen Gardiner did tell her, however, that "if thou love thy husband well, go to him, and give him good counsel, to utter such naughty fellows as he knoweth, and I promise thee he shall have what I can do for him." Gardiner then used his powers over the keeper at Marshalsea to have Marbeck's wife allowed access, under the condition that "ye search her both coming and going, lest she bring or carry any letters to or fro, and that she bring nobody unto him, nor any word from any man."[100] During Mary's reign, the Protestant Laurence Saunders also seems to have been cut off from his wife, though by his own insistence. According to a letter, Saunders enjoined her not to "come to the [prison] gate where the porter might see you. Put yourself not in danger where it needs not. You shall, I think, shortly come far enough into danger by keeping faith and a good conscience."[101]

Marbeck's and Saunders's wives seem to have supported the choice of their husbands to remain stalwart in prison, though cases existed—how many is uncertain—revealing conflict between prisoners and their visiting family members who wished them to recant or do whatever else it took to gain release. One of the more famous episodes, recounted by William Roper, involved the visit of Dame Alice to the Tower, where she confronted her husband Thomas More with the choice he had made. "I marvel," Roper quotes her saying, "that you, that have been always hitherto taken for so wise a man, will now so play the fool to lie here in this close, filthy prison, and be content thus to be shut up amongst mice and rats, when you might be abroad at your liberty, and with the favour and good will of the King and his Council, if you would but do as all the Bishops and best learned of this realm have done."[102] More, "with a cheerful countenance," attempted to argue otherwise, and even expressed amusement when Alice showed concern that he would be suffocated in such a close chamber.[103] Of greater personal pain to More, however, was the letter he received from his daughter Margaret Roper, who attempted to persuade him to take the oath; he replied that nothing "touched me never so near, nor [was] so grievous unto me, as to see you, my well-beloved child, in such vehement piteous manner labour to persuade unto me, that thing wherein I have of pure necessity for respect unto mine own soul, so often given you so precise answer before."[104]

Along with keepers, another relationship within prison existed between religious dissidents and fellow prisoners who had committed more criminal offenses and were seen as ripe for evangelical outreach. When the Marian Protestant John Porter, for example, was allowed for a time to walk among other Newgate prisoners "which lay there for felony and murder," he "[heard] and [saw] their wickedness and blasphemy, [and] exhorted them to amendment of life and gave unto them such instructions as he had learned of the Scriptures"—all of which ensured his last, fatal return to the dungeon. A more important and visible prison presence was John Bradford, who, during the same period, gave money to his fellow inmates and once a week "visited the thieves, pick-purses, and such others that were with him in prison, where he lay on the other side, unto whom he would give godly exhortation, to learn the amendment of their lives by their troubles."[105] The conversion of common criminals also served to uphold the truth of the cause, and to provide good propaganda in the process. One pamphlet described how the Catholic George Nichols converted a highwayman in the 1580s, while according to another narrative, James Fenn claimed responsibility for the gallows speech of a pirate, who stated that "he died a Catholic, and blessed the providence of God that had brought him to a place where he had met with such holy company as taught him to be a Christian." While some prisoner conversions, it should be said, may have been opportunistic and feigned,[106] others were genuine—as was the case when one newly Catholic felon in 1588 combined religiosity with criminality and proceeded to destroy all the "books he could come by [which were] set out by her Majesty for the advancement of the gospel."[107]

Other prisoners who were perceived as requiring either conversion or direction in correct doctrine were fellow religious dissidents, for not all prisoners incarcerated for religion were of the same persuasion. A Marian inmate such as Stephen Cotton may have written to his brother from the bishop's coalhouse in London that "be you most assured, good brother in the Lord Jesus, that we are all of one mind, one faith, one assured hope in our Lord Jesus," but given the range of orthodox and unorthodox beliefs coexisting at the time, this was most definitely not the case. The King's Bench seems to have been an especially fertile place for Anabaptists and Freewillers, which inspired John Clement to write a treatise in 1556, complaining that he saw "a wonderful sort of sects swarming everywhere, not only of Papists . . . but also of Arians, Anabaptists, and all other kind of heretics, which . . . go about the country deceiving many a simple soul, to whom the depths of Satan's subtlety is not known, and bringeth into sundry sects and schisms, causing them to divide and separate themselves from the true Church of Christ."[108]

The variety of heretical beliefs scandalized "true professors," such as Cranmer, Ridley, Latimer, and John Bradford, with the latter conducting prison debates with the Freewiller Henry Hart. In a letter that Hart himself might have written to his followers in prison, a warning was given to avoid non-Freewillers whenever possible—perhaps in response to the fact that a few such followers did, in fact, go over to the other side.[109] Most famously, John Philpot—who also took time in prison to write on the issue of infant baptism—spat at a prisoner of Arian persuasion, an act for which he would write a forceful and unrepentant apologia. Rather than set Arians straight, however, Philpot enjoined his readers to beware "Satan's whelps," "who be more crafty than the others, and more damnable, and for that the diligenter to be avoided."[110]

Prison disputations also became noteworthy at the end of the century, especially between Catholics and Puritans such as the Jesuit Paul Spence and Robert Abbot, who debated in the early 1590s from Worcester jail. Indeed, the famous debates conducted in the Tower between Edmund Campion and his Protestant opponents functioned within a

set period of time, as long as garnishes were paid to propitiate the jailers. The confusion that occurred in prisons as the result of sudden
political turmoil or a change of regime also allowed a prisoner to escape,
as when Edwin Sandys received a visitor, who informed him, "Master
[Sandys], there is such a stir in the Tower, that neither gates, doors, nor
prisoners are looked to this day. Take my cloak, my hat, and my rapier,
and get you gone; you may go out of the gates without questioning: save
yourself, and let me do as I may." Sandys refused the offer, however, with
the reason that "I know no just cause why I should be in prison; and thus
to do, were to make myself guilty."[39]

Some Catholics, such as the priest William Freeman, opted to remain in prison despite the enjoinments of friends and colleagues to use
various opportunities to escape. Freeman, however, "would never con-
sent thereto, unlesse yt might be with likeinge of his keeper, to whom
he supposed an escape might be cause of troble, & matters of scandall
to Catholykes abroad: or else peradventure bycause he was not willinge
to let goe so goode an occasion of martyrdom offred, of which yt may
seeme he had some desire."[40] Indeed, as Peter Lake and Michael Questier have pointed out, some prisoners, or at least Catholics at the end
of the century, chose to remain within the prison walls, which served as
protection as well as punishment from the outside world. While never
exactly a pleasant experience, prisons were often so lax and permissive
that individuals could, more often than not, move about freely, receive
a stream of visitors, and join together in communities of likewise religious persuasion.

Within prisons, levels of segregation often existed, between English
subjects and "foreigners," men and women, or individuals who could pay
for amenities and those who could not. Dukes, after all, could not be
expected to reside with beggars, and were therefore housed—again, if
they paid—in chambers known sometimes as messuages, where they
lived with their wives, children, and servants. During their first seven
months in the Tower, Thomas More and John Fisher were accorded
such privileges of rank and imprisoned either in the Bell or Beauchamp
Towers, where they were allowed reasonable food, exercise, visits from
the outside, and personal servants—all of which were slowly taken away
as time went on and the noose of official harassment gradually tight-
ened. Wealthy Catholics also found good accommodations in the Fleet
during Elizabeth's reign, while those of lesser standing had to content

larger context where challenges to beliefs and doctrines were constantly being parried in prison between hostile camps. Questions concerning attendance and recusancy were also at the forefront in places such as the York Castle jail, as were Protestant sermons that Catholics were forced to listen to periodically.[111] The result of all this activity probably harmed the government's case more than it helped; while recantations did take place, and were staged with great fanfare,[112] disputations only served to harden positions and create even more of a climate in which religious communities could flourish in solidarity and evangelism. In this sense, as Peter Lake and Michael Questier have written, "Far from being simple sites of official repression and constraint, the prisons became arenas of ideological conflict."[113]

With prisoners able to debate, receive visitors, or walk freely among themselves, it is not surprising that communities were strengthened by incarceration, with encroaching martyrdom experienced as a group phenomenon that fed upon and was strengthened by its own deeply collective nature. In the 1530s the Charterhouse monks were housed together in Newgate, where they received brutal treatment that only served, according to Hugh Latimer, to "indurate [rather] than ... mollify" them.[114] It was important that leaders appear among them to represent pillars of strength, or at least to distribute mass. John Bradford, for example, not only dispensed the communion bread and wine to his followers—and is said to have withheld it from others of more unorthodox persuasion—but also functioned as a model for others in the displaying of his own fortitude. Other "prison groups" later on included Congregationalists, who followed Robert Fitz, their leader, until his death in prison,[115] while the Brownists flourished for a time under Robert Brown, who died in prison at the age of eighty.[116] Recusants and priests, as mentioned, were often thrown together in Elizabeth's time, and were able to receive mass either openly or secretly. In the 1580s the aforementioned Wisbech became so notorious as a holding-pen for Catholic priests that one commentator called it "as dangerous as a seminary college, being in the heart and midst of England," while the Jesuit Henry Garnet praised it as "a college of venerable confessors of the faith." All the confidence that the Wisbech Catholics projected as a group, however, did not prevent serious dissension from breaking out, as they proceeded to fight over—and in the process influence—matters pertaining at that time to the archpriest controversy.[117]

Apart from actual contact with keepers, helpers, or other inmates, prisoners connected to the larger world through their writings, which constituted perhaps the most important element in their incarcerated existence. Not only did their letters and treatises provide consolation or describe their condition to others in dense and tortured scribblings, but so did the prison walls offer themselves up as a kind of blank space for graffitied self-testament. Recusants and priests in Elizabeth's time, for example, carved their initials or religious emblems on the walls of the Tower, as John Gerard discovered when he first entered the Tower and was placed in Henry Walpole's old cell, on whose walls were chalked the orders of the angels: "at the top above the Cherubim and Seraphim, was the name of Mary, Mother of God, and then above it the name of Jesus; above that again the name of God written in Latin, Greek, and Hebrew characters."[118] In other cases, the margins of Bibles or other religious texts could invite additional scrawls of consolation, as was the case when Henry Garnet smuggled into the Tower a breviary for Robert Southwell, who used a pin to scratch in the words "Jesus," "My God, and my all," and "God hath given himself to thee, give thyself to him." In addition, Garnet wrote, "One can also see there are many numbers, similarly scratched with a pin, and I fancy they must be signs pertaining to the examination of his conscience, whether general or particular."[119]

But it was writing letters that most memorialized the prison experience and contributed to strengthening resolve, thus fortifying communities within and outside the prison walls. The restrictions and conditions of jails often made the act of writing difficult, however, as prisoners suffered from lack of sunlight or from close confinement. "That I have not written unto you erst, the cause is our strait keeping and the want of light by night," John Philpot wrote, while another time he complained from Newgate to a friend that writing was difficult in his "dark closet," though other times he was able to persist, and write from a "coal-house of darkness out of a pair of painful stocks."[120] Another major problem in composing letters or treatises from prison was the frequent deprivation of writing materials, though servants could be used to smuggle in ink and paper; as Ridley wrote an imprisoned Cranmer—whose lack of writing concerned him—"If you have not what to write with, make your man your friend. And this bearer deserveth to be rewarded, so he may and will do you pleasure."[121] Even if writing materials could be smuggled in, however, the risk was always great, not only to the smuggler, but to the prisoner. Writing from the Tower to his mother and friends, John Bradford warned them to take care of the letter that they were receiving, "for if it should be known that I have pen and ink in the prison, then it would be worse with me."[122]

According to Thomas More's great-grandson, the approximately 150,000-word treatise entitled the *Dialogue of Comfort*, which was composed entirely in prison, was "for the most part written with no other pen than a coal."[123] More himself, while able at times to use ink, nevertheless was known to complain of the coal, or charcoal pencils, he was largely forced to preserve and ration, along with the ever-present problem that he "lack[ed] paper."[124] During Elizabeth's reign—and for purposes of secrecy—John Gerard had to make do with a writing agent more crude than coal, when he composed letters in lemon juice, "so that no writing should appear on the paper except when it was moistened"; eventually, however, he came to prefer writing in orange juice, which proved a more amenable fluid for his purposes.[125] Protestant prisoners in Mary's reign similarly endured hardship, as they were compelled to write letters and treatises with coal, window lead, or their own blood[126]— all of which was extraordinary in light of the fact that while prisoners often complained of having to cut short their writing because of such limitations,[127] their letters nevertheless could extend, when later printed out, to fifty-two closely worded pages in length.

Another difficulty for writers was the limitation or full restriction on books, which often forced them to rely on memory when it came to referencing certain works. Confiscation of reading material, along with prisoners' own writings,[128] had always been standard prison policy. In a petition from 1529, John Field, who was imprisoned illegally on orders of Thomas More, requested of the privy council to have a Greek vocabulary, the works of St. Cyprian, and More's own *Supplication of Souls* restored to him after they had been seized.[129] More later suffered the same fate, when Richard Rich and others entered his cell at one point "to fetch away his books from him."[130] As a result, More was unable to consult important authorities such as the early fathers, ancient philosophical sources, or Juvenal or Terence, all of which resulted in a dearth or shakiness of citations. It was the Bible, however, that was perhaps the most essential confiscated text, and an especially potent weapon when withheld from the prisoners, since it served as the key text of consolation, meditation, and solidarity.[131] But the absence of a Bible would not have been a completely acute loss, since even the most illiterate of the population had a modicum of familiarity with scriptural references, and individuals such as More or the Marian Protestants knew the Bible so thoroughly that they could virtually pack their writings with its presence, despite its absence from their cells.

Prisoners used their letters to reach out to a circumscribed audience of followers, who would disseminate and read them in taverns, conventicles, and places overseas; while the writers may have been preaching to the converted, the cause they shared with their readers was never entirely free from external threat or internal apostasies, and thus needed strengthening. Thomas More, for example, was writing from a distinct minority position, due to his refusal to take the oath;[132] as for the Marian Protestants, it was by no means clear or inevitable that their followers would remain stalwart, especially in the face of royal and social pressures. "You are at this present in the confines and borders of Babylon, where you are in danger to drink of the whore's cup, unless you be vigilant in prayer," John Philpot wrote his sister. "Take heed the serpent seduce you not from the simplicity of your faith, as he did our first mother Eve."[133] Letters were thus a way in which leaders could fortify communities, provide consolation and prayer, and in the process reconfirm the necessity of staying together as a community. This was exactly what Paul had done in his letters from prison to the Philippians, for example, and Tudor prison writers—Catholics and Protestants alike—knew it.[134]

Letters from prison could also provide a forum in which to expound to the wider world on theological positions—as was the case in the 1530s, when John Frith informed his followers about points on which he had been questioned concerning transubstantiation and purgatory.[135] More's *Dialogue of Comfort* and other writings also served this purpose, while twenty years later, Ridley would similarly increase his stature and define his theology through written disputations that included a fictional conference undertaken with "Antonian," a stand-in for Stephen Gardiner.[136] The fact that the writer was composing his work from prison only lent him further credibility and authority to instruct others in theology and offer counsel from a position, paradoxically, of strength. In a 1556 letter, for example, John Careless advised Agnes Glascock on what to do after she had gone to a Catholic mass; "[the] thing that is done cannot be undone," Careless wrote, "and you are not the first to have offended, neither are you so good and so holy, as hath at a time slipped forth of the way. Therefore I would not have you to be so much discomforted as I hear say you be." In harsher tone, John Philpot told the lapsed Ann Hartipole that Rome "hath bitten you by the heel and given you a foul fall." "What meaneth it that you are so suddenly departed from Jerusalem into Jericho," he wrote, "to be a companion of thieves and idolaters, to the utter overthrowing of that good which you have professed?"[137]

While the angrily prophetic tone of Protestants such as Philpot tended to differ from the writings of Catholic priests, for example, the basic meanings and points of reference conveyed in letters crossed confessional lines. Prison itself, for example, offered to the writer rich metaphors, many of which were taken from Paul: it was a desert of temptation, a place of sheep preparing for slaughter; it was a pit of alchemical fire that turned base metals into gold (or transformed the sinning individual into the martyr for Christ, as the bread was transformed into the body); it was a "black cross [helping] us to more whiteness,"[138] a place to learn to "loathe the world"; earth itself was a prison which each person was forced to endure in turmoil.[139] Prison also served as a point of rhetorical contrast—and again borrowed from the language of Paul, especially in Galatians—in comparing the darkness of the dungeon to the light of heaven, the body in chains to the spirit free. Inversions and contrasting dualities are utilized heavily, in the manner of Paul's or Cyprian's epistles: "When they imprison our bodies," John Philpot wrote at another point, "they set our souls at liberty with God; when they cast us down, they lift us up."[140] "The prisons stink," John Hooper wrote, "but yet not so much as sweet houses, where the fear and true honour of God lack." He continues:

> I must be alone and solitary; it is better so to be and have God with me, than to be in company with the wicked. Loss of good is great; but loss of God's grace and favour is greater. . . . I shall die then by the hands of the cruel man: he is blessed that loseth this life full of miseries, and findeth the life of eternal joys. It is pain and grief to depart from goods and friends; but yet not so much, as to depart from grace and heaven itself.[141]

Prison also reinforced a sense of election, though it should be pointed out that jailed writers enjoined their coreligionists not to follow the same path as they, aware as they were that imprisonment and martyrdom was not meant for all. Still, even those on the outside—especially those on the outside—faced threats and temptations of a more insidious nature, and were urged to hold fast in the face of the harassments and enjoinments of persecuting authority. John Bradford was especially explicit that his coreligionists move against the ever-hurtling wave of worldly sinfulness and instead follow biblical models of suffering, beginning with "Abel, and come from him to Noah, Abraham, Isaac, Jacob, Joseph, the patriarchs, Moses, David, Daniel, and all the saints in the Old Testament; and tell me whether any of them found any fairer way than ye find now."[142] Just as God allowed "the old popish doctrine to come again and prevail" in order to test the faithful, "so did he with the Israelites, bring them into a desert, after their coming out of Egypt . . . where [they now lacked] that which they had in Egypt." Thus, "in peace, when no persecution was, then were you content and glad to hear me, then did you believe me: and will you not do so now, seeing I speak that, which I trust by God's grace, if need be, to verify with my life?"[143]

Beyond the Old Testament, a key text that breathed through letters from both Catholics and Protestants was the Acts of the Apostles, which provided a standard of comparison in its story of Stephen's martyrdom, Peter's imprisonment and miraculous escape in Jerusalem, the persecutions of Herod, and the missions of Paul. With the Marian Protestants especially, the letters of Paul were also important as literary models, as they followed the writer's epistolary structure of opening with a prayer and a greeting, following with words of comfort and exhortation, and ending with a final farewell. Paul's preoccupation with the community of Christ, as well as his idea of a muscular faith, forged in bondage and combat, were also themes that carried special and obvious resonance to writers who were exhorting themselves as much as they were upholding their followers on the outside. Equally important were the treatises of St. Cyprian, who, like Paul, was particularly clear about the approach Christians should take in the face of persecution. For Thomas More, Cyprian proved illuminating in his recounting of the story of Celerinus, who "for nineteen days [was] shut up in the close guard of a dungeon . . . racked and in irons; but although his body was laid in chains, his spirit remained free. . . . His flesh wasted away . . . but God fed his soul."[144] Thus, just as Christ turned to Thomas and said,

"Look at my hands," so did Celerinus, still alive, "in his glorious body shine the brightness of his wounds."[145]

For all the formal conventions followed by the prison writers, letters finally carried more personal considerations of family, which stood as a counterpart to martyrdom's singular calling. The martyrs were themselves aware of what they were leaving behind, and not all proceeded with complete confidence. In a letter to Lucy Harrington, Laurence Saunders wrote that "[if] God make me worthy to be his witness at this present . . . it is enough for me to say to you, that I have a poor wife and child, whom I love in the Lord, and whom I know, for my sake, that you will tender when I am departed hence." In another letter, Saunders thanked Harrington for her "friendship and tender good-will towards my wife," and requested further that she "[take] care and charge of my said poor wife; I mean, to be unto her a mother and mistress, to rule and direct her by your discreet counsel."[146] Nicholas Ridley, on the other hand, attempted to strengthen the resolve of Robert Glover's wife, who was facing the prospect of her husband's martyrdom: "Be hearty now . . . to your husband and declare yourself to love him in God, as the true faithful Christian woman unto her husband is bound to do," Ridley wrote. "[S]eeing him your husband, which is set by God's ordinance to be your head, is ready to suffer and abide in adversity by his Master's cause, and to cleave to his head Christ, see likewise that you do your duty accordingly, and cleave unto him your head: suffer with him that you may further his cause."[147]

Cloaked within the shroud of exhortation and comfort to the community were words of parting to family and supporters as the prisoner accepted the inevitability of his own martyrdom. In a letter to Augustine Bernher, John Bradford asked him to "commend me to my most dear sister, for whom my heart bleedeth. . . . I think I have taken my leave of her for ever in this life, but in eternal life we shall most surely meet." His mother he addressed directly: "When the wind doth not blow, then cannot a man know the wheat from the chaff," he wrote, "but when the blast cometh, then flieth away the chaff, but the wheat remaineth, and is so far from being hurt, that by the wind it is more cleansed from the chaff, and known to be wheat."[148] For Bradford and others, prison not only served as a kind of preparation stage for martyrdom, but was also part of a larger continuum, as well as a self-contained drama in its own right.

The liminal state to which one was rendered by incarceration allowed for individuals, now cut off from the larger world, to loosen themselves from their previous attachments as well as their former identities; in this sense, imprisonment served as a rite of passage involving one's own death as an individual and rebirth as a future martyr, as he or she was challenged in a series of tests by jailers, torturers, or the conditions of prison life itself. Imprisonment was only the beginning, however, as it would lead in turn to the very different tests that imbued examinations and finally executions; in the meantime, letters would continue to be enriched and given legitimacy by having emerged from prison, with its attendant suffering and violence. As Hugh Latimer wrote: "I have learned by experience . . . that God never shines forth more brightly, and pours out beams of his mercy and consolation, or of strength and firmness of spirit, more clearly or impressively upon the minds of his people, than when they are under the most extreme pain and distress, both of mind and body, that he may then more especially show himself to be the God of his people, when he seemed to have altogether forsaken them. . . . So that we may say with Paul, 'When I am weak, then am I strong; and if I must needs glory, I will glory in my infirmities, in prisons, in revilings, in distresses, in persecutions, in sufferings for Christ.' I pray to God that I may endure to the end."[149]

CHAPTER FOUR

"In the hands of Caiaphas"

Interrogations and Trials

ONE OF THE ESSENTIAL MOMENTS IN THE PERSECUTION PROCESS occurred during interrogations and trials, which served as the central forum where prosecutors and defendants could plead their cases before a large public or send a message that would presumably fragment the authorities and deter any waverers from turning toward disobedience. In this sense, trials were not so much legal forums—though authorities in all reigns did attempt to proceed under the fiction of law—as theatrical and propagandistic displays reflecting clashes not between right and wrong, but between different constitutional, political, and religious understandings. Between these clashes, there could be no room for resolution or compromise on the part of the monarch's representatives or the determined martyr-to-be; the only option for both sides was defendant recantation, crown pardon—both of which were relatively rare at this point in the process—or death. Since trials were controlled and directed from the top, the authorities generally won the immediate battle in gaining recantations or guilty verdicts. In the long run, however, more strongminded defendants and their followers from the other side could also take control of their circumstances and display strategies of resistance—

bold speaking, counter-interrogating, equivocating, modeling themselves on Paul or Jesus before their tribunals—that made government
victory somewhat pyrrhic in the end.[1]

In examining the larger patterns over the course of the century, one
cannot speak of a clear progression from heresy into treason trials, or
from ineffective to effective legal enforcement of conformity. Despite
the shared continuities in confronting and handling dissident challenges, each reign struggled with its own set of concerns, which necessitated that trials be shaped according to particular contingencies and
circumstances; each reign, in turn, achieved success or failure according to the conditions and limitations under which it was functioning,
and in line with the different threats it perceived as arrayed against it.
While all monarchs placed obedience, for example, at the forefront of
their concerns—which most every subject throughout the century, from
Anabaptists to Catholic priests, professed—obedience carried different connotations and levels of commitment throughout the century:
obedience to the Act of Supremacy under Henry, to the Book of Common Prayer under Edward, to the restored church of Rome under Mary,
or to the supremacy and Church of England once more under Elizabeth. Strategies of interrogations—questions asked, answers given—all
shifted accordingly.

If heresy or treason trials are to be seen as showpieces or official displays that projected state power and were intended to secure public relations victories for the crown, it was Elizabeth who was probably most
successful in using trials to shift public perception, especially in the
1580s, when the threat from Spain was greatest. It was during this period
that English Catholics became increasingly divided among themselves
as they were faced with the decision to outwardly conform or pay fines,
or go further and embrace the more radical tenets of the Jesuits, who
could, by association, cast them all as highly suspicious, if not outright
seditious. Yet trials, like prison writings, could also backfire on the authorities, a fact which Edmund Bonner even recognized in the 1550s
under Mary, when he requested in a letter to Reginald Pole that trials
be moved from St. Paul's, where they were becoming too public and
contentious, to quieter quarters, such as the parish quarters at Fulham
Palace. Bonner was implicitly recognizing a fact of sixteenth-century
heresy or treason trials, which was their potential to serve as spaces in
which defendants displayed a range of assertive strategies and thus pre-

pared the ground for their own martyrdom. Interrogations in this sense constituted a test of faith, serving as a great distiller that early on took away the more wavering souls and left only those with the real stuff of martyrdom standing. Though they were comparatively few in relation to the larger number of individuals who recanted, those on trial were significant enough to cause deep and understandable concern to the authorities, who viewed them as souls lost forever, despite all attempts at persuasion. Even worse, not only did these obstinate defendants cast themselves out of the true church and true country, out of the light of the monarch's protective and jealous glow, but they also used their trials to transform rebellion into a God-sanctioned act of providence.

Martyrologists, such as John Foxe or the later Catholic propagandists, also understood the dramatic potential of trials to illuminate their cause, and proceeded to utilize and edit surviving transcripts, and include them as literary centerpieces of their works.[2] One result, as will be seen, is a bias against the interrogator, whose sympathetic personality or occasional acts of kindness tend to be omitted in favor of a portrayal that fits into a stereotype of the demonic persecutor—the sixteenth-century Decius or Diocletian.[3] Equally biased are the interrogation records written by the examinees themselves; the 1546 account or "spiritual autobiography" of Anne Askew, for example, was probably close to the truth in its details, though some comments may have been added, and the later version, edited by the fiercely Protestant writer John Bale, carried further hagiographic embellishments that also modified answers which he deemed were unbecoming to her sex.[4] Bale was himself a playwright, as was John Foxe, and their accounts of interrogations were shaped by the literary tropes and conventions of mystery plays, "tyrant plays," and general biblical dramas, which continued to flourish well into the sixteenth century, not to mention the account in Matthew and Mark of Jesus' trial.[5] In addition, one could also view accounts of examinations as literary dialogues that fit in with the larger humanist tendencies of the age, most notably in the writings of Thomas More, who influenced, albeit in a limited way, the approach that some interrogators would take toward heretics.[6] In the end, however, despite the literary accretions and the fragmented records, one is able to attain a partial glimpse of the way in which the law worked (or was evaded) through interrogations and trials, and the clash of individuals seeking to gain victory over each other concerning the greatest issues of the day.

Sixteenth-Century Interrogations: Procedure and Weaknesses

Interrogations were part of the fabric of life in sixteenth-century England, as successive monarchs attempted to keep watch over their subjects' inner doctrinal beliefs along with outward behavior in matters such as church attendance.[7] Questions put forward at visitations, for example, were highly important in taking the religious temperature of a community, and countless informal interrogations took place on the initiative of bishops, with the help of lower-level functionaries, church-wardens, and other religious monitors. But trials—heresy trials, treason trials—were the central events of the religious dramas that unfolded, and it is in the records of these particular interrogations where a more nuanced and complex picture emerges of the relationships and negotiations between authorities and religious dissidents, who reveal through them their own specific personalities and motivations.

The questioning of suspects could vary in character, though the process for the most part began with preliminary, extra-judicial sessions before the privy council or informal private conferences in bishops' or the lord chancellor's chambers. One of the more striking aspects of these sessions was the length to which questioners were willing to go in arguing with the defendant at this point, and in using the forums as a kind of pressure valve to persuade, intimidate, and threaten those defendants into submission. During the reign of Mary, for example, John Philpot was examined at least thirteen times before the final session that would condemn him, while Richard Woodman underwent, by his own estimate, thirty-two preliminary interrogations.[8] That there were so many examinations in the first place attests to their central aim, which was not to punish or even make a point, but to extract a written abjuration or to get the suspect to name fellow associates. These abjurations or confessions were sought for a number of reasons, one of which was a genuine desire on the part of authorities to bring a lost sheep back to the flock;[9] for many interrogators, however, the issue came to be seen as one of law and order and sheer crown loyalty, as a denial to confess was construed as willful insubordination to the government's policies. A confession, it should be added, also made the authorities' task easier, especially during preliminary examinations, in that the burden of proof at trial lay on their shoulders, requiring them to summon witnesses, gather evidence, draw up articles, and marshal their arguments in a process that did not necessarily turn in their favor.

Torture was sometimes employed during this preliminary or extra-judicial stage of questioning, though its ostensible purpose was to extract from the suspect incriminating information rather than a confession or recantation. In the Elizabethan period especially, when the practice reached unprecedented levels,[10] the guilt of those stretched on the rack was presumably established before torture had been used, even if guilt rested simply on the fact of one's being a priest. A justification that authorities had for employing torture was that it involved matters of state, not conscience; according to William Cecil, in his treatise justifying the practice, no Catholics were tortured over questions, for example, of transubstantiation or the mass, but were instead dealt with over conspiracies or personal actions, such as bringing papal bulls into the realm. Moreover, Cecil would continue to insist with others that torture functioned under the law and was sanctioned by the privy council—neither of which prevented individuals such as Richard Topcliffe from inflicting pain freely and without warrant, in the understanding that their methods were sanctioned from on high.[11]

In heresy trials, if a recantation was not secured in preliminary examinations or through the threat or reality of torture, the matter would move on to the bishop's consistory court, which began with an official opening statement followed by the presentation of articles, witness statements, and evidence.[12] Though the defendant could try to plead his own case at trial, the only options available to him were, again, a recantation of his beliefs or a verdict of guilty, with the latter leading to a formal sentence of condemnation. The bishop of the particular diocese where the case was being tried served as the primary interrogator, though he could be joined by other bishops as well as chancellors, deans, lawyers, various members of his entourage, and secular officials, such as justices of the peace or members of the privy council.[13]

For cases concerning Catholics charged with treason, trials were entirely secular, and were presided over by commissioners of oyer and terminer, who argued their side before a petty jury that consisted theoretically of men of rank and wealth who had been selected for their duty by the crown.[14] After the grand jury's first formal presentation of the indictment, the defendant was asked to raise his right hand, face the court, and make a plea of guilty or not guilty, even though he had not been given the chance to view the indictment beforehand. There followed the presentation by the king's (or queen's) learned counsel, which usually consisted of the attorney-general, the solicitor-general, and a king's serjeant, and the presentation of evidence in the form of incriminating letters, previous examinations, and depositions from witnesses. The defendant was then questioned, though he was given few opportunities at this point to articulate his defense, nor could he call his own witnesses to the stand. At the end of the trial, the jury was dismissed to deliberate the case, and then returned when a verdict was reached; if the jury rendered the defendant guilty, then the presiding magistrate asked him if he had anything to say before he was to receive judgment "according to the law," which gave him the opportunity to plead for the king (or queen's) clemency. If this failed—and it usually did—then one of the judges proceeded to detail the grisly punishment he would face.

It was, perhaps, inevitable that judicial and legal lapses would appear in an age of political and religious upheaval, and while the defendants, as will be seen, found themselves subject to abuses and biases, trials and interrogations were not altogether unfair procedures. Acquittals, for example, sometimes occurred, though rarely. As Geoffrey Elton once demonstrated, between 1532 and 1540 only 38 percent of the 883 defendants charged with treason were actually executed; this number, however, is taken from the mass of indictments that include individuals whose cases were eventually dismissed or rejected by the crown, and therefore does not capture the percentage of individuals who lasted throughout a treason trial and were exonerated. Indeed, if the actual number of people sent on to trial for treason is factored in, the acquittal rate drops to 10 percent—a low number that could reflect either the crown's care in taking only those of probable guilt to court, or evidence of the odds stacked against a defendant in finding vindication and freedom.[15]

Fundamental political and religious changes not only contributed to the decline of traditional ways in which religious dissidents were taken through the trial and interrogation process; they also led to an increasing fragmentation in understandings of the law and its respective place or legitimacy in temporal and ecclesiastical realms. Henry's break with Rome, for example, meant that procedures and laws—above all, canon laws—took a back seat to a newly assertive common law,[16] and were in a state of flux that would not work itself out for decades. Even Mary, who restored Roman Catholicism and its canon law, continued the pattern of leaving the secular governmental authorities in charge of determining the commissions and controlling the actions of the judging bishops in heresy trials.[17]

Legal confusions therefore prevailed and were evident at most religion-related trials, where defendants who clung to older laws did not recognize the grounds under which they were now being tried, as was the case with many Marian Protestants who refused to accept the "foreign" canon law of the courts that were pursuing them, or Elizabethan Catholics, who questioned the common law treason charges against them, when in fact—or so they believed—their real crime was religion. Competing systems of law and legal ideas were not limited to the canon and secular realm, however, and also could include a more abstract but vehemently stated loyalty to God's law, or the law of one's own conscience, especially as it conflicted with temporal, worldly law imposed by the monarch. This was not a new issue in the history of the church, but it took on different connotations in the sixteenth century, when the idea of conscience was pushed to the forefront in trials throughout the century, with defendants having to face stark and unprecedented choices in allegiance. Ultimately, these shifts in court jurisdiction and procedure, as well as legal understandings, point to an uncertainty that undermined the power of the government and its instruments of enforcement and prosecution. The inconsistencies and weaknesses of the court system opened up opportunities in which defendants challenged the grounds of the proceedings and laid claim themselves, quite validly, to the true law. There was thus a great deal of grappling back and forth about the legality of the proceedings and the charges under which the defendants were being tried; while prosecutors in various reigns were convinced of their legal and jurisdictional powers, the challenge to their authority nevertheless put them on the defensive, and often turned the trials into actual debates rather than simply displays of state-imposed might.

The Magistrate

Since accounts of interrogations have entered the historical record primarily through martyrologies that take the defendant's point of view, the questioning authorities are presented in the full and sinister colors of persecution, as caricatures who must accord with their dubious scriptural and early church predecessors. In reality, interrogations were a complex process led by men who could variously turn irate, frustrated, bullying, sympathetic, skillful, or buffoonish in utilizing methods and tactics to bring the defendant around to their side. Though these figures are well known, it is difficult to gain a full sense of who they were, not least because they are portrayed with such bile by their enemies, whose accounts often constitute the only surviving documents of such examinations. Historical accuracy was not always the goal of such writers, especially when their narratives could be shaped toward particular rhetorical ends, as was the case, most notably, with John Foxe, who presented his own narrative as a battle between darkness and light, evil and good. Thus the Marian commissioner John Story is described by Foxe as the "white child of the mother church," a "hydra," "an arch-enemy to Christ's gospel," a "persecutor of God's people," and a "bloody Nimrod," while other interrogators are used to contrast (Romish) pomp and ceremony and the apostolic simplicity of those under examination. In another Foxe account, the bishop of Rochester, for example, is described as greeting the widow Margery Polley by "rising up out of the chair of his majesty, in the high swelling style, after his ordinary fashion," and then proceeding to "dash the silly poor woman" to pieces with a pretentiously worded accusation.[18] Perhaps unsurprisingly, one of the worst culprits to Foxe is Cardinal Wolsey, who is portrayed as greeting the Protestant Robert Barnes by saying, "Is this Dr Barnes . . . had you not sufficient scope in the Scriptures to teach the people, but that my golden shoes, my pole-axes, my pillars, my golden cushions, my crosses did so offend you, that you must make us 'ridiculum caput' amongst the people?"[19] While he was allegedly speaking these words, Wolsey, in Foxe's description, sat "in his whole pomp, mitred . . . enthronised, his chaplains and spiritual doctors in gowns of damask and satin, and he himself in purple; even like a bloody Antichrist."[20]

Even in the biased and febrile depictions of Foxe, however, or in the Catholic narratives by William Roper or William Allen, interrogators are often individualized—if only to be demonized—and portrayed as impassioned advocates of orthodoxy, albeit a wrong one.[21] What is missing from these accounts, as well as the work of later (and recent) historians, is an examination of these interrogators on their own terms; rather than constituting mouthpieces for high policy, or serving as attack-dogs for the state, interrogators were, in fact, acting understandably and rationally, as even their enemies had to admit at times. Interrogators did not view themselves as persecutors, or even as prosecutors; rather, in cases of heresy they took on roles as defenders of the true religion, confronting not Christians but dangerous religious deviants, while in treason cases, especially in Elizabeth's reign, they were convicting conspirators against the crown rather than singling out an innocent community of Catholics. Moreover, all interrogators believed to some extent or another that they were working under the aegis of order in the realm, and that the law imbued them with the responsibility of ensuring the stability of England—a responsibility that they professed and took very seriously, even if they did not always follow legal guidelines in practice.

This respect for the legality of the proceedings, or the attachment to a legal pretext, was due in part to the background of many interrogators, who had been extensively versed in the law, or were at least proficient in the exercise of it. Thomas More, for example, had gone through Lincoln's Inn, one of the four colleges that constituted the Inns of Court,[22] and as lord chancellor presided over the Court of Chancery, while Thomas Cromwell had begun as a solicitor and a member of Gray's Inn—which was also Cecil's alma mater—as well as a member of parliament and legal councilor to Wolsey.[23] John Story, so excoriated by Foxe, began his career as a lay brother of the Greyfriars and went on to hold the first patent as regius professor in civil law at Oxford under Henry and, for a time, Edward; upon Mary's accession—and after a falling out with the Edwardian regime—Story again returned to the post, only to resign and become chancellor under Bonner in London, where he earned his malignant reputation.[24] As overseers of the consistory court, bishops, as well as lay lord chancellors such as More and Audley, were also expected to be fully knowledgeable in the canon law, even as its hold on the realm was fatally weakened. While this was less the case after the break with Rome, when a new generation of bishops was ordained, many Protestants, such as Cranmer, had deep backgrounds in canon law to the point where their knowledge made them especially able theorists and critics against it.

Under Elizabeth, when heresy trials gave way to treason trials and the more obstinate Catholics were recast as traitors, the presiding judges consisted of serjeants-at-law, who numbered an exclusive brotherhood of ten and were "created" at the bar of the Court of the Common Pleas.

Having come up through the Inns of Court, the serjeants-at-law were appointed to the King's Bench or Common Pleas—the forums for treason trials—and considered to be the top jurists in the field, as their opinions, recorded in the yearbooks, were alone responsible for shaping the common law in the realm.[25] But in treason and other cases, serjeants-at-law also faced emerging competition in the attorney-general and solicitor-general, crown law officers who had been similarly immersed and advanced in the law, and who shared in the same judicial appointments. Like the serjeants-at-law, solicitor- and attorney-generals were expected to keep alive their connections with the Inns of Court which had trained them, though they lived apart and were considered to have achieved an eminence in the law that went far beyond that of the Inns' teachers.[26]

Despite their training and the primacy with which they placed the law, interrogators could lapse, however, into a kind of tortured legalism—or so it was perceived by the opposition. This was especially the case when it came to facing down Protestant defendants, whose adherence to the one clear law of God and conscience was contrasted by writers, such as John Bale, with the specious legal encrustations that clung to interrogators along with all the other hollow ceremonialism associated with the Romish church.[27] According to Foxe, when in 1531 the draper Thomas Patmore found himself in trouble for speaking against the saints, for example, he was brought before Stokesley, and became "so wrapt in the bishop's nets that he could not get out," which resulted in his having to abjure and pay a fine to the king of one hundred pounds.[28] The prevalence of entrapping and subtle questions—the "crafty couching of . . . interrogatories," as Foxe put it—had early on been a well-known complaint by the laity, leading to a "Supplication against the Ordinaries" made in 1532, which attempted to remedy entrapping or overly subtle questions and may have been inspired by the trials of Thomas Bilney, described by A. G. Dickens as reflecting "the rigid, merciless legalism of the system at its worst."[29]

The attempt to snare a defendant through legal means worked less well, however, when the defendant was himself trained in the law. In the case of Thomas More, after his problems began a series of questioners made constant efforts to hold him to a firm position and used various entrapping strategies to do so. Sometimes the strategies even worked, or at least succeeded in scoring a point of debate. During an early examination, for example, Cromwell attempted to loosen More's silence or imprecision concerning the king's supremacy by pointing out that More had once compelled men to make a stand concerning the pope's authority; when More replied that the recognition of the pope had been different, since—unlike in England—"the pope's power was recognized for an undoubted thing," Cromwell answered that people "were as well burned for denying of that, as they be beheaded of denying of this, and therefore [had] as good reason to compel them to make precise answer to the one as to the other."[30]

Pedagogical elements from training at the Inns of Court resonate through these interrogations, and training at the moot courts, which required that students set forth imaginary scenarios and spar with each other over them, was particularly evident.[31] In the famous, if controversial, conversation that Richard Rich recounted between him and Thomas More, for example, Rich followed this tradition by saying, "Admit there were, sir, an act of parliament that all the Realm should take me for King. Would not you, Master More, take me for King?" Rich then allegedly "put [the] case further" by asking that if there were an act of parliament "that all the Realm should take me for Pope . . . would you then, Master More, take me for Pope?" More, who was familiar with hypotheticals, said that while parliament could meddle in affairs of temporal princes, "to make answer to your other cause, I will put this case: Suppose the Parliament would make a law that God should not be God. Would you then, Master Rich, say that God were not God?" Rich answered no, that "no Parliament may make any such law," and later testified—controversially—that More then added the words, "No more . . . could the Parliament make the King Supreme Head of the Church."[32]

A background in the Inns of Court's moots could also be discerned in Thomas Martin's interrogation of Thomas Cranmer during trial as to whether, according to Cranmer's reasoning about supreme headship, Nero could then be considered the head of the church. Cranmer, who should have brought forth his own ideas distinguishing full headship and temporal authority, instead fell into the trap and replied that Nero was head of the church "that is, in worldly respect of the temporal bodies of man." This in turn provoked Martin to reply, "Then he who beheaded the heads of the church, and crucified the apostles, was head of Christ's church; and that he that was never a member of the church, is head of the church by your new found understanding of God's word." Martin proceeded in his brutal cross-examination of Cranmer, who seems to have collapsed in the face of the barrage:

Martin: Now, sir, as touching the last part of your oration, you denied that the Pope's holiness was Supreme Head of the church of Christ.

Cranmer: I did so.

Martin: Who say you then is Supreme Head?

Cranmer: Christ.

Martin: But whom hath Christ left here in earth his vicar and head of his church?

Cranmer: Nobody.

Martin: Ah! Why told you not King Henry this when thou had made him Supreme Head? And now nobody is. This is treason against his own person as you then made him.[33]

In the same trial, Cranmer's case was further weakened when he was made to answer for the evidence, which the lawyers ably exploited by presenting him with incriminating documents from the notarial archives that attested to his having once sworn loyalty to the pope; even though Cranmer had long explained his changeover from Rome to the king, the evidence nevertheless was damaging and bespoke an inconsistency in the defense's position.[34] Later on, during the treason trials in Elizabeth's reign, prosecutors also took advantage of evidence, or used the defendant's previous examinations and confessions against him.[35] Such was the case during the trial of the seminary priest Cuthbert Mayne, whose interrogators were able to point out that since in his preliminary examination, Mayne had stated that he brought twelve or thirteen Agnus Dei into the realm, and he only had eight or nine copies when he was captured, the rest were delivered in direct contravention of the act 13 Elizabeth c.2 against distributing such works. Later, incriminating letters were produced as well, further leading Mayne down a path that ended in conviction.[36]

For all their occasional successes, interrogators nevertheless had a difficult time in trying to break down the resilience of defendants who remained persistent in their religious convictions. Sometimes friendliness or sympathy was used as a tactic, as were bluffs and even bribes, though of no avail if the defendant was set on holding fast.[37] When attempts were made to offer bribes to defendants, the results could be particularly heavy-handed and unsuccessful, and indicative of desperation on the part of interrogators. Thomas Martin—so effective with Cranmer—attempted to persuade John Careless to recant by offering him a more earthly reward: "Thou speakest so much of the Lord, the Lord," he said, "wilt thou be content to go with my lord Fitzwalter into Ireland? Methinks thou art a goodly tall fellow to do the queen service there." Careless answered that he would be glad to do the queen service; "And if her grace or her officers under her do require me to do anything contrary to Christ's religion, I am ready also to do my service in Smithfield for not observing it, as my bed-fellow and other brethren have done, praised be God for them."[38]

Threats had a better chance of working, as was the case in 1543, when Robert Wisdom was visited in prison by Edward Whitechurch and told of the punishments he would face as a heretic—a tactic that resulted in his abjuration.[39] For others of a firmer mettle, however, threats only served to strengthen them further. During one of Thomas More's early examinations in prison, Cromwell asked whether he was aware that the king "would follow the course of his law toward such as he shall find obstinate?" to which More replied that "My poor body is at the King's pleasure, would God my death might do him good."[40] On a blunter level, the priest John Gerard, while detained in prison during Elizabeth's reign, faced Richard Topcliffe—"old and hoary and a veteran in evil"— who demanded, "You know who I am? I am Topcliffe. No doubt you have often heard people talk about me?" As he said this, he "slapped his sword on the table close at hand as though he intended to use it, if occasion arose." Gerard, however, remained unmoved.[41]

Religious dissidents, especially those willing to go to their deaths, were thus the worst possible subjects for the interrogator to examine, as even simple and illiterate individuals could frustrate all tactical, lawyerly attempts to induce them to conform. As will be seen, genuinely impassioned defendants were working from a different set of assumptions than those of their interrogators, and according to what they believed was a higher law or principle; against this shield, interrogators, in the end, could do little except use their legal weapons to entrap or bully, or, failing that, to cajole. Not surprisingly, many sessions lapsed into frustration for the interrogators, as was the case in the 1558 trial of Roger

Holland, whose examiner, Dr. Chedsey, addressed the defendant with kindness and an appeal to familiarity, only to be told, "Sir, you crave of God you know not what . . . I beseech God to open your eyes to the light of his word." When Holland was then dismissed and returned for his second examination, Edmund Bonner attempted to appeal to him by saying, "Roger, for thy friends' sake (I promise thee) I wish thee well, and I mean to do thee good." Holland still refused, despite Bonner's entreaty during his last examination that "you will not with these lewd [heretics] cast yourself headlong from the church of your parents and your friends that are here . . . [P]lay the wise man's part and come home." Ultimately, Holland chose martyrdom.

In their dealings with heretics or traitors, interrogators could in fact display a remarkable amount of patience, especially with challenging or insulting defendants. The examinations of John Philpot, above all, attest to the exhaustive lengths to which interrogators were willing to go, and while Philpot was a notable figure, interrogators could also expend the same amount of energy on lesser folk, such as the fisherman Rawlins White. Even Thomas More, who wrote the blistering *Confutation of Tyndale*, advocated moderation and patience in his *Dialogue Concerning Heresies*, which instructed clergy on how to "see through the cunning malice of heretics."[42] More knew from experience—and from sitting in at heresy trials—that heretical opinions could withstand hours of interrogation, and that if a recantation finally did come forward, then the opinions could reassert themselves afterwards; indeed, challenges to heresy, no matter how reasoned and convincing, had difficulty withstanding the more passionate oratory of a well-preached sermon, as More himself understood.[43] For him, heresy was a sickness, a diabolic infection that took insidious, labyrinthine forms in the educated and uneducated alike; moreover, heresy could become convoluted with hearsay, as individuals took in doctrines secondhand and judged clerics, for example, on the basis of this flimsy sidelong evidence. More's purpose was thus to use dialogue, or interrogation, to make the heretic "see again" by countering false knowledge with the right and true knowledge, not only through verbal persuasion but through the presentation of written evidence—Luther's works, for example—that could be countered with lawyerly, reasoned arguments.[44]

Nevertheless, the frustration that interrogators experienced, especially at the hands of obstinate and frequently insulting heretics or Jesuit traitors, often sent the process into a downward spiral. In this, Edmund Bonner displayed the hottest head, as was the case in his dealings with the Protestant John Rough, who had been to Rome and now claimed the pope to be antichrist—an assertion which caused Bonner to lose his temper and "[make] as though he would have torn [Rough's] garments." According to Foxe, Bonner then asked, "'Hast thou been at Rome and seen our holy father the pope, and dost thou blaspheme him after this sort?' . . . And with that flying upon him, he plucked off a piece of [Rough's] beard."[45] Less heated, but no less frustrating, was the 1555 trial of the bishop Robert Ferrar, which descended into near nonsense:

Bourne:	You were once abjured for heresy in Oxford.
Ferrar:	That I was not.
Bourne:	You were.
Ferrar:	I was never; it is not true.
Bourne:	You went from St. David's [Ferrar's diocese] to Scotland.
Ferrar:	That I did not.
Bourne:	You did.
Ferrar:	That I did never; but I went from York into Scotland.
Bourne:	Ah! So said I: you went with Barlow.
Ferrar:	That is true; but never from St. David's.
Bourne:	You carried books out of Oxford, to the archbishop of York, Edward Lee.
Ferrar:	That I did not.
Bourne:	You did.
Ferrar:	I did not; but I carried old books from St. Oswald's to the archbishop of York.[46]

Perhaps the most off-putting challenge that interrogators faced, however, occurred when they were on familiar terms with the defendants—a situation that was also unique in the examination of religious dissidents, many of whom had once shared beliefs and were members of the same community as those who were now questioning them. Sometimes interrogators used this familiarity as a tactic, as when Dr. Webb appealed to the Protestant John Bland by saying, "Master Bland, I knew you when ye were not of this opinion. I would to God ye would reform yourself"; Bland, however, replied, "If ye had known me of another opinion than I am of now, it was for lack of knowledge."[47]

Less sympathetic was James Brooks, who served as one of Cranmer's judges in the 1555 trial, thus continuing an antagonistic relationship that had begun in the 1530s, when Brooks had been a member, and adversary, of the conservative, anti-Cranmer faction at Oxford.[48] Thomas More similarly faced an antagonistic and prejudicial commission of judges: not only did the nineteen commissioners include Cromwell, whose dislike of More was evident, but also the Duke of Norfolk (Anne Boleyn's uncle), the earl of Wiltshire (Anne Boleyn's father), the Duke of Suffolk (Henry's brother-in-law), as well as a number of officers of the court who served as Henry's direct appointees. One of the commissioners, Thomas Audley, was not only More's successor as lord chancellor, but revealed himself as a lackey to the king when he earlier told More's stepdaughter of the necessity of adjusting one's conscience to the winds of popular opinion. As for Norfolk—who had also judged the Carthusian monks and John Fisher, and would later turn around and judge his niece Anne Boleyn—a famous conversation recounted between him and More reveals his own inclinations. "By the Mass, Master More," Norfolk recalled his saying to More, "it is perilous striving with princes. And therefore I would wish you somewhat to incline to the King's pleasure, for, by God's body, Master More, *Indignatio principis mors est.*"[49]

Over the course of the century, the relationship between interrogators and those they interrogated grew even more complicated and antagonistic, especially when religious and political affiliations shifted from one reign to another.[50] In the time of Mary, this was particularly evident with men such as Bonner, who started his career as a Wolsey protégé and firm upholder of the royal supremacy in the 1530s, only to return to Catholicism and embrace the pope once more as the church's rightful authority.[51] This inconstancy was noted by the defendants who now faced him, including William Tyms, who mentioned that Bonner had not only taken the oath of supremacy under Henry, but had written the preface to Stephen Gardiner's pro-supremacy treatise entitled *De Vera Obedientia*. In his defense, Bonner replied:

> Lo! Here is a goodly matter indeed, My lord of Winchester [Stephen Gardiner] being a great learned man, did write a book against the supremacy of the pope's holiness, and I also did write a preface before the same book, tending to the same effect. And thus

did we, because of the perilous world that then was: for then was it made treason by the laws of this realm to maintain the pope's authority, and great danger it was to be suspected a favourer of the see of Rome; and therefore fear compelled us to bear with the time, for otherwise there had been no way but one. You know when any uttered his conscience in maintaining the pope's authority, he suffered death for it. . . . But since that time, even since the coming of the queen's majesty, when we might be bold to speak our conscience, we have acknowledged our faults.[52]

By exploiting their examiners' complicated shifts in allegiance, defendants could thus undermine the interrogations and the authority which those in power were trying to establish. Gardiner, the source of *De Vera Obedientia,* and thus the most apparently hypocritical in his repudiation of the work, was particularly subject to such barrages when he returned to power in Mary's reign.[53] "As I remember," the Protestant Thomas Rose said to him, "that when this truth [of the doctrine of supremacy] was revealed unto you, you thought the scales to fall from your eyes." "Thou liest like a varment," Gardiner replied; "there is no such thing in my book."[54] During the same period, John Rogers challenged Gardiner on the same point, saying that the bishop had upheld the Act of Supremacy passed by parliament:

Gardiner: Tush! That parliament was with most great cruelty constrained to abolish and put away the primacy from the Bishop of Rome.

Rogers: With cruelty? Why then I perceive that you take a wrong way with cruelty to persuade men's consciences. For it should appear by your doings now, that the cruelty then used hath not persuaded your consciences. How then would you have our consciences persuaded with cruelty?[55]

Occasionally, the defendants' convictions combined with outrage over their questioners' apparent hypocrisy to produce frequent outbursts of impudence, as when in the 1550s the blacksmith John Fortune accused his bishop of perjury for now standing before him when once he had taken the oath repudiating the pope.[56] In the same period, Robert Smith addressed the doctors before him with the words, "Where were you in the days of King Edward, that ye spake not that which ye speak now? . . . Ye have for every time a visor: yea, and if another King Edward should arise, ye would say then 'Down with the pope, for he is anti-christ.'"[57] When William Tyms confronted Edward Tyrrel with the fact that Tyrrel had upheld the same Protestant truths as he had in the days of Edward, Tyrrel replied that he never believed those truths in his heart; Tyms replied, "then I pray you, master Tyrrel, bear with me; for I have been a traitor but a while [since Mary's accession], but you have been a traitor six years [under Edward]."[58]

Despite frequent accusations of religious irregularity, many inter-rogators could, in fact, genuinely answer for themselves, as was the case when Richard Woodman accused the bishop of Lincoln of being a turn-coat; the bishop, John White, replied that he had spent the days of Ed-ward "in the Tower, as the lieutenant will bear me record." During the same period, Thomas Haukes asked his interrogator, Dr. Chedsey, where he was in Edward's reign, to which Chedsey answered, "in prison."[59] Other ardent and consistent Catholics in Mary's reign included Dr. Drai-cot and John Story,[60] while Cranmer's examiner, Thomas Martin, also seemed a genuine, if a not quite exemplary, Catholic. After his educa-tion at Oxford, he spent much of Edward's reign in Europe, where he seems to have lived a dissolute life of brothel-visiting among syphilitic priests; while he did arrange the smuggling into England of books that attest to his Catholic sympathies, he spoke against clerical celibacy and, according to the virulently anti-Catholic polemicist John Bale, told Cranmer—his later opponent—that he was a Protestant. In Mary's reign he returned to England, where he proceeded to interrogate Protes-tants and destroy Cranmer on the stand; still, this "natural Proteus," in Bale's words, managed to live on, despite his reputation, through Eliza-beth's reign, taking the oath of supremacy and advising Burghley on orchards and various other horticultural matters.[61]

During Elizabeth's reign, interrogators displayed more constancy and could render a clean account of their pasts, since few of them had been active persecutors under Mary. Those who were, such as Richard Rich, may have retained a modicum of power, but they did not serve as active commissioners during treason trials. Indeed, the worst that could be said—and it was not said—about interrogators such as Burghley was that they had quietly sat out the reign of Mary, neither acquiescing to nor actively rebelling against her policies. Catholics under interrogation, however, did bring up the general issue of the period's confusing instability to justify their beliefs, as the following statement from Cecily Stoner, examined for her recusancy, attests:

> I was born in such a time when holy mass was in great reverence, and brought up in the same faith. In King Henry's time this reverence was neglected and reproved by such as governed. In Queen Mary's [time], it was restored with much applause; and now in this time it pleaseth the state to question them, as now they do me, who continue in this Catholic profession. The state would have these several changes, which I have seen with mine eyes, good and laudable. Whether it can be so, I refer it to your Lordships' consideration. I hold me still to that wherein I was born and bred; and so by the grace of God I will live and die in it.[62]

Examiners should not be castigated altogether for their changeability or adaptability, since they were subject, like everyone else, to the countervailing currents of a time in which religious policy, and much religious belief, was in confusion. One was not necessarily inconsistent, after all, in embracing the supremacy in the 1530s, only to become disillusioned, as the conservative Gardiner and Bonner did, by the instabilities that Protestantism wrought under Edward. Moreover, contrary to being zealous persecutors, interrogators were often reluctant in the tasks that faced them, as was the case with Bishop Cuthbert Tunstall, who was so intent on preventing the condemnation and execution of Thomas Bilney that he continued to stall, dismiss, and reconvene the court proceedings in the hope that Bilney would at some point change his mind.[63]

Interrogators were thus not faceless or demonic representatives of an all-persecuting state, despite their portrayal as such by martyrologists, but rather individuals doing their job in the face of often stubborn resistance. Indeed, their willingness to listen to traitors or give heretics a chance in the face of what was considered the greatest transgression an individual could commit, is impressive or—in the case of authorities in Elizabeth's time—understandable when issues involved genuine plots or national security threats. This is not to say that interrogators should be completely redeemed from their portrayals, nor should Henrician, Edwardian, Marian, and Elizabethan interrogators be grouped under the same equivalence. Still, all of them, in their own context, felt as if they were dealing with the worst criminals imaginable, ones who offended against church or state (or both); even though some of the interrogators may, in fact, have been motivated by careerism or unsavory principles, they attempted to pursue their task under the law as they understood it at the time.

Questions

Since religious and political uniformity was the foremost goal of all the monarchs, it was the duty of interrogators to formulate questions that would elicit the divisive or schismatic elements in the defendants' responses, and to thereby enlighten the heretic or traitor as to how far he had strayed, or fallen, from the truth. But interrogations were also dialogues, and as such existed in an unstable zone where different fundamental and essentially unresolvable truths vied with one another for primacy; indeed, notions such as uniformity refracted off each other's opposing meanings as in a hall of mirrors. The terminology between disputants may have been shared, but the foundational understandings were radically different. For example, Protestants and Catholics both agreed on the four traditional marks that defined the church, but whereas Catholics emphasized unity and catholicity (or universality), Protestants insisted on holiness and apostolicity, in a disagreement that became egregious enough to drive a wedge into the very meaning of what a church was to be. This, in turn, was exacerbated by related questions that centered around the issue of authority—of whether the head of the church resided in Rome or England, for example, or if scripture or church tradition was the sole doctrinal measure of things. Not only did life and death hinge on one's interpretation of authority, as well as on the stand one made concerning justification by faith and the role of sacraments—especially the sacrament of the eucharist—but so did the very life and death of the English church or the Roman church depend on the unambiguous victory of one correct soteriological and historical understanding over another.

Interrogators under Elizabeth professed not to care about such inner points of belief, except on the issue of allegiance to the pope, which for them translated, of course, into treason. Especially after

1570, authorities during Elizabeth's period thus implied that loyalty to Rome—and to its doctrines, institutions, and the idea of universal churchhood—had a direct corollary in disobedience to the queen—an idea which many, if not most, English Catholics denied, as they continued to profess their devotion to both the queen and to England. This could border on the disingenuous, but so could the government's claim that it was interrogating priests, in the words of a warrant issued to Topcliffe and Young, in order to attain from them "the better understanding of the trewth of matters agenst her Maiestie and the Stayte."[64] The line between internal belief and external behavior was thin, however, with the one always holding implications for the other. Simply being a priest implicated one in guilt, no matter what was said or withheld; as one interrogator said to the priest Edward Jones in 1590, "There is treason enough proved against thee in that thou art a priest."[65]

The importance placed on specific questions was reinforced by the fact that they were often drafted from the highest levels of government by royal ministers who wished to create guidelines for others and to control the process as a whole. Thomas Cromwell, for example, composed many questions—to Thomas More, or the Carthusians—while later on, William Cecil took charge of trials by overseeing the directions that the interrogations would take and even drafting, in 1583, the infamous "Bloody Question." Bishops, and even archbishop Cranmer, also played a direct hand in determining the way in which questions accorded to the government's orthodoxy and determined what did and did not constitute heresy, which they themselves had often personally formulated. Not surprisingly, throughout the records of questions and answers, one finds echoes of arguments laid down in important treatises written by Stephen Gardiner, Cuthbert Tunstall, and John Fisher, who themselves played the role of interrogator at various times, just as the defendants, including John Frith and Cranmer, also brought up points that they had earlier delineated in treatises of their own.

Early in the interrogation process, the goal was simply to extract information from the suspect: his name, his parish or diocese, his travels, his last attendance at confession, or communion. Church attendance was a particularly strong barometer that authorities used in testing the suspect's obedience to the crown. Elizabeth certainly used it in regard to suspected Catholics or recusants, but Mary, Henry, and even Edward sought to narrow down the suspect's allegiances according to the church

he did or did not attend.[66] Authorities also used these early interrogations to pin the suspect, if the matter was pertinent, to a possible affiliation with sectarian groups and controversies. One way to do this was to
interrogate the subject on the question of oath-taking—or to request
that he make an oath on the spot—which would uncover for authorities
not only disobedience to the crown, but also confirm what they perceived to be a state-rejecting Anabaptist menace.

Even in the reign of Mary, when Catholics viewed most if not all
forms and aspects of Protestantism as heresy and made no distinction in
throwing Anabaptists as well as Edwardian Evangelicals into the flames,
interrogators sometimes sought out differences among their enemies to
prove, if nothing else, their point that Protestantism only led to fragmentation and thus proof of the faith's falseness.[67] Marian interrogators, for example, asked defendants how many sacraments they believed
in; if the answer was two—baptism and the eucharist—then authorities
knew they were dealing with a Protestant. But the authorities also knew
that Protestants were themselves divided on the issue—as well as on
matters of predestination and grace—and that the division could serve
those authorities as a point of castigation useful in the prosecutory arsenal. During his examination, John Careless was asked about the conflicts that existed among varieties of Protestants in the King's Bench
prison; Careless denied any difficulties, which led his interrogator—
again, Thomas Martin—to bring up the name of another prisoner who
had disagreed with Careless's faction on such matters. Careless then
admitted that there had once been disputes in prison about the nature
of election and salvation, but that the problems were now over, and "I
was sorry that the papists should hear of our variance." Martin accused
Careless of lying, and said, "I know there is a great many of other matters between you. Tell me the truth, I pray thee; for I promise thee I do
ask thee for no hurt, but to do you good: for I think you will be burned
all the sort of you."[68]

The best sort of defendants for examiners were those who had attained positions of religious leadership among their factions or communities, since it was thought that interrogators' victory over them
would constitute a fatal blow to the head from which the body—the
followers—would subsequently crumble. Thus the Protestant William
Tyms was told by Bonner in 1556 that "I will begin with thee first, for
thou art and hast been the ringleader for these thy companions; thou

hast taught them heresies, and confirmed them in their erroneous opinions."[69] If a group's leadership was not available for questioning, then
the next best defendant would be the follower who could name his or
her fellow associates, leading in turn to the unraveling of illegal networks and also to the bolstering of the prosecution's case with witnesses.
During the same period as Tyms, the interrogator, told John Marbeck
that if only he would "be plain," and since "[t]hou art acquainted with
a great sort of heretics," it would thus be to his benefit to "open" those
heretic friends and secure his own "deliverance" and a "better living."
Marbeck refused to comply, however: "I am but a poor man," he said, and
"as for their secrets, they were too wise to commit them to any such as
I am." Later, Knight confronted Marbeck with blunter demands: When
was Marbeck last with the reformer and dean of Exeter Dr. Haynes?
What was Marbeck saying to his fellows in church "when honest
men . . . walked up and down beside you" and "ye . . . stayed your talk
till they [were] past you, [so] they should not hear whereof you talked?"
Marbeck replied that he could not in all good conscience name as heretics those men he knew were not, which brought on the interrogator's
response, "What tellest thou me of thy conscience? Thou mayest, with
safe conscience, utter those that be heretics, and, so doing, thou canst
do God and the king no greater service." Anyway, Knight added, even
if Marbeck did not name names, his friends, under examination, would
surely name him. Marbeck was then left alone to ponder the matter and
was handed a pen and sheet of paper "that thou mayest excogitate with
thyself, and write such things as shall come to mind." Instead, Marbeck
wrote that "I cannot call to remembrance any manner of the thing
whereby I might justly accuse any one of them, unless it be the reading of the New Testament, which is common to all men."[70]

Marbeck may have held out and refused to name his associates, but
others were less reticent, and proceeded to divulge information that led
to the apprehension of their coreligionists.[71] In 1521, for example, Bishop
Longland—a man of "moody violence," in Foxe's words—managed to
compel the parishioners in his diocese, through "captious interrogatories," to incriminate one another in heresy; thus did Marian Morden
turn her brother in for teaching her to say the Pater Noster in English,
while Robert Bartlett named his brother and wife for similar crimes.[72]
Edward Crome, as mentioned in the previous chapter, named his coreligionists in 1546 when he was examined, though one of those friends,

Anne Askew, refused to submit her own names, even as she was tortured on the rack in the Tower.[73] Members of conventicles or sects were especially prone to being asked these questions—who their fellows were, where they had gathered—when their number and the nature of their activities remained ambiguous to the authorities.[74] Thus, in 1561, two ex-members of the Familists proceeded to depose against their coreligionists before a Surrey interrogator, revealing the time and place of secret meetings, the number present in these gatherings, and the connection with groups in other counties.[75]

Elizabethan authorities were especially intent on extracting information from Catholics, and particularly Jesuit priests, who circulated through an extensive underground network. In the 1580s, John Gerard was asked how long he had been in the country and with whom he had been living; Gerard, however, was adamant in his refusal to name those who had harbored him. "I honour the Queen, and I will obey her and you in all that is lawful," he said. "But on this point you must hold me excused. If I name any person who has harboured me or mention any house where I have found shelter, innocent people will suffer for the kindness they have done me." In a later examination, Gerard was asked the whereabouts of the Jesuit Henry Garnet, for "He is an enemy of the state, and you are bound to report on all such men." Gerard, however, again refused to reveal any information.[76] Even more worrisome to Elizabethan authorities was international sponsorship, and where the precise source of Jesuit activities had originated. Typical was the following exchange, between Gerard and his examiners:

> "Who sent you over here [to England]?" they asked.
> "The Superiors of the Society [of Jesus]," [Gerard answered].
> "Why?"
> "To bring back wandering souls to their Maker."
> "No, you were sent to seduce people from the Queen's allegiance to the Pope's, and to meddle in State business."[77]

In examinations and trials that dealt solely with issues of heresy, one of the most important questions sought the defendant's position on the sacraments and especially the meaning of the mass and transubstantiation. It was not that authorities were interested in the sacramental beliefs of the defendant per se, but rather the subject's attachment (or detachment) to the institutional hierarchy—the Roman Catholic Church—upon which those sacraments rested. For Catholics such as More, the papacy lay at the heart of the seven sacraments, which even Henry, in 1521, had asserted when he wrote *Assertio Septem Sacramentorum*, the work that would grant him the title of Defender of the Faith. To downgrade the sacraments from seven to two, or to deny transubstantiation—as Protestants did—was, from a Catholic perspective, to turn away from Rome's doctrinal and moral hegemony, which had been established through centuries of tradition. It meant that one was literally and figuratively "emptying out" the church—though radical Protestants, such as John Hooper, would say "cleansing out" the church—of all its vestments, chalices, stone altars, and monstrances, as well as its sacramental structure.[78] In this sense, the question cut to the heart of the issues at stake, and revealed the defendant's potential antinomianism; to claim grace to be a thing not sacramentally delivered, but directly received by God's love alone—as the more radical Evangelicals did—carried implications that challenged all intermediaries, including social and political institutions such as the kingship itself.[79]

During the Marian persecution especially, questions concerning the sacrament of the mass were thus pushed to the forefront in an unprecedented way, especially as they centered around three core points: the real presence, or whether the consecrated bread and wine constituted the body and blood of Christ; the priest's ability to effect transubstantiation through his consecration of the host; and the belief in the mass as a sacrifice. Behind these questions, however, lay broader issues concerning the meaning of the words "Hic est corpus meum" ("This is my body"), whether Christ's body was located in heaven or on the altar, if it could exist in two places, and how wicked individuals or—in echo of a timeworn debate—even unwitting creatures such as mice—could partake of the body of Christ. Again, the responses varied: the most sophisticated ruminations on the real presence from a Protestant perspective came from Cranmer and Nicholas Ridley, both of whom had written important treatises on the subject[80]—not to mention the 1549 and 1552 prayer books in Cranmer's case—though they were deprived of their freedom to explain their ideas in their disputations and trials. Still, what they had once written did find echoes in lower-level interrogations. To claim, as many Protestants did, that the sacrament was a sign which conveyed what it signified—or a seal of the divine promise—was a direct echo of the 1552 prayer book, while Thomas Haukes also borrowed from Cranmer in denying the real presence on biblical grounds, because Jesus never taught the doctrine, and "[n]either Peter nor Paul ever taught it, neither instituted it so."[81] During the same period, the weaver Matthew Plaise also expressed the more radical Cranmerian position of the 1553 prayer book, when he stated that "the bread was nothing but a sign, token, or remembrance"[82]—a position that also seemed to reflect Cranmer's evolving stance toward acceptance of a complete Zwinglian memorialism.

Other defendants presented their own kind of counterarguments: when Nicholas Sheterden was asked whether the statement "This is my body" was to be taken as scriptural proof of the real presence, Sheterden replied, "Then, belike, when Christ said, 'This cup is my blood,' the substance of the cup was changed without any other meaning, and so the cup was changed, not the wine." "Not so," answered the staunchly Catholic Marian examiner Nicholas Harpsfield, who was not exactly getting Sheterden's point, "for when Christ said, 'This cup is my blood,' he meant not the cup but the wine in the cup.'" Sheterden then turned the tables and asked whether the words spoken or the mind of the priest changed the substance, to which Harpsfield replied that the priest's mind changed the substance. Sheterden then said, "if the priest then do mind his harlot, or any other vain thing, that thing so minded was there made, and so the people do worship the priest's harlot, instead of Christ's blood. And again, none of the people can tell when it is Christ's blood, or when it is not, seeing the matter standeth in the mind of the priest; for no man can tell what the priest meaneth but himself; and so are they ever in danger of committing idolatry."[83] Similarly, John Newman argued against literalness: "Christ saith, 'This cup is the new testament in my blood' . . . if he will have it so meant, then let them take and eat the cup." Moreover, if Judas, during the Last Supper, had taken in the literal body of Christ, and if the devil also dwelled within the betrayer, "I pray you how did they two agree together?"[84]

Another approach to the real presence was taken by Alice Driver, who asked her examiner, Gascoine, whether Jesus had been literal when he had told his disciples to make the bread he was offering his body. When Gascoine answered that the bread was in fact Jesus' body, Driver asked, "How could that be, when the disciples had eaten him up overnight," he could then be bodily present the next day for crucifixion? Was Gascoine saying then that Christ had two bodies—the one that was eaten and the one that was crucified? If so, "Be you not ashamed to teach the people, that Christ had two bodies?"[85] During the same period, John Bland argued that since it was impossible that Christ's blood could make a man drunk, "If a man be drunken with wine consecrated, it must be a miracle." Moreover, "The body that ye receive, ye say, is alive, because it is annexed to the Godhead, and the flesh that ye receive is lively, because it hath the Spirit of God joined to it. This division is of your new inventions, to divide the body and the flesh, the one alive by the Godhead, the other lively by God's Spirit, and both one sacrament: ye make of it a thing so fantastical, that ye imagine a body without flesh, and flesh without a body."[86]

In their attempts to reply to Protestant challenges, interrogators did not always consult treatises on the subject which might have buttressed their counterarguments. When Matthew Plaise was asked if Christ's body could be present at the mass, Plaise answered that "Christ's body was in heaven, and no where else." Cranmer had once made the same claim in his *Defense of the True and Catholic Doctrine of the Sacrament of the Body and Blood of our Saviour Christ* (1550), to which Gardiner argued, in his treatise entitled *Explication and Assertion of the True Catholic Faith,* that Christ's body was in heaven as well as at the altar, "not by shifting of place but by the determining of his will." Catholic interrogators in Mary's reign could also have consulted John Fisher's *De Veritate Corporis et Sanguinis Christi in Eucharistia,* published in 1527, in which the bishop of Rochester used arguments of tradition and the church fathers to claim, among other things, that sacraments served to strengthen a constantly challenged faith, which in turn could be given certainty by those very sacraments—a certainty which was lacking in the writings of Protestants.[87]

Questions about the real presence always circled back to issues of the true church, which caused both sides to use the early church in backing up their own cause. In his examination of Cranmer, for example, John Story said to the defendant, "Well, sir, you will grant me that there was a perfect Catholic Church before any king was christened [as a Christian]," a supposition which Cranmer had long challenged in his arguments that the church had only reached its perfection and discipline under princes, and that the English church was a restoration—a renovation, not an innovation—of the teachings of the "auncient fathers."[88] In other cases, authorities were met with counter-assertions when it came to the subject of the early church, as when Roger Holland in 1558 declared, "The antiquity of the church is not from pope Nicholas or pope Joan; but our church is from the beginning, even from the time God said unto Adam, that the Seed of the woman should break the serpent's head; and so to faithful Noah; to Abraham, Isaac, and Jacob." Indeed, "[f]or the upholding of your church and religion, what antiquity can you show? Yea, the mass, that idol and chief pillar of your religion, is not yet four hundred years old." As for the church of Rome's claim to universality and unity, "What unity was in your church, when there were three popes at once? Where was your head of unity, when you had a woman-pope?"[89]

Other Protestant defendants followed similar lines, appealing to a true, apostolic church that existed before the wicked, Rome-based antichrist. When George Marsh was urged to submit himself to the church of Rome, he replied that he did believe in "one holy catholic and apostolic church, without which there is no salvation," but it was a church "before any succession of bishops, general councils, or Romish decrees," and that it was "a little poor silly flock, dispersed and scattered abroad, as sheep without a shepherd in the midst of wolves . . . and that this church was led and ruled by the only laws, counsels, and word of Christ, he being the Supreme Head of this church."[90] With Matthew Plaise, a quotation from scripture was enough to define what a church was: "Christ saith," Plaise told the interrogators, that "where two or three be gathered together in his name, there is he in the midst among them."[91]

When asked by what authority they based their opinion, Protestant defendants inevitably appealed to scripture, as was the case when Plaise later turned to his examiners and asked, "[W]ould you have me to believe you, because you say you hold the truth? . . . That which makes me believe chiefly, is the Scripture, which I am sure is the truth indeed."[92] When Bonner's chancellor turned to Elizabeth Young and asked, "Who shall judge between thee and me?", she replied, "The Scripture."[93] Similarly, John Philpot stated to his own examiners that "For Christ saith in St John, 'The word that he spake, shall be judge in the latter day.'" According to John Newman, "I stand not to mine own opinion, God I take to witness, but only to the Scriptures of God, and that can all those that stand here witness with me, and nothing but the Scriptures." In contrast, Thomas Spurdance asked during his own examination in 1557, "ye cannot prove the pope to be authorized by Scripture," while Thomas

Haukes claimed that Catholicism taught another "gospel," of "praying to saints and to our Lady, and trust in the mass, holy bread, holy water, and . . . idols"—but this was not scripture.[94] This sort of answer infuriated the authorities, who believed a reliance on scripture alone would only bring on a range of chaotic opinions. "Ah, sir! Ye are a right scripture-man, for ye will have nothing but the Scripture," Bonner told Haukes.[95]

Authorities attempted to dissuade defendants from such ideas with arguments of their own, to little avail. In 1556, Dr. Cooke told William Tyms, "Thou speakest much of the Scripture but understand it not"; like the hunter who spends a fruitless day searching for game, so Tyms "labourest in reading of the Scriptures; thou takest the letter, but the meaning thou knowest not; and thus thy reading is as unprofitable unto thee, as hunting was unto [the hunter]." During the same examination, Bonner asked Tyms's codefendant, Drakes, how he knew scripture to be the word of God; when Drakes replied that scripture showed the way to salvation and "doth revoke and call back all men from wicked life," Bonner responded that "heathen writers have taught precept[s] of good living, as well as the Scripture, and yet their writings are not esteemed to be God's word."[96] Some Catholic interrogators, in their defense, brought up one of Thomas More's primary arguments, which was that Protestants did in fact judge and base their knowledge on the church, which had established the scriptural canon they all recognized; "There is like surety and like certain knowledge of the word of God unwritten as there is of the word of God written," wrote More, "sith ye know neither the tone or the tother to be the word of God but by the tradition of the Church." To this, however, the orthodox Protestants appealed to tradition as well—that is, the *traditio quinquesecularis,* or the tradition of the church's first five centuries, which they depended on as an objective standard that supplemented scripture, and deflected charges of scriptural subjectivism, as a fundamental basis of authority.

At the core of many (though by no means all) Catholic arguments lay the defense of the church of Rome's universal authority, which for them the royal supremacy shattered by claiming headship for itself and thus creating, in William Allen's words, "the very gap to bring any realm to the thraldom of all sects."[97] In order to counter this fragmentation, the church, Allen believed, must hold an autonomous position with its own rights and powers, if it can have any claim to being universal; this was the principle Thomas More had died for—that the pope alone ultimately held superior spiritual power over secular and political authorities, that he alone had power to interpret scripture, and that only he could convene general councils.[98] It was the extent to which Catholics believed this universal church to have powers over the secular government, including the powers to depose kings, that was never entirely agreed upon by the community, especially later in the century; it constituted the key point that coursed through all the questions presented by Elizabethan authorities when they confronted their defendants on the stand.

Earlier in the century, the pope had been portrayed in woodcuts and pamphlets as the antichrist, but by the time of Elizabeth he thus took on an identity as a political foreign power and enemy of state. It was therefore important that in the interrogation of Catholics, particularly priests, the question be asked whether the accused acknowledged the queen as lawfully holding supremacy in matters both temporal and spiritual. Catholics could answer in the negative and deny the queen's legitimacy altogether, in which case they would be declared traitors and sent on to their deaths; such was the case with the priest James Bell, who denied the queen's supremacy, "for she hath not to iudge in spirituall causes and matters of fayth; but the Pope is to deale in those matters, and under him byshops and priests." As for his allegiance in case of war between England and Rome, Bell replied, "We ought to take parte with the Church of God, for the Catholicke religion."[99] Other Catholics, meanwhile, could also state, in accordance with the 1570 papal bull of excommunication, that Elizabeth was the queen—just not the lawful queen—which did not help their cause very much.

After 1580, Pope Gregory XIII attempted to make matters easier by allowing Catholics to grant the queen temporal legitimacy, but the question they had to answer before Elizabethan authorities conjoined both temporal and spiritual legitimacy, linking them together inextricably. A related question asked whether the defendant acknowledged the pope's power not only to excommunicate, but also to depose the queen. Again, this was an impossible question for Catholics to answer one way or another, for if they agreed, then they were traitors, and if they disagreed, then they were not Catholics. Some defendants tried to get around this, the most famous being Edmund Campion, who answered, even while being racked, that the question was irrelevant to his trial and more appropriate to the "schools." It was a decent answer, and it was repeated by others, but it did not, of course, save them in the end.[100]

The range of questions posed to Catholic priests—who were the primary targets of persecution under Elizabeth—was captured well in the preliminary interrogatories presented in written form to John Fynch in 1584. The questions began with details about his travels, including whether he had been overseas (he had not, he claimed), and where he had stayed within England during past six years (he was legally not bound to answer, he said). From there, the interrogatories moved to more religious grounds, asking if he had taken part in the mass ("I have harde Mass, I thanke God. I may not tell where, and I cannot tell how often"), and what he thought of the bull of excommunication ("I have hard sometyme of that bull; but I know no certentie thereof, therefor I cannot answer"). To the question as to whether Elizabeth was head of the church, Fynch declared outright that "The Pope's Holynes is head of the whole Church in earth; and it is impossible that the Queene or any other woman or layman should be Head of the Church," though he also added, "I . . . do professe my selfe her subject."[101]

Eventually, Fynch was faced with the most hated question of all— the "Bloody Question" devised by Cecil in 1583, which was overtly political and thus worked against the Catholics' claim that they were being persecuted solely for religious matters. The question was perhaps best expressed by Richard Topcliffe, when he asked the priest John Gerard,

> What would you do if the Pope were to send over an army and declare that his only object was to bring the kingdom back to its Catholic allegiance? And if he stated at the same time that there was no other way of reestablishing the Catholic faith; and commanded everyone by his apostolic authority to support him? Whose side would you be on then—the Pope's or the Queen's?[102]

Responses varied, though rare was the answer of one young priest who, soon after the Armada, declared "that, if an army be sent into the realm, he will take part with that army and will persuade as many catholics as he can do the like." Coming from a priest—a spiritual father of an indeterminate flock—these were strong words indeed, and resulted, perhaps rightfully, in the man's death.[103] John Gerard, for his part, answered that "I am a loyal Catholic and I am a loyal subject of the Queen. If this were to happen, and I do not think it at all likely, I would behave as a loyal Catholic and a loyal subject." Of course, this did not answer the question at all, as Topcliffe himself, flying into a "violent rage," well knew.[104] At the same time, the question was not, it should be said, permitted at trial; restricted to preliminary interrogations, it was not covered by statute as a formal offense, but served instead as a psychological and, in William Allen's words, "odious" sledgehammer by which authorities could win a cheap propaganda victory and justify executions on the grounds that "[martyrs] were worthy of death for other causes, though not for that whereof they were condemned."[105] Still, the "Bloody Question" illustrates, in stark colors, the pressing concerns of Elizabethan authorities, especially after 1580; like all questions throughout the century, no matter how different in content and emphasis, it constituted a test of orthodoxy and loyalty, which made the asking of it as important as the answering.

The Accused

For all their pretense of legality, sixteenth-century trials were inherently biased against the defendant, who not only was given little time to prepare his own case or take notes during trial, but also was often dragged from a debilitating months-long stay in prison to the proceedings, where he was both denied legal counsel and refused permission to face his accusers, whoever those often unknown accusers were. As the Protestant Ralph Allerton told his commissioners, "If I cannot have mine accusers to accuse me before you, my conscience doth constrain me to accuse myself before you."[106] Even when the trial came to a close, the defendant was allowed little time to answer for his charges—as was the case during the final trial, in 1555, of Nicholas Ridley, who was given exactly forty words to rebut all the charges against him. While some defendants did succeed in presenting effective legal challenges or at least seizing control of the debate, others, especially those less learned or confident, thrashed about helplessly as they were thrown from one intimidating authority to the next. In the trial of John Lambert, mentioned in chapter 1, the defendant was forced to face the vision of a king "with his brows bent, as it were threatening some grievous thing to him"; when asked his name Lambert replied, "John Nicholson, although of many I be called Lambert," as Henry thundered, "What, have you two names? I would not trust you, having two names, although you were my brother." Lambert then attempted to redeem himself with a long, praiseful speech to the king, which Henry angrily interrupted by telling him to shut up and get on with it: "I came not hither to hear mine own praises thus painted out in my presence; but briefly go to the matter, without any more circumstance."[107]

The same weaknesses in heresy trials also applied to treason trials, with the complaints of Robert Persons giving ample testimony to the injustices in the system. As in the bishops' consistory courts, defendants were allowed no legal counsel, which was unique to England, since even the papal regulations for the Inquisition had allowed counsel to the defense;[108] an inability to review the charges beforehand also made it extremely difficult to marshal one's arguments. "How is it," Persons wrote, "that [the defendant] especially if he be bashful and unlearned, in so short a time as there is allotted him for answering for his Life without the help of a Lawyer, Proctor or other Man that may direct counsel, or assist him in such an agony; how can he see all the parts or points that may be alleged for his defence being never so innocent"?[109]

Hostile or biased witnesses were another element that contributed to the unfairness of trial procedure, as was the quality—in secular treason trials—of jurors; as Persons put it, it was difficult to make his own case against "the . . . malice, ignorance, or little Conscience or care of twelve silly little men." While some degree of fairness existed on the part of those jurors who did not always follow the government's bidding,[110] it is also true that justices of the peace and others who held direct office under the crown were allowed to serve on juries, as were members who had just finished serving on the same case as indicting grand jurors. Perhaps as a result, and because jurors were locked away to deliberate their verdict without benefit of food, drink, fire, or even furniture to sit on, the judgment often, though by no means always, came swiftly, as was the case with Robert Southwell, whose jury conferred for all of fifteen minutes before handing in its judgment of guilty.[111] If the jury, however, decided on an acquittal, then it could be sent back again to rethink its judgment; thus did Thomas Cromwell threaten and bully the jury which initially judged the Carthusian monks not guilty, until he finally got the verdict he wanted, while in John Fisher's trial, he made it known "what verdict they must return; other ways [he would] heap such danger upon their own heads, as none of them were willing to undergo."[112]

Not only were interrogators, witnesses, or jurors hostile, but the defendant also found himself in a generally cramped environment, surrounded by the noise, murmurs, and hecklings of a largely hostile audience. Arriving in court, he was also required much of the time—like Lambert—to stand or kneel, though old age or infirmity could allow him to successfully petition for a chair, as was the case with Thomas More and Hugh Latimer. Meanwhile, the pressure to recant was fierce and constant, as was the intimidation that bore down on him like a wilting beam of heat from the interrogators. Even the use of Latin during disputations and parts of interrogations—though English would be the primary language of the proceedings—worked against the defendants. During his own disputation, Latimer requested that in light of his rusty Latin, he read out his answers in English, while John Philpot interrupted Bonner, who was in the middle of reciting a prayer in Latin, to speak in English—a tactic which might have also carried an element of playing to the audience.[113]

Defendants were not powerless, however, and could utilize a number of strategies to resist the onslaught and make their own case known. Indeed, a self-consciousness pervades their behavior in court, reflecting an awareness of the theatricality of their moment, as even the simplest gestures could project a heroic defiance to their followers. Thus, Cranmer, at the beginning of his trial, tipped his cap to the royal interrogators Thomas Martin and John Story, and pointedly put it back on before James Brooks and other clerical interrogators, who represented Rome; even more, Brooks was sitting under the pyx that held the sacrament—the body of Christ—which Cranmer, according to the Catholic position, was scorning. Nicholas Ridley seems to have taken the hat-tipping to extreme levels; though he did doff his hat at the reading out of his examining bishops' names, he put his hat back on when the pope and the papal legate were named, and continued the gesture until finally his hat was seized from him.

Meanwhile, the last of the three Oxford martyrs, Hugh Latimer, appeared at his own last trial wearing, in Foxe's words, "a kerchief on his head, and upon it a night-cap or two, and a great cap (such as townsmen use, with two broad flaps to button under the chin), wearing an old thread-bare Bristol frieze-gown girdled to his body with a . . . leather girdle, at the which hanged by a long string of leather his Testament, and his spectacles without case depending upon his neck upon his breast."[114] While Latimer was, by that time, ill and aged, and probably suffering from some kind of mental collapse as a result of his long imprisonment, he was nevertheless able to use this self-presentation as a way to avoid having to answer to the last charges made against him, and instead read from a simple, informal statement of his beliefs, from which he re-asserted his position denying the supremacy of Rome and the corporal presence in the eucharist.[115] Later on, during and after the 1580s, Jesuit priests could similarly make statements in their dress or comportment; John Gerard, for example, put on "my Jesuit gown and cloak" whenever he was summoned from prison to appear before the interrogators—an act for which "boys laughed at me," but which only confirmed his loyalty to the old faith.[116]

Just as writers such as Foxe portrayed interrogators as weighted down with false and jeweled abstruseness, so did they present defendants—and defendants present themselves—as simple-speaking harbingers of the truth. Tanners and weavers, for example, knew how to exploit the humbleness of their station before the pomp of authorities, while Anne Askew used the subjectness expected of her sex to plead, disingenuously, that she was "but a woman."[117] When Julius Palmer's interrogator pulled rank and said, "Thou art but a beardless boy, start up yesterday out of the schools," the statement backfired in his unwitting acknowledgment that Palmer possessed the holy spirit and displayed what Paul, in 2 Corinthians, called "the simplicity that is in Christ."[118] Hugh Latimer was probably the model of holy simplicity, having used homeliness of speech to his advantage from the reign of Henry on, in distinguishing himself as one of the best preachers of the century. During his trial, such qualities were on display, as he answered his interrogators with bluntness, interrupted their syllogistic Latin arguments with a "Will you give me leave to speak?"—in English—and finally declared outright that he would never turn in his faith, and that he only prayed that Queen Mary would turn instead.[119]

Despite their simple-talking personas, dissidents could also rise to combative levels and spar with their interrogators on highly legalistic and theological levels, especially when they had received training in the law. Often the defendants questioned the very legality of the proceedings, as was the case, most famously, of Thomas More, who managed to get three of the four counts against him dismissed, and vigorously pleaded not guilty to the fourth, which claimed—falsely, More stated—that he had spoken against the supremacy in a private conversation with Richard Rich. And indeed, More's case was a good one, argued with the assurance and expertise of one of the century's best lawyers; not only did he not commit any overt act of treason, he stated, but silence was no crime and it certainly did not contain malice as defined by Henry's recent treason statutes.[120] Still, as one writer has put it, while More challenged his indictment on the grounds that it was based upon a repugnant statute—and though the trial itself was a clash not of right and wrong, but of different political and constitutional theories—he did accept his verdict in the end, because "Law was law, after all, even if, by the standards of eternity, it was wrong."[121]

In the time of Mary, Protestants also challenged the legality of their trials in various ways. John Bland, for example, refused to answer questions concerning transubstantiation and the sacrament of the mass until he saw the law which compelled him to answer; as he said at another point, "I pray you let me have a counsellor in the law, and I will make my answer according to the law." When told that he was being judged by canon law, Bland—whose Protestantism did not recognize laws that originated in Rome—answered, "I doubt whether it be in strength or no."[122] The most sophisticated challenger of the canon law in general was Thomas Cranmer, who did not comport himself well during his own trial, though he managed to reiterate one of the main themes of his writings, which was the incompatibility of the papal canon law and the common law; since "Whosoever sweareth to both must needs incur perjury to the one," Cranmer stated, the entire proceedings of the court were, in effect, meaningless.[123] Of all the Marian defendants, however, John Philpot seems most to have come into his own over the course of his thirteen examinations, all of which were marked by some sort of challenge on legal grounds. During a private examination with Bonner, for example, Philpot stated that according to St. Ambrose, "the disputation of faith ought to be in the congregation, in the hearing of the people, and that I am not bound to render thereof to every man privately, unless it be to edify." Thus, Philpot continued, "as the said doctor said unto Valentinian the emperor, so I say to your lordship: 'Take away the law, and I shall reason with you.'" This did not go over very well with Bonner, who next faced Philpot in the archdeacon's house, alongside three other bishops; but still Philpot stated that "I have learned to answer in matters of religion, in ecclesia legitime vocatus, in the congregation being thereto lawfully called." Philpot—who studied law extensively at Oxford, when the later Marian persecutor John Story resided there as regius professor of law—went on to claim that he could not be put on trial for conscience, nor could he be tried in a diocese that was not his; instead, he said, "I ought by the law to be sent to my [own] ordinary, if I require it, and not to be punished by you that are not mine ordinary."[124]

Catholics in Elizabeth's reign also used the law in their defense, sometimes with success. When the tide turned in Elizabeth's reign and Edmund Bonner was placed in the dock, for example, he based his own case on a loophole in the statute law, specifically, that he had not, in fact, taken the oath of supremacy after all, because the bishop who had administered it back in Henry's time was not rightly constituted. As a result of his objection and an ingrained respect for the law by the authorities, Bonner was released from the charge, though not from imprisonment in the Marshalsea, where he eventually died. Though his case involved recusancy and not a formal treason trial, Edmund Plowden, one of the greatest barristers of the day, also attempted, in 1569, to legally make his case on the basis of conscience—one of the first times the term "conscientious objection" was used in English law. Upon having to swear on the book of subscription which included the Act of Uniformity, Plowden stated that "he could not subscribe, but belief must precede his subscription."[125]

Others, especially Catholic priests, also defended themselves on the basis of law, though with less success. When it came time for John Story to be placed on trial in 1571—after being kidnapped in Europe and brought back to England—he refused to make a plea of guilty or not guilty, since he "was not the queen's subject, nor had [he] been there these seven years, but was the subject of the most catholic and mighty prince king Philip, king of Spain, to whom he was sworn."[126] Taking another tack, the priest Edward Jones denied, in 1590, the charge that he had arrived from overseas and "did contemptuously come into this realm of England"; "I came not contemptuously into this realm," he stated, "but to save souls. And whereas there is a penalty appointed for the not observing of a law (as do this, or pay this sum of money, or suffer this punishment) there is no contempt." Later, Jones brought up the statute passed in the reign of Edward which had stated that treason must be proved by voluntary confession or the testimony of two witnesses; "Here," he said "is [neither] two witnesses nor voluntary confession." When Richard Topcliffe, who was present at the proceedings, challenged this point, Jones turned to a justice and replied, "I am to be tried by the law, & therefore I pray you, my Lord Chief Justice, let me have the law." Still, the jury found Jones guilty, though he was further able to argue his case on a legal basis—this time, again, concerning conscience—when he was given his chance to respond. "I crave the mercy of Queen Elizabeth," he said, "that as she caused it to be published in pamphlets, which I have seen both in English & Latin, that none of her subjects should suffer the pains of death for their consciences, so no treason being proved against me but that I am a Catholic Priest, which is only conscience, I crave the favour of a subject & the mercy of Queen Elizabeth." Furthermore, he continued, while Mary's pursuit of heretics had at least been sanctioned "by a law made and received & put in execution by all Princes Christian whatsoever . . . [w]hat may be said after in the reign of Queen Elizabeth when so many Priests & Catholics are butchered by a peculiar law made by herself & never heard of before?"[127]

Catholic priests—and Jesuits especially—were particularly frustrated at treason trials which prevented them from disputing. The disputation had always been extremely important to such individuals, constituting as it did a large part of their seminary training on the continent, as well as a key element in their missionary purpose. Primed to fight the enemy on his own terms, Jesuits learned scripture, as well as Hebrew and Greek, to attack the Protestants for the "sophistical" mangling of biblical meanings.[128] But Elizabethan authorities were not interested in disputing during interrogations and trials, which were ostensibly freighted with political concerns; disputations did exist, but they were kept out of the parameters of treason cases. An exception was made in the case of Edmund Campion, who was allowed to undertake a series of disputations against Anglican clergy, in order to demonstrate, in Thomas McCoog's words, that the government "was not afraid of a discussion." The result of the debates, which centered around justification of faith, the real presence, and other points, was somewhat unclear, though it was said that Campion did well enough that Bishop Aylmer requested that the following scheduled sessions be canceled. Shortly after the cancellations took place, Campion was tried at Westminster, condemned, and executed. According to Laurence Humphrey, who was set to take part in the debates, "It was [the cancellation], perhaps, [where the authorities] smelt out that a different course was to be taken with the Jesuits, and that they would have to plead not for their religion, but for life, and be accused not of heresy, but of treason."[129]

Despite the ways in which rules could be changed midstride, the accused often succeeded in turning on their questioners and putting them on the defensive. According to Foxe's somewhat dubious or exaggerated account, in 1558 Richard Smith took such an aggressive stand against his interrogators on issues such as patristic authority that one of them, the chancellor of Exeter, "fell in such a quaking and shaking . . . that he was fain, stooping down, to lay both his hands upon his knees to stay his body from trembling." At one point during his examination, Smith questioned Bonner on the matter of of baptism and its accompanying accessories, such as ointment:

Smith: That is a shameful blasphemy against Christ, so to use any mingle-mangle in baptizing young infants.

Bonner: I believe (I tell thee) that if they die before they be baptized, they be damned.

Smith: Ye shall never be saved by that belief. But I pray you, my lord, show me, are we saved by water, or by Christ?

Bonner: By both.

Smith: Then the water died for our sins; and so must ye say, that the water hath life; and it being our servant, and created for us, is our Saviour. This, my lord, is a good doctrine, is it not?[130]

Later in the examination, Bonner lost his temper and threatened Smith that "thou shalt be burnt at a stake in Smithfield, if thou wilt not turn," to which Smith replied, "And ye shall burn in hell, if ye repent not." During the same period, Thomas Haukes had a similar exchange with Bonner, to the point where it became unclear who was the examiner and who was the examinee. After being asked what so offended him, Haukes replied:

Haukes: The cross of wood, silver, copper or gold, etc.

Bonner: What say ye to that?

Haukes: I say it is an idol. What say you to it?

Bonner: I say every idol is an image, but every image is not an idol.

Haukes: I say, what difference is there between an idol and image?

Bonner: If it be a false god, and an image made of him, that is an idol; but if an image be made of God himself, it is no idol, but an image, because he is the true God.

Haukes: Lay your image of your true God, and of your false god together, and ye shall see the difference. Have not your images and feet go not, eyes and see not, hands and feet not, mouths and speak not?—and even so have your idols.

Chedsey   [another interrogator]: "God forbid," saith St. Paul, "that I should rejoice in any thing else, but in the cross of Christ Jesus."

Haukes: Do ye understand Paul so? Do ye understand Paul?[131]

Defendants also resorted to outright proclamations of their beliefs, even going further in their boldness (and some would say rudeness) than the injunction in 1 Peter to "Always be prepared to make a defence to any one who calls you to account for the hope that is in you, yet do it with gentleness and reverence." William Tyndale had himself early on advised those under fire to "play Paul" and confront the fallen with their sins, even if their defense approached insulting levels. In this he found precedence, again, in the apostles, and fervently identified with them through Jesus' words, "[T]hey shall lay their hands on you, and persecute you, delivering you up to the synagogues, and into prisons, being brought before kings and rulers for my name's sake." As Brad Gregory has pointed out, while such figures were therefore willing to offer themselves up, lamblike, to their persecutors, they could also display a militancy and judgment more in line with the Old Testament than the New. In the early 1540s, Nicholas Shaxton, before he turned from Protestantism back to Catholicism, thus declared before his examiners, "Good brethren, remember yourselves, and become new men, for I myself was in this fond opinion that you are now in, but I am now become a new man," to which Wolsey replied, "Ah, are you become a new man? Wo be to thee, thou wicked new man, for God shall justly judge thee." Later in the century, John Gerard knew that as a known priest he was already compromised, which allowed him to forthrightly answer Topcliffe's question about whether he had reconciled others to Rome. "Yes, I have reconciled people to the Church," Gerard said, "and I am sorry I have not brought this blessing to more." When Topcliffe then asked how many Gerard would have reconciled if he had the chance, Gerard answered, "A hundred thousand. And more than that, if I could."[132]

"Dark Speaking"

The practice of bold declarations coincided with another strategy, which was to reply to interrogators with equivocation and casuistry. Though Catholics—or Jesuits—have been most associated with the practices, recent historians have given more attention to the ways in which Protestants also used dissimulation for their own purposes.[133] It was the goal of every interrogating authority to bring on a recantation, which was supposed to be a formal submission and acknowledgment of the heresy to which one had previously succumbed, often with an added stipulation that involved a recommitment to the religious positions of the government. Since bishops were theoretically held responsible for all the sheep in their flock, they particularly made it a point to claim, and not without some truth, that for every obstinate heretic in their diocese, they had succeeded in urging many more to submit, repent of past waywardness, and "revoke their errors."[134]

Not every recantation, however, was genuine, and while authorities could attempt to counter any hedging by ultimately drawing up formal, explicit, and specific articles of faith to which one had to assent and sign, defendants in an examination could continue to evade by blurring the meanings behind their words—even if those words seemed, on the surface, to accord exactly with the government's line. Recognizing this tendency, authorities urged defendants to speak truthfully and without any reservation or ambiguity. Thus, Bishop Cuthbert Tunstall, for example, asked Thomas Bilney and Thomas Arthur during their trial to state their beliefs "with their hearts,"[135] while Thomas Cromwell, in 1535, dealt with the Carthusians by telling them that they were no longer to equivocate before the king's oath, but to speak in "open language, plainly and simply, [that] you affirm and approve what is put before you."[136] For this reason, questions were often structured so that the defendant was limited to a simple monosyllabic answer, with no room to dissemble or debate. Such was the case in 1557, when Ralph Allerton was presented with thirteen articles and had no choice but to answer all in the affirmative, though he was given leeway to explain himself on one point.[137] Unsurprisingly, the use of the yea or nay question also happened to work very much in the defendant's disfavor, as was the case with Cranmer, whose affirmative answer to the sixteen highly prejudiced articles presented against him at trial appeared as a damaging admission of guilt.[138] Included among the questions was article six, which stated, "Item, that he shamed not openly to glory himself to have had his wife in secret many years," which Cranmer answered by writing, "And though he so did, there was no cause why he should be ashamed thereof," thus indirectly affirming the immoral implications presented by the question.[139]

Individuals who did succeed in submitting to their interrogators and later recanting nevertheless found themselves tortured by conscience; after Thomas Bilney had recanted and carried the faggot at Paul's Cross in the late 1520s, for example, he was said, in Hugh Latimer's words, to have been "in such an anguish and agony that nothing did him good, neither eating nor drinking, nor even any other communication of God's word; for he thought all the whole Scriptures were against him, and sounded to his condemnation."[140] In Mary's reign, John Snell of York was also so tormented after his own recantation that he drowned himself, while Peter Moon, after initially recanting, almost did the same, before he recanted his recantation.[141] Still, many individuals throughout the century continued to dissimulate, and apparently did so without wracking themselves with guilt or facing serious repercussions later on from their previous coreligionists.[142] As Susan Wabuda has pointed out, one of the most notorious recanters was Edward Crome, who rescinded his stated beliefs twice and even named names, though he suffered relatively few recriminations by his former associates.[143] Others chose simply to stay quiet, possibly recant when confronted, and outwardly conform while maintaining their inner beliefs; for them, there was no shame in emulating Nicodemus—the Pharisee in the gospel of John who came to see Jesus only at night, thus keeping his faith a secret—as it could simply constitute a valid option of biding their time until the religious climate shifted in their favor. A significant number of individuals who received noteworthy positions in Elizabeth's reign had spent the years under Mary in this manner, not embracing a martyr's death or fleeing to the continent, but staying quiet; such was the case with large numbers of privy counselors, including Burghley, and at least six bishops who were appointed within the first two years of her reign.[144]

Equivocation was not without controversy, however. Among Protestants during Mary's reign, exiles from the continent such as John Ponet followed Calvin's strong condemnation of Nicodemus,[145] and with their emphasis on personal confession and conscience over Catholic penance and confession, found the dissembling of one's faith hypocritical, if not morally repugnant.[146] Equally vehement were the anti-Nicodemite writings of the Protestant George Joye, whose 1544 work, *Present Consolation for the Sufferers of Persecution for Righteousness,* also counselled readers to openly embrace the cross of suffering, "[setting] the example of Christ before our eyes."[147] But the concern that was expressed with dissembling was also a testament to its continued existence, if not prevalence, as Marian crypto-Protestants did what it took, short of changing their hearts' belief, in order to protect their goods and lives.[148]

Among the strategies of evasion, one common tactic at interrogations was to hedge under the guise of the Apostolic Creed, as was the case when Elizabeth Young was asked her stance on the sacrament of the altar and answered: "I believe in God the Father Almighty, the Son, and the Holy Ghost, three persons and one God. I believe in all the articles of my Creed," and "all things written in the holy Scripture, and all things agreeable with the Scripture, given by the Holy Ghost unto the Church of Christ."[149] This still did not exactly answer the question about the mass, however. During the same period, John Bland told his examiner, Nicholas Harpsfield, "I am not ashamed of my faith: for I believe in God the Father Almighty, maker of heaven and earth, and in Jesus Christ his only Son our Lord, etc., with all the other Articles of the Creed." Harpsfield, however, could not get Bland to extend the Creed with the words "and upon all the holy scriptures, sacraments, and holy doctors of the church, and upon all the general councils that ever were."[150]

In the reign of Elizabeth, Protestants more radical or extreme—or traditional to the extreme—also resorted to Nicodemism when facing the authorities, as when Familists were given permission by their leaders "to denie before men all theire doctrine, so that they keepe the same secrete in their hearts."[151] Justification for this was sought in the scriptures, and specifically Jesus' injunction in Matthew 7:6 to "give not

that which is holy unto dogs, neither cast your pearls before swine."[152]
This tactic was also consistent with Familist notions which placed emphasis on the privacy of belief; as one writer put it, "Let that which is secrete to God only, whereof no proof can be made nor lawfull witnesse broughte, abide to the coming of the Lorde, which shall open all the secretes."[153] It was thus almost logical—or consistent—that Familists would sanction equivocation, recantation, and reservation as a way to protect the kind of extreme interiority which lay at the heart of their faith. Not surprisingly, this caused the authorities some consternation, for it undermined the very meaning and purpose of interrogations themselves, and cast doubt on the confessions of others. As J. W. Martin once put it, "If the Familists' conformity was delusive, might not that of the 'church papists' be also?"[154]

Sixteenth-century Jesuits have been most closely identified with casuistic practices, but as Peter Marshall has pointed out, earlier Catholics, such as John Forest, were already using such devices fifty years before.[155] By no means were all Catholics in favor of these methods, or of dissimulation in general.[156] Increasingly, however, with the establishment by William Allen of the Catholic seminary at Douai, in France, Catholics turned to the Spanish Jesuits, and specifically Martin de Azpilcueta, for textbook lessons on the art of evasive speaking, and went on to produce booklets of their own for the edification of fellow priests in England.[157] Under these influences, Robert Southwell, Robert Persons, and Henry Garnet thus advised their coreligionists on how to approach interrogators truthfully, without resorting to lying. Though Catholics had already faced the quandary of what to do when it came to facing the Act of Uniformity or attending Protestant churches,[158] the problem of answering the more difficult and indeed impossible questions was in its own distinct category, and demanded a different set of considerations.

Catholics learned to distinguish, and justify themselves, according to varying levels of interrogatories, ranging from the legitimate question, which should be answered, to the question asked with evil or illegitimate intent, in which case equivocation or a different kind of truth could be employed.[159] Reserving or adding a clause was another way to evade authorities, especially when it came to the taking of oaths; long before the Jesuits, in the 1530s, for example, John Houghton and his fellow Carthusians had already figured out how to take the oath of succession by adding the clause "as far as it is lawful"—an addition that Cromwell later refused to accept.[160] Later on, such reservations turned inward, as individuals were told to withhold certain phrases while "speaking" them in one's mind. According to writers such as Henry Garnet, Jesus implicitly sanctioned the practice when he was asked about the date of the end of the world and answered that he did not know; surely, Garnet wrote, he was reserving an extra proposition in his mind. Catholics thus learned to use reservation, especially withholding the phrase "Non . . . ut vobis servisset," which was used famously by Edmund Campion when he denied his name was Campion "to serve your purposes."[161] Less extreme, and more typical, was the "no" answer given by William Freeman when asked if he was a priest, since "yt was no denyall of his faith, but only of his state."[162] Mental reservation was also encouraged among lay people, as when Robert Southwell told a woman that she could say that she had not seen a priest, as long as she reserved in her mind the phrase that she had not seen the priest "in order to betray him."[163]

Another tactic available to defendants throughout the century—and a kind of equivocation in its own right, though it carried a long tradition behind it—was to resort to passivity and silence. According to Mark 15.2–5, when Pilate asked whether he was king of the Jews, Jesus answered, "You have said so"; when confronted with further charges against him, "Jesus made no further answer, so that Pilate wondered." This mode of evasion and silence would give early Christians a reputation for stubbornness and obstinacy—"pertinacia et inflexibilis obstinatio," in Pliny's words—which in turn justified authorities' decisions for executions.[164] While not following active defenses of faith as Paul had enjoined, silence reflected a calculated and even defiant inaction appropriate to martyrs awaiting their fate and using the courtroom to "give themselves up" to the harsh sentences imposed by these sixteenth-century Pilates.[165]

There were many varieties of silence, however. A defendant could use silence as a wedge by refusing to answer questions until he was given the legal justification for his trial; thus Robert Ferrar refused to answer certain articles and questions directed toward him, "till he might see his lawful commission and authority."[166] Defendants could also express a kind of silence in refusing to take an oath, which nevertheless carried an implication of guilt, especially with Anabaptists, who did not recognize oaths to the state. The most famous case of silence in the century occurred in the case of Thomas More, whose refusal to take the Oath of Supremacy—to simply say yes or no to it—infuriated and puzzled the government. One of the reasons More took such a tactic was to avoid being sentenced according to the recently passed laws of treason, which had broadened the crime to include malicious speech against the king, along with an outright denial of the supremacy; instead, More wrote, "I had fully determined with myself neither to study nor meddle with any matter of this world, but that my whole study should be upon the passion of Christ and mine own passage out of the world."[167] Eventually, upon his sentencing, More did make an outright denial of the supremacy, but only after using everything in his legal arsenal, including his silence, to defend his case—all of which constituted a kind of equivocation in its own right.

Most individuals who were on trial remained adamant that they were innocent of treason, especially Catholic priests who believed they were martyring themselves for religious rather than political reasons. But their insistence on loyalty to the crown could also be heartfelt. In his speech before his judgment, Edmund Campion, for example, said that if "our Religion do make us Traitors we are worthy to be condemned; but otherwise [we] are and have been as true subjects as ever the Queen had."[168] During the same period, Christopher Bales announced at the scene of his execution, "Good people, you are come hither to see a man die, but why or wherefore you know not. A traitor! But now wherein a traitor? In that I am a priest, and seek to reconcile souls unto Almighty God according to my office and calling."[169] The implication behind such declarations, though it was not stated outright, was that the queen herself was the traitor to her own being as queen, by refusing the kind of reconciliation to orthodoxy with which monarchs, beginning with Constantine, had long been entrusted. "I am no traitor," Thomas Spurdance earlier asserted in 1557, capturing another aspect of the dilemma; "for I have done, I think, better service to the crown imperial of England, than you." He continued, "There is no man alive (I thank God) that can accuse me justly, that ever I was disobedient to any civil laws. But you must consider, my lord, that I have a soul and a body, and my soul is none of the queen's, but my body and my goods are the queen's. And I must give God my soul, and all that belongeth unto it; that is, I must do the laws and commandments of God: and whosoever commandeth laws contrary to God's laws, I may not do them for losing of my soul, but must rather obey God than man."[170]

Condemnation

The process by which defendants were condemned differed according to the particular trial they faced. In treason trials, a verdict of guilty or not guilty could be appealed by way of a plea for clemency, while at the end of heresy trials, defendants were usually presented with a series of articles to which they had to subscribe. Unsurprisingly, in many cases, the articles were skewed against the defendant, as in the case of Julius Palmer, who refused to affirm articles that conveyed not his own beliefs but "horrible, heretical, damnable, devilish and execrable doctrine."[171] In other cases, however, the articles were carefully tailored to the defendant's specific offenses, and were based not only on examination records and witness testimonies, but also, as in the case of the Protestant Alexander Seton, their previous sermons.[172]

If the defendant agreed to the articles, a formal condemnation was read that included an excommunication—in Mary's time—and a statement detailing how he or she would be handed over to the secular authorities for burning. The formal reading of a condemnation was a highly charged moment, for not only was the defendant being expelled from the church, but his expulsion also portended the finality of execution, or death. John Frith's sentence in 1533 began with the declaration that the bishop of London "lawfully and rightly . . . with all godly favour" proceeded against Frith, who had "heard, seen, and understood and with diligent deliberation weighed, discussed and considered" the arguments presented against his heresy, but still persisted in those "damnable opinions, contrary to the doctrine and determination of the holy church." "We therefore . . . [are] not willing that thou who art wicked, shouldst become more wicked, and infect the Lord's flock with heresy[.] . . . We do judge thee and definitively condemn thee," the statement continued, before coming to the final condemnation of heresy:

> [We declare] that thou hast been and art, by law, excommunicated, and do pronounce and declare thee to be a heretic, to be cast out from the church, and left unto the judgment of the secular

powers . . . most earnestly requiring them, in the bowels of our Lord Jesus Christ, that this execution and punishment, worthily to be done upon thee . . . that it may be to the salvation of thy soul, to the extirpation, terror, and conversion of heretics, to the unity of the catholic faith, by this our sentence definitive, or final decree, which we here promulgate in this form aforesaid.[173]

The condemnation was not always so formal, however. In 1557, according to his own account, Richard Crashfield had exasperated the chancellor, one Dunning, to such an extent that Dunning, in Crashfield's words, said, "'When were you at your parish church? These two years and more you have stood excommunicate: wherefore you are condemned!' And so I was condemned." Sometimes, bishops added asides of their own, as was the case with George Marsh, whose bishop read the sentence and then declared, "Now will I no more pray for thee, than I will for a dog."[174] Authorities were also known to interrupt the reading in order to urge the defendant to recant at the last minute; before he was condemned, George Marsh faced his interrogators and members of the audience, all of whom urged him to recant after the presiding bishop finally recited the familiar words, "Non disputandum est cum haeretico,"[175] and began to read the formal condemnation. According to Foxe,

> . . . [W]hen the bishop had read almost half [of the condemnation], the chancellor called him, and said, "Good my lord, stay, stay; for if ye proceed any farther, it will be too late to call it again;" and so the bishop stayed. Then his popish priests, and many others of the ignorant people, called upon Marsh, with many earnest words to recant; and, amongst others, one Pulleyn a shoe-maker, said to him, "For shame, man, remember thyself, and recant." [When Marsh refused to recant] the bishop put his spectacles again upon his nose, and read forward his sentence about five or six lines, and there again the chancellor with a glavering and smiling countenance called to the bishop, and said, "Yet, good, my lord, once again stay; for if that word be spoken, all is past, no relenting will then serve." And the bishop, pulling off his spectacles, said, "I would stay; and if it would be! . . . How sayest thou? Wilt thou recant?" Many of the priests and ignorant people bade [Marsh] do so, and call to God for grace;

and pulled him by the sleeve, and bade him recant, and save his life. To whom he answered, "I would as fain live as you, if in so doing I should not deny my master Christ."[176]

Though some last-minute recantations did occur, the chances in general that a defendant would recant, after having lasted through numerous and grueling examinations, was slim, and in fact, resolve was only strengthened at the end. When Thomas Wats came into the consistory court for the last time and was asked to deny his statements of faith, he only responded, "God keep me from the doctrine that ye would have me to come unto, which ye have now declared. And I beseech God that I may persevere in that I have done; for I will stand to mine answers." Shortly after, the condemnation was read, and Wats was delivered to the sheriff.[177] Equally defiant was Thomas Haukes, who answered the bishop's urgings to recant by declaring, "[I]f I had a hundred bodies, I would suffer them all to be torn in pieces, rather than I will abjure or recant."[178]

Defendants could also use these extremely tense moments to make a heroic—or impudent—last stand before the authorities and audience. One of the most startling declarations, for example, occurred when Bonner formally told John Philpot that he was now "haereticum, obstinatum, pertinacem, et impoenitentem" and Philpot suddenly interrupted by saying, "I thank God that I am a heretic, out of your cursed church; I am no heretic before God. But God bless you, and give you once grace to repent your wicked doings, and let all men beware of your bloody church."[179] Later in the century, Catholics would take on similar stances of defiance, as when the priest Edward Jones declared that "I rather submit myself to any death whatsoever before I will forsake the Catholic faith."[180]

No formal condemnation was read in treason trials; instead, the judge received the jury verdict before asking the defendant, "What hast thou to say for thyself, why thou shouldst not have Judgment to die?" The defendant could then choose either to challenge the verdict on legal grounds or plead for mercy.[181] In 1581, Edmund Campion used his own moment to speak before the verdict was rendered by challenging the indictments against him on the grounds that the charges were based on "Presumptions and Probabilities." "The constitutions of the realm exact a necessity, and will that no man should totter upon the hazard of like-lihoods," he stated; moreover, "if all were cut off, that hath been weakly or untruly [charged] against us, there would indeed rest nothing that might prove us guilty." The only case that the government had in its favor rested on the priests' unwillingness to take various oaths, for example, to the Act of Uniformity; but what validity were oaths if they could be taken "untruly" by a murderer, a "detestable Atheist, a profane heathen? . . . On your consciences would you believe them?" In the end, however, a guilty verdict was rendered.[182]

Only the monarch's pardon could discharge the defendant from death, which usually did not happen; instead, the judge, after hearing the defendant's case and perhaps dismissing him for a few days, read out the punishment that was to be exacted. In the case of John Fisher, the judge ordered, in a somewhat standard statement, the gruesome punishment that met traitors, but even here resistance to authority took place, as the defendant could use the opportunity of his condemnation or jury verdict to echo, in a kind of *imitatio christi,* the forgiving words of Jesus. As Fisher put it after his condemnation, "I have no more to say, but only to desire Almighty God to forgive them that have thus condemned me, for I think they know not what they have done."[183] At the end of the century, too, the priest John Fynch received his sentence of guilty by "looking upon the Iudge with a cherfull countenaunce and [in a] lowd voyce said, Benedicam Dominum in omni tempore, semper laus eius in ore meo, and turning hyme selfe to the people, [adding] the next verse following, In Domino laudabitur anima mea, audiant mansueti et laetentur."[184] But self-assertion as well as munificence could be contained within the bounds of forgiveness, as individuals wished to demonstrate their holy indifference to the wiles of authority; when confronted by Richard Topcliffe's insults, for example, the priest-harborer Swithin Wells at first responded in kind, until he composed himself and said, "Good sir, forgive me. . . . At this time, Mr Topcliffe, you should not use such speeches to drive me to impatience. God pardon you and make you of a Saul a Paul . . . by your malice I am thus to be executed, but you have done me the greatest benefit that ever I could have had. I heartily forgive you."[185]

Authorities knew this was happening, yet the trial and its verdict had given them no choice but to move ahead with the next stage in the process. Such was the case, for example, with Hugh Latimer in 1555. Standing before the tribunal, aged, infirm, and oddly dressed, he was read his sentence; afterward he asked one more time to defend his beliefs before the court, and then, somewhat disingenuously, requested that he be allowed to appeal his case to the "next general council" in Rome. But Bishop White, one of his examiners, refused. Ordering that the church be cleared so that Latimer would not have to contend with the jostling crowds on his way out, White turned to the secular authority present, who was to carry through the punishment. "Now he is your prisoner, master mayor," White said, and handed Latimer over.

CHAPTER FIVE

"Whither goest Thou?"

The Execution

AUTHORITIES SOUGHT TO EXECUTE THE REALM'S MOST TROUBLE-some religious dissidents in order to maintain stability or to expunge divisive and mutinous individuals from the world, but to be beheaded, burned, hanged, or quartered also carried a resurrectionary potential, as the executed lived on as martyrs in the eyes of their followers.[1] If one examines only state papers and other government documents, then a certain rational and bloodless efficiency emerges as the characteristic of top-down directives to kill, just as it could be easily assumed that the government's orders were met with general consensus among the people, which was not the case at all. People, and perhaps even a majority of them, may have enthusiastically cheered on executions or witnessed them as a kind of theater no different from any other of the numerous executions of the time; yet the behavior of many of the executed in the face of their gruesome fates attested to a bravery that impressed many in the crowds. Rather than inspire a uniform acquiescence among the larger population, the government's pursuit of dissidents to their grim death thus only created or perpetuated an ambivalence on the part of the public; while the nature and extent of that ambivalence differed according to popular sentiment and circumstance, it was nevertheless present among enough of the people so as to make the government's victory pyrrhic, at best.

Rather than functioning as a display of state-controlled power, the theater of execution was thus a contested site, involving a negotiation between three poles of power: the official authorities acting in the name of the crown and guiding the hand of the executioner; the martyr, who turned the drama of death to his own advantage; and the crowd of spectators toward whom the display was ultimately directed, and who influenced the event through their various responses. No side was ever fully dominant: while the autonomy of expression and carnivalesque element of the crowd wielded its own undoubted power, the role of the state should not be underplayed, especially in its ability, in V. A. C. Gatrell's words, to "implant the law's presence, power, and moral messages in the collective mind."[2] The presence of the victim acting in agency and subverting officially sanctioned death to his own purposes nevertheless complicated the mix, turning the spectacle, according to Peter Lake and Michael Questier, into one that carried the potential "for a whole range of gestures and counter-gestures, a serious set of exchanges between state, victim and audience, as inherent in this essentially theatrical way of dispatching the felon and embodying the power of the state."[3]

Though control of the proceedings shifted among participants, it was the martyr who focused all attention and stood at the center of the drama; the ways in which the victims acted and responded were therefore essential, as they well knew. By self-consciously modeling their plight on the passion narrative, or giving stake-side speeches, or dressing and behaving in a particular way, martyrs were able to subvert the authorities' intentions, which was to silence and obliterate them. In this sense, the infliction, by the officials, of torture and punishment did not break down the victim's self—as Elaine Scarry, for example, has argued[4]—but rather strengthened and transcended that self through pain and with full knowledge of the martyrological history behind it. For those about to be put to death, execution served as a kind of alchemy, as the base material of human, flesh-based sinfulness was transformed into the metal of spiritual purity, just as the burning body of the Marian Protestant Robert Samuel, according to Foxe, "did shine in the eyes of them that stood by, as bright and white as new-tried silver."[5] Rather than quench the majesty of martyrdom, the humiliation of an exposed and gruesome death only strengthened that majesty further, as it was now transformed and reinvented into the ultimate *imitatio christi*.

In examining the shifting roles played by authorities, martyrs, and crowds, it is therefore important to take not one side but many, placing oneself in the middle of the action from a confusing perspective that shifts from the stage to the audience and back again. Still, one's perspective remains limited, determined as it is by records either written long after the fact or shaped according to self-conscious literary and hagiographic forms pasted together from secondhand or hearsay accounts. It seems, for example, that remarkably few individuals actually recanted or emotionally broke down at the stake or gallows; but one must also bear in mind that it is in the interest of many writers—such as John Foxe, or the Catholic pamphleteers—not to present their heroes in such a light. In addition, while those about to be executed may have come prepared with elaborate and rehearsed final speeches, some of those speeches could also have been shaped later on to produce more dramatic and powerful effects.[6] However, accounts of executions provide a glimpse into the general dynamic of such ceremonies, which contained mishaps and confusion under the veneer of law and the crown; more important, such accounts also attest to a central fact of executions, which was not that they were simply displays of state power or set pieces for one individual's embrace of martyrdom, but rather collective affairs, dependent on all the actors involved.

Religious Executions in a Larger Context

Executions of religious dissidents constituted only a small percentage of overall executions in the sixteenth century, and, in fact, paled next to those involving murderers, counterfeiters, pirates, adulterers, and robbers. As Raymond Mentzer writes, "the use of the death sentence for heresy was neither singular nor extreme when compared to its application for other felonies."[7] It is difficult to determine, in light of the vague statistical evidence, the cumulative number of individuals, religious and criminal, executed throughout the century; the official notation in cases of treason of "susp.," meaning "to be hanged," does not indicate if executions were actually carried out, or whether a pardon was granted during the period of limbo between condemnation and execution. Keeping this in mind, according to one estimate, the period from 1530 through

1630 may have witnessed the execution of up to 75,000 individuals, with anywhere between 18,000 and 20,000 put to death between 1580 and 1610, a rate which, if applied proportionally to contemporary population rates in the United States, would add up to the equivalent of about 46,000 deaths per year.[8] Other estimates, however, have claimed that under Henry alone between 800 and 2,000 people were put to death annually—which in itself would lead to a figure from anywhere between 32,000 and 80,000 total executions brought about in his reign—an inordinately high number, which should provoke some caution.[9]

Whatever the precise figures, a substantially larger number of individuals were put to death in sixteenth-century England, a fact due in part to the Tudors' increasing the amount of penal legislation and expanding laws already in place.[10] Indeed, directives to various justices and other law officers suggest that the Tudors believed that not *enough* people were being put to death—though later on in the century, alternatives to the death penalty were presented, for example, in sending felons off in galley ships.[11] Executions, however, were not steadily consistent over the course of the century, but could increase in times of political crisis or economic hardship. According to one estimate, in Devonshire during the year 1598, seventy-four individuals were put to death—a large number that could be attributed to the fact that the region had been suffering from an economic downturn due in part to rising grain prices.[12] As for religious heretics or traitors, numbers varied in accordance with royal policy, which itself could be subject to extenuating factors such as national security crises or internal political revolts.

Executions in general were thus a deeply ingrained, even quotidian, reality for sixteenth-century English people, who were aware that long tradition lay behind the spectacle they were viewing. Even so, the legal process which preceded death for religious dissidents, whether they were cast as heretics or traitors, differed from the norm, which in itself placed their fate outside the bounds of the normal, at least from others' perspective. In heresy cases, after the condemnation was read out in consistory court by the presiding bishop, the prisoner was then turned over to the sheriff and justices; while the church remained a presence at the execution site, and, in fact, had the last word at the death scene, it was constrained by its inability to kill, and thus depended on the supplementary presence of secular officials to carry out the task. Treason trials, however, were entirely secular affairs, ending with a verdict by the jury followed by one of the presiding judges reading out the type and terms of punishment; representatives of the crown were then put in charge of seeing that writs or warrants for execution were in place, as the prisoner was to be handed back to his jailer, to wait out the uncertain period before his execution.

The punishment of burning at the stake had been utilized for a variety of offenses throughout the Middle Ages, though it was primarily utilized for women convicted of poisoning, witchcraft, adultery, or treason.[13] The first act passed in England that specifically ordered the punishment of burning for heretics, male and female, would come later, during the reign of Henry IV, when the 1401 statute *De haeretico comburendo* was drawn up, stipulating heresy as a secular offense, to be actively pursued by bishops with the punishment of burning carried out by the secular arm.[14] Burning for heresy was thus a gender-inclusive punishment, unlike the penalty extracted on traitors, which tended to relegate women to fates such as hanging, while men were ordered to be drawn and quartered as well as hanged—a practice that seems to have begun in 1241, with the death of one William Maurice on charges of piracy, though it became legally enshrined with the Statute of Treason of 25 Edward III, passed in 1351.[15] According to Blackstone, such gender discrepancy in punishment was necessary in that "decency due to the [female] sex forbids . . . exposing and publicly mangling [of] their bodies." It was also the tradition—though not always followed—that women were strangled with a rope or chain before they were burned, to release them from the suffering; such preventive measures did not, however, prevent the women burned at Guernsey in 1556, according to Foxe, from torment, since "the rope brake before they were dead, and so the poor women fell in the fire."[16] Members of the nobility or those more prominent were spared from such options altogether, garnering the more honorable treatment of a beheading, by ax or by sword, conducted usually on a permanent scaffold set up on Tower Hill or within the Tower itself; though the chosen place was meant to shield the victim from the larger public's gaze, crowds could still be large, and the parboiled heads were later posted, usually on London Bridge, for all to see.

The act of burning also carried heavy theological implications, as did the throwing of a traitor's bowels and still-throbbing heart into a fire after they were removed from the body. Burning was an act of cleansing and purification, appearing in the injunctions of Deuteronomy; fire also carried alchemical associations, according to Malachi 3:2–4, which described the Lord's coming as a "refiner's fire," which would turn his people to "gold and silver, that they may offer unto the Lord an offering in righteousness." Later on, Marian Protestants would also bring in the sacrificial aspect of fire and offer themselves up as "burnt offerings," in direct reference to the Old Testament. One of them, Hugh Latimer, had himself, however, once likened fire to heresy itself, for just as "the nature of fire is to burn and consume all that which is laid in the fire . . . the nature of false doctrine is to condemn, to bring to everlasting damnation; that is the nature of false doctrine."[17] In the Middle Ages, fire in Christian doctrine could also stand in for hellfire as well as purgatory— an idea which continued throughout the early modern period, with the flame-assailed victim representing the individual's thrust downward into the diabolic underworld. As one writer has put it, fire represented expulsion, as "The flames of hell reach[ed] up to the earth and fetched down the heretic who was forfeit to them."[18]

The significance, aside from the deterrent effect, of disemboweling and quartering a body hearkened back to the medieval belief that treasonable or heretical ideas were literally contained in every bodily part, thus necessitating that bowels, entrails, and genitals be removed piecemeal before being thrown into a purging fire.[19] In 1606 Edward Coke, in his judgment of the Gunpowder Plot, would claim that such "Godly butchery" carried biblical precedents and meanings, as victims' "members" should be separated from corruptible blood. Coke in general perceived symbolism in every detail of the traitor's bodily deconstruction. The purpose of drawing and quartering, he wrote, was to show that the victim was unworthy "to tread upon the face of the earth whereof he was made: also that he hath been retrograde to nature, therefore is he drawn backward at a horse tail"; hanging was necessary because "being hanged up by the neck between heaven and earth" would show him to be unworthy of either realm, while his head was to be cut off since it had "imagined the mischief." In addition, the victim was to be castrated to show him "unfit to leave any generation after him," and his heart removed since that is where he had "harbored . . . such horrible treason." Finally, leaving the body or its remains to hang on a gibbet evoked the ancient biblical idea of associating an exposed body with shame, cursedness, and infamy, in accordance with the prophetic enjoinings of Jeremiah. "Their carcasses will I give to be meat for the fowls of the heaven, and for the beasts of the earth,"[20] he declared, in forecasting the doom of the Jews; their bones shall be "spread before the sun, and the moon, and all the host of heaven . . . they shall not be gathered, nor buried."[21]

The punishment of drawing and quartering also took on significance in that it signaled to the crowds that the victim was in fact dying for treason rather than religion.[22] But the charge of treason was a government designation propounded most loudly by William Cecil, meant in part to shield the crown from being accused of the kind of religion-related persecutory excesses of Mary's reign; it is important to point out that Catholics themselves—or rather, Catholic priests or Jesuits, who were the primary targets—went to their deaths fully believing that the cause for which they were dying was religion. A great many, though by no means all, of their fellow English Catholics believed so, too, and would provide a ready, if numerically small, audience for the subsequent martyrological narratives written by Thomas Worthington or Richard Verstegan.

Approximately 125 Catholic priests and sixty recusants (including a total of three women) were executed as traitors in Elizabeth's reign, primarily in the 1580s, when threats emanating from abroad were strongest.[23] While intolerance toward Puritans, Separatists, or Anabaptists was high and manifested itself in imprisonments, for example, actual executions of heretics—namely, Anabaptists—under Elizabeth probably amounted to six.[24] While not a particularly high number in relative contemporary terms, Elizabeth's executions nevertheless reflected a continuation of the entirely new persecutory wave of the period. Before 1500, Lollards or Wycliffites were the only heretics who posed any kind of challenge to the authorities, and the burning of Sir John Oldcastle in the early fifteenth century forced them underground.[25] Yet this was not quite the same as what happened in the next century, when truly challenging opposition movements emerged, leading to a marked increase in religious executions.[26]

Numbers varied across reigns, however. Aside from Elizabeth's reign, it has been generally accepted that Henry put to death approximately eighty-one heretics and traitors over the course of his regime, while Edward burned only two, and Mary executed somewhere under three hundred Protestants. The class and gender composition of those executed varied from reign to reign. After the break with Rome, Henry tended to pursue individuals whose capacity to influence others made them noteworthy and dangerous; certainly Thomas More and John Fisher were among this group, but almost more important were the Carthusian monks, many of whom were in closer contact with common English people.[27] Later, after the passage of the Act of Six Articles, Henry would turn more concertedly to Evangelicals and others, but even then he would pursue those, such as Anne Askew, whose influence—in her case, at court—was notable and threatening. It was during Mary's reign, however, that executions became almost indiscriminate, with the majority consisting of young people under thirty, and nearly 20 percent constituting women; indeed, the famous "Marian Ten"—most notably the bishops Thomas Cranmer, Nicholas Ridley, Hugh Latimer, John Hooper, and others—were a distinct minority, as were members of the gentry classes, with the great mass of deaths occurring among weavers or various tradesmen.[28]

Fewer women were executed for heresy or treason than men, due in part to propriety, a desire to prevent sympathy for the victim, or a general belief that held women less accountable for their beliefs, even if, like Eve, they were the source of temptation and sin. During Henry's reign, Anne Askew was the only noteworthy woman killed specifically for heresy, while under Mary, perhaps one-fifth of the nearly three hundred executed were women. Under Elizabeth, Catholic women could not be executed even if they begged for it—as was the case with eight women who "with open outcries and exclamations" unsuccessfully sought to die alongside the Catholic layman Ralph Milner, whose crimes were the same as theirs.[29] Despite this gender rule, three women would nevertheless be executed under Elizabeth's watch, including, most famously, Margaret Clitherow, whose fate was to be crushed to death by rocks.[30]

The Tudors were not alone, however, in executing individuals on religious grounds, but rather functioned within a larger context of heresy executions throughout a Europe affected by the upheavals of the Reformation. The number of individuals who were executed under Mary was, in fact, small compared with the number executed under Francis I of France or Charles V of the Holy Roman Empire, not to mention the one thousand who perished under the Duke of Alva's "council of blood" in the Netherlands, which lasted from 1567 through 1574. As William Monter has pointed out, during the period from 1520 through 1565, approximately three thousand executions on religious grounds were carried out in the German regions, the Low Countries, France, Italy, and

Spain, as well as England.[31] While this number does not account for the periods of persecutions during Elizabeth's reign which culminated in the 1580s, it nevertheless reveals that the number of religious executions in England, from Henry through Mary, accounted for something like 7 percent of the total individuals killed throughout Europe.[32]

In a world where thousands were executed, the question arises as to the extent that audiences viewed the execution of religious dissidents as different from the killings of adulterers, counterfeiters, or husband-poisoners. The act of witnessing a charred or dismembered or hanging body, at least in London, was not in itself shocking, especially when such punishments were nearly everyday occurrences. Rather, the varieties of responses tended to rely, at least initially, on one's attitude toward the victim and his or her offense. For many the heretic was, if not a criminal, then certainly a sinner, and for those already inclined against the burning victim, little sympathy would be had for someone who was seen to have clung tenaciously—and despite opportunities of recantation—to his heresy. Even worse to others were traitors, such as Catholic priests, who had allegedly colluded with international and papal powers to overthrow the queen and the church of which she was supreme head. In this sense alone—for the egregiousness of their acts—religious dissidents' deaths *were* perceived as different, with treason considered the worst crime that anyone could commit against the crown, just as heresy was its equivalent to the church and, by extension, the crown with which it was allied.

While it is difficult to estimate crowd size, the presence of representatives from all levels of society attests to a great deal of attention paid to the event; unlike executions of common felons, the proceedings against heretics and traitors were, more than anything else, directed to the whole realm, and treated accordingly. This is not to say that the state's presentation of executions met with a uniform response across reigns. In the 1520s and even 1530s, for example, the still largely Catholic public seemed to have been more enthusiastic about the burning of Protestant heretics, while Mary's reign elicited a more ambivalent response to the executions of those who had only recently held the highest ecclesiastical positions, under Edward. Burnings under Mary, in fact, actually caused a shift in opinion among the public which, while it did not suddenly embrace Protestantism, was affected enough by the sheer volume of those burnings, and the use Protestants made of them. As for

Elizabeth, executions were largely accepted by the crowds. Even so, though they did not succeed in creating the kind of backlash that had occurred under Mary, enough priests were put to death—and faced their deaths bravely—that the Catholic community, small as it had become, sustained itself and received an infusion of life under such newly minted saints as Edmund Campion.[33]

Duties of State

Though they acted in the name of the crown and the laws of the realm, the officials charged with carrying out executions consisted of individuals rather than faceless personnel, and as such were subject to biases, sympathy, ambivalence, and even conflict regarding their duties. Unsurprisingly, resistance could set in when it came time for sheriffs and others to execute members of their own communities, a few of whom they personally knew; the fact that many of the officials retained their positions through changes in the monarch—and the religious policy—in power made their tasks to expedite what seemed to be ever-changing policy all the more difficult to fulfill. It is therefore necessary to tease apart these officials and the specific tasks with which they were charged. Although the roles that they played at executions tended to be well-defined, the duties that faced them were not always easy and could often be improvisationally handled, especially in the sixteenth century, which lacked systematic means of enforcement and administration.

Executions could be complicated undertakings, requiring a degree of planning that involved hiring executioners, choosing the site and the date of execution, enlisting officials to preside over and control the crowds, and clerics to preach the last sermon. Every execution was, theoretically, to be instigated on the authority of a warrant or writ, which was usually drawn up by a member of the privy council or, later on, the solicitor-general, and then delivered to the jailer or sheriff. According to a writ of 1587, for example, "it shall not be lawful for [the lieutenant, jailer, or other official] to execute that condemned person without any more a-doe, but the Queen's expresse direction there is to be expected."[34] Occasionally, however, executions proceeded without any writs, as was the case in 1557, when eight individuals only recently apprehended were put to death without any warrant for burning. According to Foxe, the practice was not unusual, as other justices, "without any lawful writ of discharge or order of law, have unlawfully and disorderly burnt the servants of Christ . . . especially at Salisbury, and at Canterbury, and Guernsey."[35] In 1558, three heretics were also burned at Bury St. Edmonds in Suffolk, and though their execution was reinforced by a writ, it had been released two weeks before Mary died, during a period when she was known to be "past remedy of her sickness."[36]

While local officials, such as mayors, justices, and sometimes members of the privy council, played prominent roles in the execution drama, it was primarily the job of the sheriff to expedite the details, from bodily handling of the prisoner, to bringing order in the crowd, and to clearing the site after the execution had taken place.[37] Often, the sheriff had to bear the financial burden as well, and indeed, wood, gunpowder, stakes, or temporary gallows were not cheaply acquired.[38] Equally onerous was the cost of hiring horses, carts, and other accouterments to transport, when necessary, the heretic or traitor (or his disemboweled quarters) to various parts of the realm, which was necessary in light of the law that required executions to take place in the county or parish where the treason or heresy had occurred.

Along with jailers and executioners, sheriffs were closest to the prisoner, taking him from court to jail, and notifying him, writ in hand, when it came time to die. It was the sheriff, in fact, and not the executioner, who was the real angel of death, accompanying the prisoner on his last walk (or ride) to the stake or gallows. The sheriff also had a distinctly legal role in the proceedings, ensuring that a proclamation was posted or read out during executions, which justified the punishment in accordance with the law;[39] in addition, the sheriff often presented to the condemned a document offering pardon in return for his conforming or recanting his beliefs, a practice which continued right up to the moment of death. "Here is a letter from the Queen," one sheriff said to William Hunter in Mary's reign, when the young man was being prepared for execution; "If thou wilt recant, thou shalt live, if not, thou shalt be burnt." Hunter, however, refused the offer, and proceeded to his death, even though he was again given the chance to recant, this time by the officiating priest.[40]

Sheriffs generally fulfilled these functions with a degree of diligence, despite the reluctance many felt toward the duties and expenses of the office as a whole. As will be seen, it is not clear how many sheriffs were resistant to aiding in the execution of heretics or traitors based on their own religious sensibilities, but the maintenance of order, rather than religiosity or even crown loyalty, seems to have preoccupied them above all. This meant preventing any instability from breaking out at the execution site, especially if the victim chose to make a last, possibly incendiary speech before a riled crowd. In 1540, for example, the Evangelical Robert Barnes began a lengthy stakeside exhortation, denying, among other things, the slander that he had once referred to the Virgin as a "saffron-bag"; after Barnes had reiterated his belief in Mary, the sheriff then interrupted him and said, "You have said well of her before."[41] Fifteen years later, John Bradford also brought on trouble when he lay face down before the stake to pray, until the sheriff told him to "Arise, and make an end; for the press of people is great." When, at another point, Bradford asked God to forgive the sheriff for interrupting him, one of the sheriff's officials exclaimed, "If you have no better learning than that, you are but a fool, and were best hold your peace."[42] During the same period, another sheriff said to George Marsh, when he was beginning to exhort the crowds, "[W]e shall have no sermonizing now,"[43] while Christopher Wade, during his execution, was eventually interrupted by the sheriff, who said, "Be quiet, Wade! And die patiently." Traitors in Elizabeth's reign could also cause trouble in their last acts and speeches, as was the case with the priest Ralph Crockett, who began to state that he died "for religion and coming to execute his function of priesthood," until the sheriff and justices cut him off and reminded him that his crime was treason.[44] Indeed, in one case, a priest named William Dean was thought to be so inappropriate in his speech that the sheriff had his mouth gagged with a cloth.[45]

Sheriffs were also charged with the task, in cases of treason, of ensuring that the prisoner was not yet dead after being hanged, so that the next phase of drawing and quartering alive could be carried out. This created some confusion in the crowd, not least because the exact point of death was sometimes uncertain. When the priest James Bell was hanged in 1595, for example, some thought he was dead, until it came time for his disembowelment, when "his hart trembled in the exequtioner's hand, & . . . leaped thrice out of the fire: & his head chopt off, his mouth gasped twice."[46] In this case the crowd showed compassion toward the sufferings of the prisoner, though at other times, people enjoined the sheriff to cut the victim down immediately, so he could be more alive to his own disembowelment—as was the case with the priest Cuthbert Mayne, whose status as a priest made executioners ensure that his death was all the more prolonged and gruesome.[47]

The sheriff did not work alone, of course, but was accompanied by a horse-mounted entourage of bailiffs, constables, or even non-officials, including, in the 1555 case of George Marsh, "a great number of poor simple barbers with rusty bills and pole-axes," who were temporarily hired for the execution to ensure stability.[48] In addition, distinguished members of the commission or the privy council were often present to help supervise the functionings of the event, as well as lend their magisterial presence as representatives of the crown. In 1555, for example, Sir John Raynesforde of Essex was thanked by the privy council "for his good service in assisting lately the Shirief of Essex in the execucion of sundry offendours." Another letter in the same period enjoined the then-Essex commissioner Richard Rich to thank on the queen's behalf "Edward Bery, gentleman, and dyverse other of the Hundred of Rocheforde in Essex."[49]

Special access areas at the execution site were occasionally set aside for these members of the nobility or council, especially in the executions of traitors, who were, again, seen as more directly related to the state than heretics. Among those who observed the 1535 deaths of the Carthusian monks were the earl of Wiltshire, the Duke of Suffolk, and other notables,[50] while all "private" executions—or those held within the walls of the Tower—were attended primarily by gentry and nobility. Heretics, especially prominent ones, also garnered a significant audience, particularly among royal councilors who could also, as representatives of the king or queen, grant powers of pardon; such was the case at the execution of Friar Forest in 1538, when, according to Foxe, "a scaffold [was] prepared for the king's most honorable council, and the nobles of the realm, to sit upon him, to grant him pardon."[51] A few years later, at the Smithfield execution of Anne Askew, the lord chancellor, Wriothesley, was joined by the Duke of Norfolk, the earl of Bedford, the lord mayor, and others. At least one of them seems to have been somewhat new to the event, when he expressed fear that the gunpowder traditionally given to the victims to speed up death would cause fiery faggots to "come flying about their ears"; the earl of Bedford, however, explained to the man that since the gunpowder was laid not under the faggots but "only about [the victims'] bodies," there was no danger.[52]

Clerics were also expected to lend their presence, especially as preachers, to all executions, including those for the lowliest criminals. It was an absolutely necessary part of the protocol that a sermon be given before the execution, not only to remind the prisoner of his sinful ways, but to control, shape, and determine the event before the public gaze. To preach at an execution was as important—if not more important—than preaching a key sermon at Paul's Cross: it was a central pulpit for enjoining the victim to repent in order to face death and God properly, while giving clerical sanction to the state's judgment and justice.[53] Execution sermons, especially, tended to follow a stereotyped pattern, first detailing the offender's sins and then justifying the worldly and eternal punishment he or she would face; at the execution of the blind young woman Joan Waste, for example, Dr. Draicot—who had also been her chief examiner—stood at the pulpit and, according to Foxe,

> [inveighed] against divers matters, which he called heresies, [and] declared unto the people that that woman was condemned for denying the blessed sacrament of the altar to be the very body and blood of Christ really and substantially, and was thereby cut off from the body of the catholic church; and said, that she was not only blind of her bodily eyes, but also blind in the eyes of her soul. And he said, that as her body should be presently consumed with material fire, so her soul should be burned in hell with everlasting fire, as it shall be separated from the body, and there to remain world without end; and said, it was not lawful for the people to pray for her. And so with many terrible threats he made an end of his sermon, and commanded the bailiffs and those gentlemen to see her executed.[54]

The fact that executions were conflictual, difficult spectacles is especially evident in the skirmishes and accusations that frequently erupted between clerics, such as Draicot, and those about to be executed. Not surprisingly, deathside preachers representing a different confessional faith were not only disliked by those about to be executed, but they were also viewed as demonic figures representing the last temptation—an offer to live—which had to be overcome, and with the utmost vehemence. When, in 1555, the Protestant George Tankerfield, for example, was approached by a priest and enjoined to believe in the sacrament of the altar, Tankerfield cried, "I defy the whore of babylon: fie on that abominable idol. Good people, do not believe him; good people, do not believe him."[55] During the same period, a priest approached William Hunter with an offer to recant, only to be told, "Away, thou false prophet."[56] The conflict was no different in Elizabeth's reign; only the players and their faiths had been reversed. In 1584, for example, the priest James Bell told a Protestant minister present at his execution to sermonize that "I will not believe thee, nor heare thee but against my will," while Bell's fellow priest, John Lynch, similarly told his sermonizer to not bother him, "For I ame not of your religion, neither will I be for any thinge that yow can say."[57]

Contrary to the stereotyped roles they embodied, many preaching clerics had, in fact, been involved in complicated, personal relationships with those about to die. Anne Askew's preacher, for example, was Nicholas Shaxton, who had once been an ardent and especially close co-religionist; during one of her examinations and before she was to be tortured, Shaxton had even shown up at prison to urge her to recant as he had done, though, in Askew's words, "I said to him that it had been good for him never to have been born; with many other like words." At the execution, Shaxton stood at his pulpit six feet away and condemned her, though she pointed out the scriptural errors he had made and said, "he misseth, and speaketh without the book."[58] During Mary's reign, Nicholas Ridley and Hugh Latimer also confronted a familiar face in Richard Smith, an Oxford divine who had taken part in their recent disputations; speaking for fifteen minutes, Smith exhorted the two former bishops and told them they were committing suicide and not embracing martyrdom—a statement which Latimer and Ridley sought to dispute, though they were refused.[59]

The most decisive official presence at the site was, of course, the executioner, whose position did not attract many volunteers. While some executioners seem to have filled the office as a hereditary position, especially after the sixteenth century, the executioner was, traditionally, a disreputable figure who was sometimes a felon himself. Most executioners went nameless, as was the case with one figure who was described in the records as simply the "hangman of Newgate" and was renowned for executing the Catholics John Felton, John Payne, and others.[60] Many had to be recruited from abroad, as was the case with Anne Boleyn's executioner, a French swordsman from Calais; such imports were due in part to England's lack of skilled swordsmen, and to a reluctance by authorities to have the queen beheaded by commoners such as Catwell.[61] Other executioners, primarily those charged with quartering, were temporarily recruited from the ranks of cooks or butchers—a fact which accounts for many a botched job, and for a reluctance on the part of the populace to come forward for the job in the first place. It was a cook who was enlisted to execute the priest Thomas Prichard in 1587, and proceeded to "most cruelly mangle" him. Prichard was even compelled to help out his clumsy killer, to the point where he "reised himself and putting owt his hands cast forward his own bowells cryinge out 'Misere mei.'"[62] Sometimes bailiffs were used as well: in 1557 one such figure by the name of William Swallow was recruited for the job of executing George Eagles, who had been convicted as a traitor and was to be hung and quartered; taking a cleaver—"such as is occupied in many men's kitchens, and blunt"—Swallow proceeded to "hackle off [Eagles's] head, and sometimes hit his neck, and sometimes his chin, and did foully mangle him, and so opened him." Eventually, Swallow managed to get around to Eagles's heart and bowels, which was customary, before cutting him into quarters, after which he stored them briefly at his home before having them transported on to various parts of the realm.[63]

The punishment of burning was perhaps the easier task to carry out, in the sense that it was undertaken by a number of men—usually the sheriff and his assistants—with possibly some help from a blacksmith whose duty was to tighten the chain around the victim's body, fastening it close to the stake. Even so, burnings did not always proceed smoothly, subject as they were to a number of complicating factors. As will be seen, sympathetic crowds could attempt to interfere with the process—or, by the same token, they could help the executioner by throwing in sticks themselves. Worse was a variable climate and damp, green wood, which could prolong death and cause particularly gruesome suffering to the victim. When, in 1533, John Frith was tied to the stake with another individual, for example, "the wind made his death somewhat longer, which bare away the flame from him unto his fellow that was tied to his back."[64] A similar fate met George Marsh in 1555, when "by reason the fire was unskillfully made, and that the wind did drive the same to and fro, he suffered great extremity in his death, which notwithstanding he abode very patiently."[65] One of the worst and most famous deaths by fire, however, was suffered by Nicholas Ridley, who was chained to the stake with his coreligionist Hugh Latimer; though Latimer, perhaps in light of his age and infirmity, died fairly quickly, Ridley took much longer to expire, even though he had been given a bag of gunpowder to speed up his death. His sympathetic friend and brother-in-law George Shipside, who was allowed to stand nearby, unwittingly made matters worse by stirring up the fuel, leading Ridley to exclaim, "Let the fire come unto me; I cannot burn."[66]

Before committing the deed, executioners often descended to their knees and asked the condemned for forgiveness, which was usually given, as was a small sum or a garment intended as a fee for carrying out the duty.[67] In 1595, for example, the priest William Freeman spent his last moments "jestinge awhile merely with the hangman, forgevinge hym his death, & puttinge money into his hand for his rewarde,"[68] while in the same period another priest even attempted to convert his executioner by telling him the apocryphal story of Paul's executioner being saved when the martyr's blood fell onto his garments.[69] Certainly, executioners could become rattled by the tasks they were entrusted with, especially when the victim demonstrated a remarkable degree of fortitude befitting a martyr. In the late 1580s, during one drawing and quartering session, the executioner was stunned when he plucked out the heart of Edmund Jennings and still the priest kept praying, to St. Gregory; "God's wounds!" the executioner cried, "His heart is in my hands, and yet Gregory is in his mouth."[70] For their part, individuals about to be executed were generally accepting of their executioners; the Carthusian leader John Houghton embraced his own executioner,[71] while Thomas More famously told his to "Plucke up thy spirites, man, and be not afraide to do thine office; my necke is very short."[72]

In reviewing the officials and clerics present at executions—the individuals who moved behind the scrim of officialdom—a question recurs concerning the degree of enthusiasm or reluctance they might have harbored in fulfilling their tasks. On a theoretical level, authorities carried absolutely no doubt about the necessity of burning heretics, especially when those heretics were seen as "contagious," threatening to infect numerous others. As Edmund Bonner wrote, "As one thief may both rob many men, and also make many thieves, and one seditious person may allure many, and annoy a whole town or country . . . such evil persons, that be so great offenders of God, and the commonwealth [should be killed], lest they corrupt other good, and honest persons."[73] During Henry's reign, Thomas More also expressed his conviction that heretics should be extirpated and "overwhelmed in the beginning," lest they continue to seize more souls from Christ.[74] Indeed, while More believed in using rational and moderate tactics to compel heretics to recant if they persisted in their beliefs, then he also felt no compunction in sending them straight to the fire.

In practice, however, genuine reluctance in burning heretics or traitors could manifest itself among sheriffs, justices, and even high council members. Certainly, a lack of zeal is evident when casting calls went out seeking individuals who could play executioner, or even sheriff, but whether this reluctance was due to religious reasons or a general unwillingness to carry out a thankless job is difficult to discern. In some cases, a religious impulse does show through on the part of the sheriff, as was the case with the hostile official who was in fact committed to his duty: one told the Protestant Dirick Carver in Mary's reign that "If thou dost not believe on the pope, thou art damned body and soul."[75] In another example, this time reflecting sympathy, Foxe alleges that a sheriff, Thomas Sutton, was loathe to execute the Protestant Elizabeth Cooper, with whom he had once been friends, "the more for the gospel's sake"; even so, he was "enforced by other persons . . . much against his own conscience, which he now earnestly repenteth."[76] In general, a marked pattern of resistance did become more noticeable as the executions continued through the reign of Mary, when the Protestant burnings seemed to backfire. While few, if any, directives were issued from 1553 through 1555, for example, by 1557 sheriffs were receiving letters from the privy council asking why they were putting off executions—as was the case with the sheriffs of Essex and Colchester, and with the sheriff of Hampshire, whose procrastination in the job of executing was called "very strange."[77]

By the same token, during Elizabeth's reign no person could be found who was willing to execute the priest Richard Daye, though whether this was due to community sympathy for the condemned or to the disrepute of the job is, again, difficult to judge. Finally, after a few weeks, a butcher finally came forward to offer himself up for the job at a price of forty shillings.[78] A vocal minority of contemporary writers, including John Foxe, were themselves often ambivalent about the benefits of execution,[79] and it was fairly common for individuals in positions of authority to be hesitant as well. In 1550, during the reign of Edward, a "certain friend" visited John Rogers and pleaded with him to use his influence with Cranmer to prevent the death of the Anabaptist Joan Bocher; "even though she might infect a few by living," the individual argued, "she would confirm many more if she were punished with death." Rogers—who in the next, hostile reign would himself burn—remained firm in his belief that the burning should go ahead, as, in fact, such a death "was the least agonizing of all the punishments and sufficiently mild."[80] Even Edward, the young king, was said to be reluctant to sign off on the execution warrant of Bocher, which necessitated the intervention of Cranmer, who finally convinced Edward to sanction the execution.[81] In the more profligate reigns of Mary and Elizabeth, however, some reluctance was expressed by the highest councilors and bishops in the land. In the 1550s, Catholics such as Reginald Pole[82]— and Charles V's ambassador, Simon Renard [83]—expressed a dislike for executions, and in a letter to Pole, Edmund Bonner even offered up his view that burnings should be carried out secretly, so as not to stir up the crowd; moreover, Bonner added at another point, conducting executions with as little fanfare as possible would reduce the need for secular assistants, who were beginning to show themselves unwilling to fulfill their duties.[84] Meanwhile, though officials were perhaps more enthusiastic under Elizabeth to put to death those that they considered traitors, not Catholics, even Francis Walsingham preferred banishing or imprisoning priests, and only executing "a few for example's sake."[85]

The Crowd

Whereas sheriffs, bailiffs, council members, executioners, preachers, and future martyrs all tended to know and accept the role they were to play, crowds were a different matter, carrying the potential to throw a wrench into the best-laid plans.[86] The presence of multitudes reinforced the idea that the execution was, again, a fundamentally collective affair, impossible without their active, directing presence; just as the throng that cried before Jesus "Crucify him!" or lined the road to his death were central in the passion narrative, so were sixteenth-century crowds indispensable to the execution process as a whole. It was for the crowd that such displays were directed in the first place; not only were they to deter those wavering individuals in the audience, but they were meant, in David Nicholls's words, to serve as "a morality play staged by magistrates for the edification of the populace, acting as an exemplar and warning to all potential wrongdoers."[87] Still, as Peter Burke writes, "audiences do not always react in the way the playwright expects, or wants, and the crowd did not necessarily interpret proceedings in the same way as the authorities."[88]

With crowds packed in densely around the site, executions, especially in the case of burnings, were almost intimate affairs, with people standing only feet away from the stake and its surrounding bundles of wood and furze. The crowds were comprised of all segments of society, including children, and numbered in the hundreds, if not thousands; indeed, entire communities turned out for the event, which could carry a riotous element, though without the level of merriment of later execution crowds. In many ways, the execution crowd was not an audience so much as an ambiguous congregation of many faiths and confessions, standing before exhorting preachers and martyrs who battled it out for its favor. Although people were drawn to the event for its spectacle, religious elements were intimately connected to the drama, not simply making it a display of ghoulish voyeurism, but also a kind of liturgical passion play from which themes of guilt, sin, judgment, justice, punishment, repentance, and sacrifice could be played out.

The woodcut illustrations which accompanied Foxe's *Acts and Monuments* literally depict the crowds as faceless, while the eerie, quiet depictions in Richard Verstegan's *Theatrum Crudelitatum* tend to omit them altogether. But in reality, crowds were not passive or invisible observers, especially since they often played an indirect part in the execution by their shouts of encouragement or discouragement to the hangman.[89] When the priest Richard White was hanged in 1582, for example, people protested that the hangman should let White die as fast as possible, rather than prolong his miseries by cutting him down too soon and making him face the next stage of his punishment.[90] By the same token, crowds could enjoin the executioner to cut down the hanging victim immediately, in order that he not be rendered insensible for what was to come. Crowds could also take part directly in the action, as executioners themselves; it was thus a fairly common practice for a few sympathetic individuals to pull on a hanging man's legs, to expedite death, while individuals could also help by making sure the wood was properly turned and burning in order to ensure that their friends die more quickly. This was the case in Mary's reign, when friends of the Protestant John Hullier, "perceiving the fire to be ill-kindled, caused the sergeants to turn it, and fire it to that place where the wind might blow it to his face." Death by burning could also be quickened by giving the victims aforementioned bags of gun-powder to place under their arms, as was the case with Hugh Latimer and Nicholas Ridley, though Catholics would later claim that by doing so they were aiding false martyrs who had cheated death.[91]

Often, the government did not have great difficulty in summoning a crowd's anger against a heretic or traitor, though audiences, for differing reasons, were more enthusiastic in certain periods than in others. The burning of heretics in the early 1530s, for example, backfired in many respects on the government, but enthusiasm was not lacking for many— perhaps the majority—in the audience. Indeed, sometimes the ire of the crowd surpassed the state's and became difficult to control, as was the case in 1532, when Thomas Bennet went to the stake amidst a raging horde, one of whom cried out to him, "Ah! Whoreson heretic! Pray to Our Lady and say *Sancta Maria, ora pro nobis,* or by God's wounds I will make thee do it!" Crowds in this time could become especially baiting, as everyone, with right and might on their side, wished to participate in the killing; such a scenario took place in 1532 with Thomas Harding, whose burning was expedited by hostile, stick-throwing children weaving in and out of the throng.[92]

Spectators seem to have been especially enthusiastic in the time of Elizabeth, however, when a nascent nationalism began to color the tone of those who cried out "traitor" or "God save the queen" to the executed. The Catholic layman Robert Widmerpool, for example, was denied his last speech when the crowd heckled him and refused to even let him speak,[93] while earlier, in 1571, the crowd "gave a shout" after John Felton's severed head was raised high by the executioner.[94] In the same year, John Story was given a similarly hostile send-off as he passed the crowds on the way to his execution. What is especially interesting here is that many people along the way remembered his role as one of the major persecutors in Mary's reign, fifteen years previously, and were motivated by a desire to see justice (or vengeance) done. One member of the crowd reminded Story that he had been responsible for the death of John Bradford; "O Story, Story! Thou art a strange Story," the individual cried, "remember master Bradford, that godly man; his blood asketh vengeance on thee, Story." Another yelled, "Story, Story, the abominable cup of fornication and filthiness, that thou hast given others to drink, be heaped up topful, that thy plagues may be the greater at the terrible day of God's wrath and vengeance, unless thou ask mercy for thy filthy, corrupt and stinking life." Story's execution was also the occasion for balladeers, one of whom recited a doggerel with words that included the rhyme, "Your holy father, the pope/Cannot save you from the rope."[95]

Despite such enthusiasms, a crowd sympathetic to the victim was always a concern of the authorities, especially in the time of Mary, when executions accumulated in number. At one point, Reginald Pole even exhorted Londoners in 1557 that "When any heretic shall go to execution, he shall lack no comforting of you, and [encouragement] to die in his perverse opinion . . . by those that come out of your house." A 1558 proclamation, issued in anticipation of Roger Holland's death, attempted to address this problem when it stated that "none should be so bold to speak or talk any word unto [Holland and others], or receive any thing of them, or to touch them upon pain of imprisonment"; nevertheless, Foxe writes, the crowd "cried out, desiring God to strengthen them."[96] At other times, orders were sent out to sheriffs to arrest anyone who displayed a measurable sympathy toward the burning heretic, and though the law was only occasionally enforced, there were instances of arrests, as was the case in 1557, when a Norwich man was flogged through the marketplace as punishment for having protested the cruelty of executions by burning.

If a prisoner was sent to die in the place where he had gained a following—which was a common practice—sympathetic communities could be especially unwieldy; when, in 1555, Dirick Carver arrived in the town of Lewes, in Sussex, "the people called upon him, beseeching God to strengthen him in the faith of Jesus Christ."[97] In hotbeds of Protestantism, such as Colchester, sympathetic crowds could generally get out of hand, as did one gathering in Mary's time—numbering in the thousands, according to one estimate—which turned out to shout its prayers and encouragement to a group of coreligionists being burned.[98] The atmosphere became even more charged if the victim had once been an especially prominent and well-liked member of the community, such as a bishop. John Hooper, for example, was sent for execution to his old diocese of Gloucester, where, according to Foxe, a crowd of seven thousand sympathizers came to greet him, and later prayed as he died; similarly, Rowland Taylor, the former bishop of Hadleigh in Suffolk, was met in the streets on his way to the stake by crowds who cried, "Ah!

Good Lord! There goeth our shepherd from us, that so faithfully hath taught us, so fatherly hath cared for us, and so godly hath governed us!"

The increasingly sympathetic behavior of crowds in Mary's reign did not necessarily indicate that England had become a Protestant realm; however, executions in some ways served as a catalyst in turning people away from her policies and associating her Catholicism with persecution. Indeed, the sight of a collective group—even prominent officials, women, and a former archbishop—going stoically to the flames was shocking enough to elicit admiration for the victims, if not quite an embrace of the cause for which they were dying. During the burning of John Laurence in 1555, for example, young children cried out, "Lord, strengthen thy servant," before he was finally consumed in the fire, while in the same period, George Marsh went to his death to the exclamations of the people that "This man goeth not unto his death as a thief, or as one that deserveth to die."[99] Some individuals even approached the stake in order to receive the martyr's blessing, while the horrific burning of Latimer and Ridley brought about the sudden conversion of one Catholic in the crowd, Julius Palmer, who would himself become a martyr for the Protestant cause one day. A similar sympathy—and even conversion[100]—was experienced at times in Elizabeth's reign, despite the overwhelming hostility of the crowd; at the execution of the priest William Freeman in 1595, the audience seemed to consist primarily of Protestants, though "never a one of the standers [made] any clamoure, or spake any word against hym, but some there were that revyled the exequtioner & said yt were no matter yf he went in the other's case." Others in the crowd, meanwhile, "noted much the hardness of [Freeman's] knees, and sayd, 'surely he was a good man & used much prayer.'"[101]

Sympathizers could even go further, seizing pieces of their martyrs' bloody garments, body parts, or burnt remains. Whether the desire was for a relic or a souvenir, the problem could be a major one for the authorities; according to a letter by Robert Southwell, guards in the Elizabethan period had to be posted around the gallows after the execution had taken place to prevent spectators from lunging at the corpse on the scaffold.[102] At the death of William Hart, crowds jostled each other to get hold of "either his shirt or shoes or some part of his clothes" to the point where officials were forced to imprison many of them afterwards,[103] while the intestines of Alban Roe and Thomas Reynolds were somehow stolen out of a boiling cauldron, and the heads of Richard

Thirkill and William Hart were seized from their respective posts.[104] A demand for relics was not unique to Catholics, however, with Protestants seizing remains of their own—-a fact which the Catholic polemicist Miles Huggarde later pointed out as evidence of those followers' hypocrisy.[105] One gory scene recounted by Foxe describes the aftermath, in 1556, of John Hullier's burning: "His flesh being consumed, his bones stood upright even as if they had been alive. . . . Of the people some took what they could get of him, as pieces of bones. One had his heart, the which was distributed so far as it would go; one took the scalp, and looked for the tongue, but it was consumed except the very root."

Individuals who had been in attendance at executions could be diligent in committing what they were seeing to memory, and composing cheap pamphlets, broadsheets, poems, and songs to convey their experience as witnesses. John Foxe based his own execution accounts on eyewitness testimonies, though some of those accounts—such as that of James Bainham's wife, Joan—could be subsequently shaped and embellished by the martyrologist himself.[106] Later on, at the execution of Edmund Campion, Thomas Alfield attended with "many good Catholic gentlemen"—including a student from Gray's Inn named Dolman, who took notes[107]—and proceeded to write up a report that subsequently influenced all later accounts of the saint's death.[108] Another Catholic sympathizer witnessed the execution of Robert Southwell and conveyed what he had seen to the noted Jesuit Henry Garnet, who included it in a letter.[109] Ambassadors or foreign dignitaries also sent on written accounts of executions, though their actual presence at the event is not entirely certain: a letter to Charles V by the imperial ambassador Eustace Chapuys, for example, described how "Yesterday there were dragged through the length of this city three Carthusians and a Bridgettine monk, all men of good character and learning, and cruelly put to death . . . only for having maintained that the Pope was the true head of the Universal Church. . . . The monks [had] maintained their cause most virtuously." Like Simon Renard, another imperial ambassador twenty years later, Chapuys's report, in fact, reveals both sympathy for the victim and— ignoring what the emperor was doing in his own backyard—an appalling sense of the barbarity to which England had descended.[110]

In the end, however, no execution ever inspired the crowd to riot or truly threaten the crown, though elements were present that made the event vulnerable to disorder, from the presence of neighbors and sympathizers to the expression of various rituals loaded with incendiary potential. Throughout the century, and no matter how notable the martyr it made, England maintained a cohesiveness, if not a unity, and an attachment to crown power that prevented such charged events as executions from lapsing into general displays of religious violence or war. In many ways, England was also saved by its own religious confusion and policy changes or ambiguities; violence, after all, demands the drawing of hard, partisan lines, and though extremists could be found on the far edges, the vast majority of individuals—to paraphrase one contemporary commentator—remained neither Protestant nor Catholic, but somewhere in the "neutered middle," at least until the reign of Elizabeth. The France of 1572, due to its own specific historical conditions, was a religiously galvanized country, as Huguenot faced off against Catholic and each side was supported (and inflamed) by powerful forces among the nobility; the fact that England in its official policies and public sentiments existed on less demarcated ground paradoxically prevented groups from mobilizing and sweeping that great neutered middle along with them.

As for the longer-term impact of the executions, while attention immediately after the deaths of Thomas More, John Fisher, and the Carthusians was keen—especially overseas[111]—it was unclear at first what their deaths exactly meant, especially to Catholics. In any case, heroic as More may have been, very few others were about to meet their deaths over a refusal to take the oath. Evangelicals and sectarians put to death under Henry carried too small a base among the masses—clustered as they had been in conventicles or small circles—to inspire any kind of widespread reaction of anger. The same held for Anabaptists under Edward. As for Mary, not enough of a strong Protestant movement yet existed to create a true threat at the execution site, though the range of emotions which executions inspired, in response to what was perceived as a harsh and arbitrarily enforced policy, eventually created a backlash—albeit one which developed over time. Finally, by the time of Elizabeth, the association of Catholicism with treason, and of the state with the true religion, had become so powerful that few would have dissented greatly from the surge of crowd sentiment. The fact that Elizabeth's executions were selective, with priests the primary victims, further focused the crowd's ire on specific individuals whose guilt was meant to be perceived as clear and undoubted. In this sense, and despite their occasional protestations, crowds ultimately tended to accept the punishment or justice being displayed before them; while not totally quiescent, audiences were thus contained, their autonomy checked by the shadow of the king or queen which they knew always hovered over them.

Golgotha

Just as one must recover the individuals who resided under the generic category of "sheriff" or "audience onlooker," martyrs must be seen as men and women who were propelled by their own peculiar motivations, theology, and external and internal circumstance at the same time that they were affected by broader gender considerations or sociohistorical processes.[112] For all their differences, however, and their deep religious distinctions, individuals about to die tended to work from the same script, which was based on biblical and early church precedent and utilized the same references and language. As Brad Gregory has pointed out, models of faith and suffering above all dominated their understanding and therefore their behavior, as they faced the most momentous task—the task of dying, of turning death into triumph— that lay before them. While Anabaptist martyrs, for example, therefore differed in profound theological ways from Catholic martyrs, the refrains to which they kept returning were the same, as they turned for comfort and justification to such passages as Psalm 116—"Precious in the sight of the Lord is the death of his faithful ones"—to the Sermon on the Mount, with its exhortation that even though "they will hand you over to be tortured and will put you to death . . . the one who endures will be saved."[113]

For martyrs, the execution scene was the ultimate stage, allowing them to witness their faith before others and to fashion themselves in ways that circumvented the authorities' control. To argue that they utilized various strategies to do so, however, should not diminish their genuine and frequently heroic embrace of martyrdom; many, in fact, were certainly aware of Augustine's dictum that "not the suffering but the cause, makes a martyr," and so were careful in resisting the temptation toward complete self-theatrical glory. Yet individuals about to be executed did not exist in a hermetic realm of scripturally imbued interiority either; they knew that they were being given an opportunity, a forum, for their last moments on earth, and that they were addressing— and possibly inspiring and persuading—an audience that was national as well as international. The act of martyrdom, as they well knew, was thus a deeply public one, and it was up to them to find ways in which to seize the high ground from the authorities present. In this sense, exe-cutions of religious dissidents also differed from those of felons in that the stakes, finally, were that much higher, as persecutor and persecuted battled for the soul of present and future audiences.

Some accounts, for dramatic purposes, collapse the time that lapsed between condemnation and execution; in reality, however, a period could pass before the punishment was to be meted out. This allowed the pris-oners time to think, to write letters, to pray, or—in the case of Lati-mer, Ridley, and Cranmer—to be formally stripped of their episcopal offices.[114] While some individuals spent their last days in "joyful me-ditation" or in a state of prayerful calm, others approached their im-pending deaths with more difficulty. Thomas More, for example, thought and wrote a great deal about his forthcoming death, and remained deeply preoccupied with the relationship between suicide and martyr-dom; while martyrdom, according to More, could constitute the ulti-mate *imitatio christi,* the desire for self-sacrifice could also be pursued out of pride and vainglory, and even compel the so-called martyr to pro-voke another to sin, in goading that person—the executioner—to mur-der.[115] More was also one of the more pain-haunted of future martyrs, and had graphically expressed these preoccupations both in letters to his daughter Margaret Roper, and in his *Dialogue of comfort against tribula-tion*; indeed, he was not entirely sure that he would be spared the pun-ishment of traitors, and it was not long before his actual death that he was told that he would be beheaded rather than quartered. In these last days, he continued to turn to the books of Job and Ecclesiastes in con-cluding that suffering, no matter what form it took, brought one more vigorously to God, and that—echoing Paul—the amount of pain one was given was no more or less than the pain one could bear. Despite these consolations, More was aware of his limitations and not always certain that martyrdom was his vocation, as he expressed at one point during his trial: "I have not been a man of such holy living as I might be bold to offer myself to death, lest God for my presumption might suffer me to fall," he wrote; "therefore I put not myself forward, but draw back," though "I trust in his great mercy, that he shall not fail to give me grace and strength."[116]

More was also haunted by dreams on the eve of his execution, as were many others, all of which attested to the fact that while the prospect of martyrdom may have been embraced, it did not come easily. During the reign of Mary, Robert Samuel spent the days before his execution experiencing dreams or visions, one of which included a foreshadowing of his burning with two women.[117] During the same period, John Bradford roused his cellmate in the predawn hours to speak of an "unquiet sleep," in which he dreamed "how the chain for his burning was brought to the Compter-gate, and how the next day, being Sunday, he should be had to Newgate, and on the Monday after burned in Smithfield."[118] Cranmer—perhaps apocryphally—is also said to have experienced a significant dream in which Christ contended for his soul, not against the devil, but against Henry VIII;[119] whether the story was true or not, Cranmer soon after attended mass, and went on to sign his sixth—and last—recantation.

Contrary to the picture often presented of individuals facing the prospect of their martyrdoms with a fully accepting serenity of spirit, approaching death was thus laden with doubt and fear as they moved through their own personal Gethsemanes. In 1555, for example, Robert Glover spent the period after his condemnation and before his execution in a state of near-despair; according to Foxe, Glover's "heart [was] lumpish, and desolate of all spiritual consolation, [and he] felt in himself no aptness nor willingness, but rather a heaviness and dullness of spirit, full of much discomfort to bear the bitter cross of martyrdom ready to be laid upon him." When he expressed this state to his friend and messenger Augustine Bernher, he was enjoined to "play the man, nothing misdoubting but the Lord in his good time would visit him, and satisfy his desire with plenty of consolation." Foxe continues:

> The next day, when the time came of his martyrdom, as he was going to the place, and was now come to the sight of the stake, although all the night before praying for strength and courage he could feel none, suddenly he was so mightily replenished with God's holy comfort and heavenly joys, that he cried out, clapping

his hands to Austen [Bernher], and saying in these words, "Austen, he is come, he is come."[120]

While some martyrs had the opportunity to meditate at length with a specific death-date in mind, others were notified only a few hours before they were to die—a practice which was not at all uncommon, as authorities sought to prevent the possibility of suicide or escape.[121] In Henry's reign, John Lambert, for example, was given little notice; taken out of prison at 8 A.M.—which was around the typical hour of death— Lambert was first shepherded to the house of Thomas Cromwell, who informed him that "the hour of his death was at hand" and proceeded to offer him breakfast before sending him off to the stake.[122] Others were told only the night before that they were to die, as was the case with Nicholas Ridley, who spent his last night at the Irishes' residency in Oxford where he had been incarcerated; while Mrs. Irish—who until now had been a somewhat nasty keeper—wept copiously, Ridley told his friend George Shipside, who was present, that he did not need companionship for the rest of the night, "For I mind, God willing, to go to bed, and to sleep as quietly tonight as ever I did in my life."[123] George Tankerfield seems to have spent his own last hours in scripturally evocative ritual acts: at the inn where he had been taken—his was a case of being transported back to his home county for execution—he asked for wine and a loaf of bread, "that he might drink that in remembrance of Christ's death and passion." Afterwards, when he sat before a fire, he "put off his shoes and hose, and stretched out his leg to the flame; and when it had touched his foot, he quickly withdrew his leg, showing how the flesh did persuade him one way, and the spirit another way."[124] During the reign of Elizabeth, the priest James Bell also spent his own last night in prayer and meditation, "wishinge (if it pleased God) more tyme to doe penaunce in; and in very few wordes exhorted all the condemned prisoners to the Catholicke fayth and to true repentaunce." The next morning, he "reioyced greatlye in God and gave Him thankes for all His benefites, utteringe these words, 'O blessed day, O the fayrest day that ever I saw in my life.' "[125]

It was common practice for authorities to order convicted dissidents, such as Tankerfield, to be returned for execution to the place where they had originally dwelled, stirred up trouble, or gained a following.

During the reign of Mary, many were transported by sheriffs back to their home county of Essex, where they were burned—and where, it should be added, the local community would presumably be deterred from falling into its own heresy. Such was the case with the Protestant linen draper Thomas Wats, who was taken to Chelmsford, his hometown, where a stake was waiting for him.[126] The policy in Elizabeth's reign was no different, though the locations could vary. In the 1580s, for example, the priests William Marsden and Robert Anderton were taken from London and executed on the far-off Isle of Wight, where they had first made their landing after living on the continent.[127]

In London itself, executions were commonly carried out at a few central public sites, most notably Tyburn, Smithfield, or Tower Hill, where permanent gallows or scaffolds were built. Tyburn and the Tower had particularly long histories, though the Tower was a more magisterial presence than Tyburn, which, despite thousands of executions having taken place there, was located near a pleasant brook, just outside a barnyard. Tower Hill consisted of an open space north of the Tower complex, which had also once served as a garbage dump for Londoners;[128] by 1597, according to the chronicler John Stow, the plain around the hill was "likewise greatly diminished, by encroachments for building of small tenements, and taking in of garden plots, timeyards, or what they list."[129] Other sites were less formal, as was the case with the burning grounds of Hugh Latimer and Nicholas Ridley, which took place in a town ditch near Balliol College,[130] while in London itself, temporary gallows were set up throughout the city at various times. Of all the execution sites, however, it was Smithfield that held dominance, especially for heretics, who faced their death in the shadow of the elm trees; the term "the Elms" would become so notorious, in fact, that it would extend beyond Smithfield and become a synonym for a number of other execution sites.

Church bells rang out when it came time for the victim to be paraded through the streets in a kind of passion scene down the Via Dolorosa. In many ways, the procession was as important as the event itself, and hundreds lined the route in order to catch a glimpse of the traitor, heretic, or—to supporters—future martyr. With his hands tied behind his back or with his feet in chains, he was publicly exhorted from atop his hurdle by a crowd which lined the route to his execution site. Thomas More, for example, famously encountered passersby asking for help; at one point, wine was even offered to him, though he replied "Christ in his passion was given not wine but vinegar to drink."[131] Frequently, the prisoner was accompanied by a preacher or, in other cases, a sheriff, who urged him along the way to acknowledge his crimes and sins, the latter being especially the case in Elizabeth's reign, when the prisoners were Jesuits or priests.[132] The condemned also had a chance to say goodbye to his family, either along the procession route or at the execution site. As he was being led to the stake, for example, William Hunter saw his father, who said, weeping, "God be with you, son." "God be with you, good father," Hunter replied, "be of good comfort, for I hope we shall meet again, when we shall be merry."[133] On his way to execution, John Rogers also glimpsed his family—a wife and ten children—who were among the crowd watching him on his way to die, while Thomas Wats enjoined his wife and six children—two of whom wanted to join their father in the flames—to hold fast in their faith.[134]

In addition to carrying with him a book of scripture or a Psalter—which was traditional practice[135]—the condemned could also dress with significance, using his clothes to convey meanings that circumvented the authorities' control. Some prisoners dressed in their finest regalia, in shirts specially sewn for the occasion, as if they were attending a high and joyful ceremony. The Welsh fisherman Rawlins White described the shirt he wore to execution as his "wedding garment,"[136] while John Bradford donned a special shirt sewn for him "by one master Walter Marler's wife," which elicited from the crowd "great admiration."[137] Nicholas Ridley dressed for his own self-described "wedding," though he was forced to shed his garments at the execution site, while others opted for more apostolic gear, as was the case with Laurence Saunders, who was dressed "in an old gown and a shirt, barefooted." On the day of his execution, Thomas More began to dress for his execution "into his best apparell," until the lieutenant of the Tower advised him to wear more modest clothes in light of the tradition that executioners were to seize garments for themselves.[138] On the other hand, during the same period, the Carthusians were pointedly ordered to wear their monastic habits as well as their traditional hairshirts, with the latter making the resulting butchery particularly difficult.[139]

It was also traditionally expected that the prisoners would distribute money to the poor along the parade route, or, in the time of Mary, to give to a priest so that masses would be said for them after their death. In 1555, for example, sympathizers offered George Marsh a purse in which he could pay a priest and "be saved"; instead, Marsh said that "he would not as then be troubled with meddling with money, but willed some good man to take the money . . . and to give it unto the prisoners or poor people."[140] Similarly, John Bradford, before he died, "gave money to every servant and officer of the house" where he had been incarcerated, before proceeding on to his death,[141] while Nicholas Ridley, when he arrived at his place of execution, distributed his clothes and various personal items to both the officers and his friends in the crowd. Meanwhile, in 1595, the priest William Freeman "went alonge the street [to the gallows] very cheerfully, & dealinge money to pore people that stoode in his way."[142] Freeman, in fact, seems to have made a great show of his procession to the execution site: emerging from the jailor's house, he "pynned upon his brest the picture of a Crucifixe made after the form of a hart, in paper," and when one of the sheriff's men noted that he seemed inordinately happy, Freeman laid his hand upon the crucifix and answered, "Yea, I have no other cause, for I dye for this."[143]

Often, the prisoner did not travel alone, but was accompanied by others also condemned, including common felons as well as other heretics or traitors. Richard Woodman, for example, was carried to the site of his death and burned with nine others,[144] while the three women who famously perished at Guernsey consisted of the mother "at the middle post," with "the eldest daughter on the right hand, the youngest on the other."[145] In an echo of Jesus on Golgotha, Foxe reports that George Eagles was executed alongside thieves and even took the opportunity beforehand to exhort them to repent; one of the thieves turned to Eagles and said sarcastically, "Why should we doubt to obtain heaven, forasmuch as this holy man shall go before us, as captain and leader unto us in the way? We shall fly thither straight, as soon as he hath once made us the entry." Another thief, however, took heed to Eagles, "earnestly bewailing his own wickedness, and calling to Christ for mercy."[146]

When he arrived at the place of execution, the prisoner was given the opportunity to address the crowd, and sometimes even take questions and undergo disputes. This was the case in 1540, when Robert Barnes was asked by one of the crowd about his opinion on saints, which produced a detailed, almost pedagogical answer, after which his stakefellow followed with a speech of his own that ended, in a somewhat typical manner, that he committed his soul to Christ, and "beseech you all to pray to God for me, and for my brethren here present with me, that our souls, leaving these wretched carcasses, may constantly depart in the true faith of Christ."[147] All in all, it was a thoughtful, dignified presentation that contrasted with the agonizing, state-sponsored fire that followed. The aforementioned William Freeman also underwent a last-minute, gallows-side disputation with his former examiner, one Boardman, who asked him whether he believed "the proceedings of the churche of England?" Freeman answered that obviously he did not, since "yf I had ben of that opinion I neaded not to have ben here now"; still, he was innocent of the "Externall acte of treason." Boardman then went on to "caville with [Freeman] about some matters in controversy, as Mediation & Intercession of Saintes, & such lyke," and tried to entice Freeman into joining him in prayer; Freeman refused, however, stating that "yow and I are divided. There was a division betwene Moyses & Aaron, God's lawfull Priestes, & Chore, Dathan & Albiron," and anyway, he had come "to dye for my faith," not to dispute. Boardman eventually let the matter drop, and said that he bore the priest no malice; the persecution of Freeman had been undertaken "in that behalf of my prince and country, & therefore I hope that yow will forgive me, & not think yll in me?" Freeman answered that he did not bear him any ill, and when Boardman wished him "eternall salvation." Freeman said, "I thanke yow, [and] wyshe the same unto yow."[148]

It was the prisoner's speech, however, which served as a set piece of the drama, and though the authorities dictated the terms and the rules—for example, that the speech was to be contained within certain limits, and not used to rile the crowd—few of the condemned individuals refused the opportunity to make their last exhortation to the world. The "last dying speech" seems, in fact, to have begun—or at least proliferated—under the Tudors,[149] and was allowed not only to heretics or traitors, but to felons and other common criminals, as J. A. Sharpe and others have recently pointed out.[150] Authorities, however, were not being particularly lenient or generous of heart in allowing the condemned to speak; instead, the speech, if it took place, was a firm part of the script as it was written by the state, with pleas for forgiveness and salutes to the crown not so subtly reinforcing the powers that be. Such speeches tended to follow a stereotyped formula, beginning with a recounting of the prisoner's early and later sins, and continuing with an expected acknowledgment of guilt, even if the prisoner had previously challenged the conviction.[151] By prostrating himself in such a manner, the condemned was thus ending the drama on a note of consensus and conveying to the audience that justice, in fact, had been done—or so the authorities hoped.

Despite attempts by those authorities to control the nature and content of speeches, however, the speaker—especially if he was a heretic or traitor, rather than a common felon—could often slip in small gibes alongside his salutes to the crown. Thomas More's last statement that he died "the King's good servant but God's first" carried a measure of self-assertion which implied that the two kinds of servants, and the laws under which they served, were deeply opposed. In the same year, 1535, John Fisher declared that "I beseech Almighty God of his infinite goodness, to save the king and the realm, and that it may please him to hold his hand over it," before adding a swipe with, "and send the king good counsel," thus implying, of course, that his present counsel was lacking.[152] Both men, however, took care to pray for their monarchs, and there is nothing to indicate that their statements were not genuinely felt. Similarly, the Carthusian John Houghton defended himself by declaring that "being about to die in public, I declare that I have refused to comply with the will of his Majesty the king, not from obstinacy, malice, or a rebellious spirit, but solely for offending the supreme Majesty of God."[153] At the end of the century, Edmund Campion also announced that he prayed for Elizabeth, "your Queen and my Queen, unto whom I wish a long quiet reign with all prosperity." Campion even went so far as to admit that "if you esteem my religion treason, then am I guilty," although it was a statement which also carried a defiant affirmation of his religion.[154] Campion, More, and Fisher were more or less able to slip past the authorities and crowds by masking dissent within their praise; others, however, were not so subtle. In 1590, the priest Anthony Middleton asked Richard Topcliffe, who was present at the execution, if he was permitted to speak; Topcliffe replied that if he spoke "to the glory of God, the honor of thy prince and country"—and not "that doctrine which thou hast taught in yonder place"—then he would be allowed his speech. But when Middleton proceeded to state that "if I had ten thousand deaths to suffer, I would suffer them for the Roman Catholic faith," he was interrupted by the howls of the crowd, yelling, "Away with him."[155]

Last speeches were also seized upon by individuals as part of a continuation of the "art of dying well" tradition, which could also be used to counteract the authorities' will.[156] Of course, officials also sought out a good death for the condemned, who were expected to face death with the proscribed amount of repentance and humility before God and the crown. However, for those about to be executed, the art of dying well meant something completely different. Where authorities wished for repentance on the part of an obstinate heretic or a traitorous priest, those same individuals were displaying, to themselves and their followers, patient suffering at the hands of unjust tormentors. Although the point of death was portrayed in the *ars moriendi* books as singularly dark and perilous—with the devil's snares lurking strongest there—the dying individual nevertheless had to bear the moment "without any contradiction but also joyously, as he should abide the coming of his good friend," or a realm of "joy and glory."[157] Speeches reflected these themes, and were only magnified by pending martyrdom; indeed, whenever the condemned declared their joy, they were echoing, in addition to the *ars moriendi*, the words of Thomas à Kempis, who wrote, "How gracious and happy is that soul that now in his life laboreth to be in that state that it desireth to be found in death."[158] Thus, in 1543, for example, Henry Filmer, Robert Testwood, and Anthony Peerson told the crowd "not to be moved by their afflictions, for it was the happiest thing that ever came to them,"[159] a statement which was appropriate for the moment of death, but also one which showed how patient endurance could win out in the face of such approaching agony, and cause the martyrs to wrest the execution drama away from the authorities' control.

The act of forgiveness was another necessity in the art of dying well, though individuals were also modeling themselves on the Jesus in Luke 23:34, who said, "Father, forgive them; for they know not what they do." The words, in fact, were often quoted, and addressed not only to persecutors in general but to specific individuals. When the preacher at John Frith's and Andrew Hewet's execution, for example, told the people that "they should in no wise pray for them than they would for a dog," Frith smiled and "asked the crowd to forgive the preacher," words which "did not a little move the people unto anger, and not without good cause." In 1540 the Protestant Robert Barnes said about Stephen Gardiner that "if he have sought or wrought this my death either by word or deed, I pray now God forgive him as heartily, as freely, as charitably, and without feigning, as ever Christ forgave them that put him to death. And if any of the council, or any others have sought or wrought it through malice or ignorance, I pray God forgive their ignorance, and illuminate their eyes that they may see."[160]

While some martyrs chose to emphasize the theme of forgiveness which prevailed in the Gospels, others adhered to the model of Old Testament prophets, going to their deaths in hard, accusatory defiance. Protestants executed under Mary were, for the most part, of this nature and, with the attention of the nation on them, exhorted accordingly: "O England, England, repent thee of thy sins, repent thee of thy sins," cried John Bradford at the stake.[161] A final, angry affirmation of faith also laced these speeches, as prisoners upheld their true church and condemned others who held fast to the wrong beliefs, all of which the Catholic writer Miles Huggarde used as evidence of the their lack of modesty appropriate to a martyr.[162] Dirick Carver, for example, enjoined his followers that "as many of you as do believe upon the Father, the Son, and the Holy Ghost, unto everlasting life, see you do the works appertaining to the same. And as many of you as do believe upon the pope of Rome, or any of his laws which he sets forth in these days, you do believe to your utter condemnation."[163] In the same period, Thomas Wats also displayed anger when he turned to Richard Rich, who was present at the execution, and told him to "beware, beware! For you do against your own conscience herein; and without you repent, the Lord will revenge it: for you are the cause of this my death."[164]

Catholics could be similarly defiant, as was the case in 1538, when Friar Forest is said to have cried out as he was dying that "if his body should be cut joint after joint, or member after member burnt, hanged, or what pain soever might be done . . . he would never turn from his old profession."[165] Later, during Elizabeth's reign, the Catholic John Story, whose speech followed the aforementioned formula, declared that "I say with St. Jerome, that ancient father and pillar of the old ancient, catholic, and apostolic church, grounded upon the patriarchs, prophets, and apostles, that in the same faith that I was born in, I propose to die in."[166] Later on, the Jesuits were notorious for their defiance, not only proclaiming their faith, but also using the opportunity to lead others in prayer, as was the case with Robert Southwell at the scene of his death.[167]

Those convicted of treason, especially during Elizabeth's reign, also used their last opportunity to deny that any treason had been committed. The Catholic John Felton, who had been condemned for posting a papal bull on the bishop of London's gate, insisted that "I take it on my death, that I never meaned hurt, or harm, or any Treason toward my prince, but only that, which I did, in setting up the Bull." Authorities present attempted to compel Felton to acknowledge that he was, in fact, "attainted of High Treason, and found Guilty, by the oath of twelve true and honest men; therefore, acknowledge thy treason, and be sorry for it, and ask God and thy prince forgiveness." Felton, however, refused to go as far as that, though he did say that "he was most heartily sorry for his fact that he was condemned for, and that he besought her grace to forgive him."[168] In 1571 John Story was also allowed to face the crowd before the gallows, and was enjoined to ask forgiveness for his treason. Story, saying that "it hath pleased Almighty God to call me to account of my 67 years," began his extremely long speech by detailing the sinfulness of his nature, and then proceeded to defend himself against the charges in his arraignment by reiterating his claim made at trial that he was no longer a subject of the realm, nor of its laws. Moreover, Story continued, he had not been as cruel as he was alleged to have been in the time of Mary, when he was on the other side, as a persecutor; indeed, when twenty-eight people had been condemned to the fire, he "moved the dean of Paul's, to tender their state." Ultimately, however, Story accepted the fate of his impending hanging and quartering, and ended his speech by asking that charity be shown his wife, "who hath four small children, and God hath now taken me away who was her staff and stay"; in addition, "now my daughter Weston and her three children are gone over to her, and I know not how they shall do for food, unless they go begging from door to door for it."[169]

The actual execution of religious dissidents was redolent of the death on the cross, just as "behind every martyrdom," according to Arthur Droge and James Tabor, "lay the self-sacrifice of Jesus himself."[170] To therefore fail at death was to fail not only at the "good death," but even more at martyrdom; it was to cast oneself aside from the joyful way in which early martyrs, such as Polycarp, had endured their sufferings, and to shrink from one's own pain as well as that of Jesus', who, in John Fisher's words, "endured [pain] for thy sake."[171] When the execution itself began, many individuals did, in fact, recoil at the pain, though this did not for the most part lead to a stakeside recantation; if they had come this far, enduring imprisonment, interrogations, trials, pressures from authorities and even family, and above all, a period of preparation for death through prayer and the support of others, then the chances were that they would make the last move to complete their martyrdom. One should repeat the fact that hagiographic reports, such as those by John Foxe, William Roper, or the Catholic pamphleteers, might have brushed over any acts of last-minute fear and sudden irresolution on the part of the condemned; still, reports even from those whose affiliations resided in the opposite camps attested to the undoubted bravery in the way many Protestants and Catholics, at varying times, faced their deaths.[172]

Even the practice of forcing individuals to watch as their coreligionists were executed did not necessarily succeed in producing a recantation or preventing those individuals from embarking down the same path. According to a Catholic account, the forced witnessing of the burnings of Ridley and Latimer by Thomas Cranmer, for example, caused the former archbishop, from the gatehouse tower, to tear off his cap, fall to his knees, and cry out in anguish.[173] The event may have led to another recantation, though Cranmer eventually, in the end, went on to his death. During Elizabeth's reign in 1588, authorities did succeed in bringing a few Catholics into conformity, including Francis Edwardes, who relented after witnessing his coreligionist Ralph Crockett being quartered.[174] Even so, for every Edwardes there were individuals such as the priest James Bell, who in 1584 was made to look on as his companion, John Finch, was "aquarteringe"; as he watched Finch's bowels being pulled out, Bell cried, "O why doe I tarrye soe longe behinde my sweete brother; let me make hast after him. This is a most happy day."[175]

This kind of joy is all the more remarkable when considering the types of executions these martyrs would face. While specific details of executions may not in themselves seem to warrant a description, it is important to note that for martyrs themselves—and for those hagiographers who would write about them—the physicality and physiology of their deaths was a key component of their story. Similarly, Thomas More insisted that one meditate on Christ's "scornful crown of sharp thorns," his "sorebeaten veins and sinews," and "the great long nails cruelly driven with hammers through his holy hands and feet," in order to approximate the full extent of his suffering on the cross.[176] Thus, the punishment for traitors, as mentioned, involved drawing them through the streets and then hanging them at a gallows, after which they would be laid across a plank or platform as their stomachs were sliced open and bowels, entrails, and heart removed, to be thrown into a fire. Occasionally, to ease the trauma, a blindfold would be provided to the victim. The process—and sometimes the actual death—would usually end with a beheading, after which the victim's parts would be quartered and usually sent on to Newgate for parboiling.

Burnings, on the other hand, were no less bloody. At the beginning, victims were chained to a stake, sometimes back-to-back if there were two or more of them, as piles of wood were placed around and under them, embedding them up to their midsections or chests. Usually, the sheriff or his men would start the fire, which would kindle around the legs before rising up their bodies—that is, if the wind did not blow the fire in another direction. If gunpowder had been given to the victim and placed under his armpits, then the explosion would kill him before the flames were to rise; if not, death could come slowly, lasting anywhere from approximately fifteen minutes to a full three-quarters of an hour. John Foxe—who Helen White once called a "master of horror"[177]—was especially vivid in his description of John Hooper in the flames, as he "knocked his breast with his hands, until one of his arms fell off, and then knocked still with the other, what time the fat, water, and blood dropped out at his fingers' ends, until by renewing of the fire his strength was gone, and his hand did cleave fast, in knocking, to the iron upon his breast." Still, Foxe continues, Hooper maintained his spiritual peace, and died amidst this horror "as quiet as a child in his bed."[178]

As Hooper's serenity demonstrates, martyrs could seize the drama from the authorities' hands and shape it according to their purposes even at the very moments of their deaths. In 1538, for example, a Suffolk man named N. Peke was put to the flames, and as he was becoming so "scorched that he was black as soot," one of the clerics present poked him in the shoulder with a "long white wand" and said, "Peke! Recant, and believe that the sacrament of the altar is the very body of Christ, flesh, blood, and bone." Peke, however, answered, "I defy it, and thee also," and, according to Foxe "with a great violence he spit from him very blood, which came by reason that his veins brake in his body for extreme anguish."[179] Enduring pain was, in fact, a mode of active resistance

rather than an example of one passively accepting in one's body the power of the state. As Brent Shaw has written about the early church martyrs, such endurance "is seen as the means by which the individual human being can withstand not just the actual tortures and bodily punishments of Roman executions in the arena, but also defeat the enemy who is identified with the Devil."[180] "Let them come at me," wrote Ignatius, with "fire and cross and contests with wild beasts, cutting and tearing me apart, racking my bones, mangling my limbs, crushing my whole body, cruel tortures of the Devil."[181]

Some martyrs chose to signal to the crowd or send a final message through gestures, with Cranmer's uplifted "unworthy right hand"— the limb which had signed his recantations—constituting one of the most famous hand movements of the century.[182] Kissing or embracing the stake before one had been chained to it was another act that drew the martyrs such as Thomas Wats and Christopher Wade, closer to Christ. As John Philpot exclaimed when he embraced the stake, "Shall I disdain to suffer at this stake, seeing my Redeemer did not refuse to suffer a most vile death upon the cross for me?"[183] It has been postulated that the similarly common sight of a martyr clapping his or her hands in the flames was not an act of gestural significance, but rather a physiological response to the violence that burning inflicted on the body; whether this is valid or not, to followers and later martyrologists, the gesture was perceived as yet another sign or miracle that the victim had triumphed over his tormentors and achieved victory of the highest calling. Thomas Haukes had even told his friends that he would raise his hands to heaven as he was being burned, to demonstrate that "a man could keep his mind quiet and patient." According to Foxe:

> Not long after, when the hour was come . . . the fire was set unto him. In the which when he continued long, and when his speech was taken away by violence of the flame, his skin also drawn together, and his fingers consumed with the fire, so that now all men thought certainly he had been gone, suddenly, and contrary to all expectation, the blessed servant of God, being mindful of his promise afore made, reached up his hands burning on a light fire, which was marvelous to behold, over his head to the living God, and with great rejoicing, as it seemed, struck or clapped them three times together. At the sight whereof there followed such applause and

outcry of the people . . . that the like hath not commonly been heard, and you would have thought heaven and earth to have come together.[184]

Executions could become especially dramatic if prisoners went to the stake in pairs or groups. A kind of ecumenical carnage occurred in 1540, for example, when the Protestants Barnes, Garret, and Jerome were executed and followed by three others, these being the Catholics Powel, Fetherstone, and Abel; the act, rather than tilting the drama in the victims' favor, above all served to display the leadership of Henry, who wished to show that he brooked no dissent from either camp.[185] During Mary's reign, many individuals were killed together: in 1557, for example, seven individuals, including Alice Benden, went together to the stake, according to Foxe, "and being ready thereto, they all (like the communion of saints) kneeled down, and made their humble prayers unto the Lord with such zeal and affection as even the enemies of the cross of Christ could not but like it." After making the invocation together, they "rose and went to the stake, where, being compassed with horrible flames of fire, they yielded their souls and lives gloriously into the hand of the Lord." If one was being burned with another, the two could console one another, as was the case in 1557 when Elizabeth Cooper was at the stake with Simon Miller; as the fire reached her and she cried out, Foxe writes, "the said Simon Miller . . . put his hand behind him toward her, and willed her to be strong and of good cheer: 'for, good sister,' said he, 'we shall have a joyful and a sweet supper.'"

The very last words spoken by the martyrs before death were final acts of assertion against authorities, even though the words, paradoxically, resonated with themes of yielding and offering oneself up in sacrifice, as Christ had done. All were directly from or evocative of scripture: the words of Jesus in Luke and Stephen in Acts—"Lord Jesus, receive my spirit"—were uttered by many, including John Hooper, Robert Glover, Roger Holland, and Christopher Wade, among others, as were the words, "Father of heaven, have mercy upon me," which were repeated by George Marsh as he was engulfed in flames. The words were important in that they transformed their speakers into scriptural figures, closely identified with the martyrs of Acts and the early church; indeed, the image of a body in deep physical torment, but a spirit in peace—or an individual shouting scripture from amidst the fire or under the executioner's knives—had an impact that ultimately ceded control, and victory, of the event over to those who seemed to suffer the most from it. Execution scenes ultimately resembled a chiaroscope of ever-shifting perspectives: from the authorities' point of view, the execution represented both earthly and divine justice at work, purifying the realm by literally burning or cutting away its obstinate heretics and traitors; the future martyr, on the other hand, viewed the event joyously as his wedding day, crying out, as one priest did, "O blessed day, O the fayrest day that ever I saw in my life." The crowd also carried within itself a multitude of perspectives which could shift back and forth, ranging from sympathy to hostility, grudging admiration for the martyr's fortitude to an enthusiasm in taking part in the execution themselves.

Just as the actors viewed executions from radically different perspectives, so did contemporary writers who chose to chronicle the events afterwards. For John Foxe, executions most dramatically and violently pronounced upon the truth of his martyrs' cause, which carried with it the providential destiny of the true church and of England. Indeed, his Protestant martyrs, by their actions, directly connected themselves with the true martyrs of the early church, just as the Church of England was a continuation of the true and apostolic church of the first five centuries, before papal Rome and its corruptions intervened. Claims such as these disgusted Catholic polemicists, such as Miles Huggarde, who famously described Protestant crowds at executions as seeing "the holy ghost in the likeness of a dove," when in fact they were witnessing nothing more than smoke-agitated pigeons.[186] For Huggarde, such pseudo-martyrs were the worst kind of impostors, insidiously usurping scripture toward their own "false and stinking" ends and leading others along with them. However, while Huggarde could attempt to prove the falseness of their martyrdom by describing the "cowardly" use of gunpowder, for example, there was no denying what all, including he, basically knew: the condemned had died, if not martyrs' deaths, then brave and even heroic ones, for the truth in which they believed.

The same problem faced Elizabethans who attempted to write against the executed Catholics, turning their fortitude into obstinacy and having them ascend the gallows mumbling "Popish prayers."[187] For such writers, it was necessary to insist that the Catholic victim had been executed—indeed, been cut apart in a specific, traditionally significant way—solely because of his treason in order for them to seize the discourse and counter any claims of martyrdom or even injustice on the state's part. Thus, Edmund Campion was said by some Protestants to have trembled before his execution and hesitated in a way unbecoming to a saint. Too many witnesses were at the event, however, and stated otherwise for such claims to hold. Waiting eagerly for their testimony in turn—and with certain rhetorical tools of their own—were the hagiographers and pamphleteers, who took those accounts and proceeded to shape them further, thus finishing the process of martyrdom that had begun with imprisonment, continued through trials, and culminated with executions.

Executions thus constituted an exchange not only between authorities, crowds, and martyrs, but also between later interpreters who shaped an essentially ambiguous event toward their own proselytizing purposes.[188] In light of this ambiguity and these vastly different interpretations, one must question the extent to which executions served the persecution process as a whole. In some ways, the display of state-sanctioned violence was sufficient enough, at least in the short run, to deter future heretics and intimidate people into obedience or conformity. Even in Mary's reign, when executions ultimately backfired and the martyrs gained the upper hand, the population was not stirred in its sympathies to the extent that a true threat was presented to the state, nor, in fact, was it at all clear that those martyrs would have the impact they eventually did. What truly set the stage for the permanent martyrdom of the Marian Protestants was not their own deaths, but rather the death of Mary and the subsequent accession of Elizabeth (and the establishment of John Foxe); as one writer has put it, while a John Bradford or John Rogers may have, in fact, achieved victory at their deaths, "whether such a victory could have endured as a lasting memory had Mary lived a further decade is another matter."[189]

Elizabeth, on the other hand, was more successful in her policies than Mary, due to the fact that her executions were relatively selective and confined, for the most part, to priests and Jesuits during times of external threat. Moreover, her strategy of relabeling such Catholics as traitors did more to galvanize a public sentiment that was becoming increasingly colored by a Protestant proto-nationalism. Unlike Mary, Elizabeth did, in fact, "live on" long enough to effect a delicate stabilization in government and policies.[190] Nevertheless, even those executions which took place under her watch succeeded unwittingly in sustaining the now-diminished English Catholic community, strengthening its members and even becoming a tool of evangelization in the hands of energizing forces, such as the Jesuits. In this sense, the execution, whether at the scaffold or the stake, belonged to the martyrs, who had reached the end of a process that had begun with the first open declaration of faith and proceeded through a series of tests—from betrayal, flight, imprisonment, through trial—all in close approximation, as they well knew, of Christ and the early church martyrs. Whereas the mass of people at some point along the process wavered before the authorities in a gray area of acquiescence, recantation, or outward conformity, for martyrs there was no alternative to conformity except death, no concessions to be made except with one's life.

The execution site constituted the gateway into the new life to come, since death, to the martyr, was not an end but a beginning, a moment to be embraced even literally, as one embraced the stake or the executioner. Of course, not all martyrs were monolithically single-minded in their approach to death and its accompanying pain. Thomas More, for example, came to the scaffold in the fullness of his personality and wit, even taking his characteristic sense of irony with him, whereas the doubtful and recanting Thomas Cranmer, in David Loades's words, also did not meet his death as a classic martyr, "but something that was in a sense greater: the man sorely tempted, whom God had finally strengthened to his glory." Paradoxically, once martyrs embraced death and underwent the execution, however, they displayed their humanity in its most exposed form, in all its bodily aspects—flesh burning, limbs torn apart, stomach sliced open ("Oh, it smarts!" cried the priest Edmund Genings).[191] At the same time, they had also ceased to become human, as they proceeded to transform pain into ecstasy, abandon their lives willingly, display absolute control on the scaffold or stake, and meet death in total certainty of their roles as God's chosen instruments. The execution was thus like a wave at its highest crest, the culmination of all that had come before; it was the highest point that all the martyrs had aspired to, and when it receded, it would leave something else behind, as the life dissolved into the hagiography, the suffering into the redemption, and the human into the saint.

EPILOGUE

ANY ATTEMPT TO UNDERSTAND THE MODERN EXERTIONS OF STATE power should consider the way in which authorities sought to impose order and control in the world that came before. While the sixteenth century should be taken on its own terms and not viewed as a prelude, one can nevertheless discern stirrings that gave rise to later developments in policing, prisons, executions, and the law, as well as changes in ideas of tolerance and intolerance, pluralism and uniformity, and the individual and the state. In sixteenth-century England, all of this was especially evident, since the very elements that it lacked—a modern bureaucracy and enforcement structure, a new conceptual or philosophical framework in which to handle dissent in its midst—needed to be developed if an effective legal and judicial system was to be worked out in accordance with changing historical conditions, and against forces with which it never had to deal before.

Tudor attempts to assert control and order over dissident religious groups ultimately worked in fits and starts, and the problem of uniformity, or the lack of it, was by no means resolved at the end of Elizabeth's reign any more than it was at the end of Henry's. Oppositional groups, such as Catholics and Puritans, would continue to cause trouble in the next century, particularly since they had gained powerful footholds at court and in parliament. Even worse, the next century would attest to a veritable explosion of religious movements that might have been extensions of previous heterodoxies, though they were far more powerful and dangerous in their revolutionary millennialism than any of their earlier equivalents.

The sixteenth century was significant in that it unleashed these tensions and these religious groups, which would not only lead in part to the civil war of the next century, but also amount to a fundamentally unresolvable problem if a rigid policy of uniformity continued. That Tudor governments were unable to contain these forces was due in part to an absence of the mechanisms available to modern states, making those governments reliant instead on an essentially personal system of enforcement, dominated by policy-making individuals at the top, to be carried out by individuals in the mid-level of officialdom, and abetted by individuals in society as a whole. The fact that all three elements were frequently out of coordination with each other—and not working in top-down tandem, as historians such as Geoffrey Elton have tended to argue—only led to further disjunctures in the goals of the government and the execution of those goals on the ground.

But even modern governments, with all their resources, cannot fully contain dissident individuals with a proclivity toward martyrdom, who take control of their own fates, and of public relations, by exploiting the spiritual power that being persecuted brings to them. Like the extremists of today who utilize the media—for example, the suicide bombers in the Middle East who videotape themselves declaring their faith before they are to die, as ritual part of their martyrdom—sixteenth-century groups also knew how to back up their martyrological claims by utilizing the technology of the printing press, creating their own training schools in the seminaries, or resurrecting long-dormant literary genres such as hagiographies and consolatory prison letters. For them, self-sacrifice was to be a deeply public gesture, played out on a stage for all to see. As for the weight of the persecutory hand that cast itself down on them, even that was to be welcomed, since its extremity only further illuminated the suffering that the martyrs were willing to bear.

Martyrdom, of course, is in the eye of the beholder, as a Catholic polemicist such as Miles Huggarde implicitly recognized when he inverted everything seen by the Protestants as righteous—bold-talking defendants, patiently suffering and lamb-like self-sacrifices, the aeriel presence of the Holy Spirit seen in the doves at the fires—into their opposite, claiming instead those things to be nothing more than obstinacy, suicidal tendencies, and pigeons. To examine the ways in which religious dissidents, no matter what their confession, seized certain strategies of resistance while maintaining, in their own eyes at least, a purity of faith, is not to diminish their very real motives. Indeed, men such as John Bradford were absolutely convinced of the truth for which they were dying, and of their destiny as Paul's heirs to spread the word and offer up witness through their sufferings. When that truth conflicted with the crown's own assertions, however, then the drama of persecution began; in a world where both sides held fast to a truth in which there was no wavering, martyrdom could only result.

The quest for uniformity on the part of the Tudors, and the desire to extinguish any groups who posed a challenge to it, was entirely logical in the context of the sixteenth century, and should not be viewed from a post-Enlightenment perspective. The idea of diversity or pluralism, which the Tudors viewed as synonymous with religious and political chaos and schism, was anathema not only to the government but to religious groups themselves, who, after all, were willing to send forth martyrs to die, not for many truths, but for the one immutable truth that they alone held. In the sixteenth century, when ancient and medieval bodily metaphors were still deeply ingrained in political thought, any element that represented division was a limb that had to be amputated, since it carried the risk of infecting and therefore killing the entire body. The fact that religious groups, however, kept persisting in upholding their cause and valiantly dying for it only made the threat all the more dangerous and insidious in the eyes of the authorities.

Above all, the pursuit as well as the evasions of religious dissidents in England raised questions about the relationship of the individual to the state and of oppositional groups to the larger society. The antagonism that arose between personal conscience and crown fealty, or God's laws and man's laws, constituted the primary battle of the century, after all, and one which had never been dealt with to such an extent before. Eventually, the opening up of the state to a grudging acceptance on a civil basis for religious oppositional groups, and a loosening of the hold of a dominant state church, resolved part of the problem, though the issue never entirely disappeared. In fact, it is misleading to assume that the modern world, which still contends with these issues, has any clearer answers about the question of individuals whose consciences and convictions vehemently clash with the government to which they owe loyalty. Whether that individual is a sixteenth-century Anabaptist or a present-day Koreshian millennialist, the question is still present and haunting, no matter how potent, how modern, the state has become.

NOTES

Notes to Chapter One

1. Any argument that centers on persecution intersects a variety of recent scholarly debates concerning such subjects as tolerance and intolerance in the sixteenth century, the emergence of modern persecution and the state, the role of casuistry and equivocation in relation to martyrological identities, and the nature and extent of religious change in the English Reformation (or Reformations). No study, however, has focused solely on the workings of religious persecution, martyrdom, and resistance as they manifested themselves in different forms, and according to different levels of effectiveness, across the course of the century. The regional studies that have proliferated in the past decades do offer a useful, if necessarily partial and tangential, portrait of persecutory activity and enforcement as they manifested themselves on a local level. Also important, if by now somewhat dated, is G. R. Elton's *Policy and Police: The Enforcement of the Reformation in the Age of Thomas Cromwell* (Cambridge, 1972), which explores policing structures and the evidence of indictments and trials in the years of Thomas Cromwell's hegemony, between 1532 and 1540. Elton's work is consistent with his larger thesis, which is that the Reformation in England was pushed through from above, by statute and proclamation, and generally accepted by the larger population. While it is true that political will ultimately propelled the Reformation forward, Elton's argument, which focuses a great deal on state papers and other official documents, tends to overlook the often powerful resistances and continued local allegiances that existed among communities throughout the century, all of which are indeed addressed in local, as well as revisionist-oriented (and very contentious) studies of Christopher Haigh and others.

2. *AM* (1583), 2047.

3. For an excellent examination of the ways in which Catholics, for example, exercised agency in the face of Elizabethan authorities' attempts to discipline and punish them, see Peter Lake and Michael Questier, "Agency, Appropriation and Rhetoric under the Gallows: Puritans, Romanists and the State in Early Modern England," *Past and Present* 153 (1996): 64–107. See also Lake and Questier's "Prisons, Priests and People," in *England's Long Reformation 1500–1800*, ed. Nicholas Tyacke (London, 1998), 195–233. For an opposing view upholding the idea of an ideologically controlling state, see J. A. Sharpe, "'Last Dying Speeches': Religion, Ideology and Public Execution in Seventeenth-Century England," *Past and Present* 107 (1985): 144–67.

4. Caroline Litzenberger writes of historians' tendency to divide sixteenth-century English peoples' religious affiliations into clear Protestant/Catholic camps: "Using such sharp distinctions hampers the accuracy of representations of the past, in that it requires religion to be trimmed of its complexities and diversities in order to fit into such strictly delineated categories. It is difficult accurately to characterize the actions, let alone faith, of either individuals or parishes using such a rigid black and white paradigm. We must find ways to accommodate myriad shades of grey." Caroline Litzenberger, *The English Reformation and the Laity: Gloucestershire, 1540–1580* (Cambridge, 1997), 1–9. For the revisionist view, see Christopher Haigh, *English Reformations: Religion, Politics, and Society under the Tudors* (Oxford, 1993), and Eamon Duffy, *The Stripping of the Altars: Traditional Religion in England, 1400–1580* (New Haven, 1982).

5. For a repudiation of the idea of the Inquisition and its often Protestant-shaped reputation, see *Beyond the Persecuting Society: Religious Toleration before the Enlightenment,* ed. John Christian Laurson and Cary J. Nederman (Philadelphia, 1998), esp. chap. 4. See also R. I. Moore, *The Formation of a Persecuting Society: Power and Deviance in Western Europe, 950–1250* (Oxford, 1987). Against Moore's extremely generalist (and problematic) approach, see also David Nirenberg, *Communities of Violence: Persecution of Minorities in the Middle Ages* (Princeton, 1996), esp. the introduction.

6. By Locke, one is particularly referring to his *Letter concerning Toleration*. See *Epistola de Tolerantia,* ed. Raymond Klibansky (Oxford, 1968). See also Richard Vernon, *The Career of Toleration: John Locke, Jonas Proast, and After* (Montreal, 1997). For standard accounts of the history of toleration, see W. K. Jordan, *The Development of Religious Toleration in England,* 4 vols. (London, 1932–40); Joseph Lecler, *Toleration and the Reformation,* 2 vols. (London, 1960). See also N. M. Sutherland, "Persecution and Toleration in Reformation Europe," in *Persecution and Tolerance,* ed. W. J. Sheils (Oxford, 1984), 153–61, and Heiko A. Oberman, "The Travail of Tolerance: Containing Chaos in Early

Modern Europe," in *Tolerance and Intolerance in the European Reformation*, ed. Ole Peter Grell and Bob Scribner (Cambridge, 1996), 30.

7. John Coffey, *Persecution and Toleration in Protestant England, 1558–1689* (London, 2000), esp. 10–14. See also the essays in Grell and Scribner, *Tolerance and Intolerance in the European Reformation*.

8. See Tertullian, "An Injunction against Heretics," excerpted in *Heresy and Authority in Medieval Europe*, ed. Edward Peters (Philadelphia, 1980), 29–30. For other patristic writers on heresy, see St. Irenaeus, *Adversus omnes haereses (Against all Heretics)*, trans. J. Roberts and W. Donaldson (Edinburgh, 1868), and St. Hippolytus, *Refutation of All Heresies*, trans. F. Legge (New York, 1921).

9. *The Political Writings of St Augustine*, ed. H. Paolucci (Chicago, 1962), 184–240. See also Coffey, *Persecution and Toleration*, 22–24.

10. Quoted in Peters, *Heresy and Authority*, 3.

11. See Geoffrey Elton, "Persecution and Toleration in the English Reformation," in Sheils, *Persecution and Tolerance*, 163–87.

12. John Fisher, "A sermon had at Paulis by the commandment of the most reuerend father in god my lord legate," in *The English Works of John Fisher*, ed. John E. B. Mayor, Early English Text Society, e.s., 27 (London, 1876), 434. See also Maria Dowling, *Fisher of Men: A Life of John Fisher, 1469–1535* (New York, 1999), esp. 90–113.

13. See Basil Hall, "Cranmer, the Eucharist and the Foreign Divines in the Reign of Edward VI," in *Thomas Cranmer, Churchman and Scholar*, ed. P. Ayris and D. Selwyn (Woodbridge, U.K., 1993), 217.

14. Sebastian Castellio, *Concerning Heretics: Whether They are to be Persecuted and How They are to be Treated . . .*, ed. Roland Bainton (New York, 1965); see esp. Castellio's dedication to Edward, 212–16.

15. David Cressy, "Different Kinds of Speaking: Symbolic Violence and Secular Iconoclasm in Early Modern England," in *Protestant Identities: Religion, Society, and Self-Fashioning in Post-Reformation England*, ed. Muriel C. McClendon et al. (Stanford, 1999), 19–42, and Margaret Aston, *England's Iconoclasts* (Oxford, 1988), 294–342.

16. For a more moderating view of Cranmer's position on tolerance, see Diarmaid MacCulloch, "Archbishop Cranmer: Concord and Tolerance in a Changing Church," in Grell and Scribner, *Tolerance and Intolerance in the European Reformation*, esp. 199–200.

17. Cranmer also played an active part in the trial of the Evangelical John Frith in 1533, as well as John Lambert in 1538. As MacCulloch points out, Cranmer also "bitterly hated" the Observant Franciscans, who were "the most effective and respected exponents of what the archbishop regarded as devilish error,

not simply on questions of systematic theology, but in their opposition to his cherished royal supremacy." One observant, John Forest, was burned in 1538, in large part due to Cranmer. See MacCulloch, "Archbishop Cranmer," 209.

18. Edmund Bonner, *Homelies sette forth by the righte reuerende father in God, Edmund Byshop of London* (London, 1555), fol. 26v. See also Gina Alexander, "Bonner and the Marian Persecutions," in *The English Reformation Revised,* ed. Christopher Haigh (Cambridge, 1987), 117–75.

19. Muriel C. McClendon, "Reconsidering the Marian Persecution: The Urban Context," in *Protestant Identities,* 199.

20. Quoted from Thomas Mayer, *Reginald Pole: Prince and Prophet* (Cambridge, 2000), 277–78; see in general 272–83. See also Mayer, "'Heretics be not in all things heretics': Cardinal Pole, His Circle, and the Potential for Toleration," in Laurson and Nederman, *Beyond the Persecuting Society,* 197–224.

21. Richard Hooker, *Of the Laws of Ecclesiastical Polity,* Book V, ed. W. Speed Hill (Cambridge, Mass., 1977), 2:16–17. See also W. B. Patterson, "Hooker on Ecumenical Relations: Conciliarism in the English Reformation," 283–303, and essays by other authors in *Richard Hooker and the Construction of Christian Community,* ed. Arthur S. McGrade, Medieval and Renaissance Texts and Studies (Temple, Ariz., 1997).

22. Edwin Sandys, *A Relation of the State Religion* (1638 ed.), 152.

23. Quoted in Coffey, *Persecution and Toleration,* 26.

24. William Cecil, *The Execution of Justice in England for maintenance of publike and Christian peace against certeine stirres of sedition, and adherents to the traitors and enemies of the realm, without anie persecution of them for questions of religion* (1583) (New York, 1936).

25. William Allen, *A true, sincere and modest defence of English Catholiques* (1584), 7.

26. Robert Persons, *A Brief Discours Contayning Certain Resons . . .* (1599), sig. 3–3v. See also William Allen, who wrote that "no Jew, no Turk, no Pagan, can by the law of God, nature or nations be forced from the name and possession of his own sect and service." *True, sincere and modest defence,* 7.

27. John Fines, "Heresy Trials in the Diocese of Coventry and Lichfield, 1511–1512," *JEH* 14 (1963): 160–74.

28. See Brad Gregory, *Salvation at Stake: Christian Martyrdom in Modern Europe* (Cambridge, Mass., 1999), 260–61.

29. See the letter from Johan Scheyfe to Charles V, which stated that "it is notorious that great numbers of Anabaptists, libertines, and atheists had come hither." *Span. Cal.,* 10:254. See also Irvin Horst, *The Radical Brethren: Anabaptism and the English Reformation* (Nieuwkoop, Holland, 1972), 97–140.

30. Coffey, *Persecution and Toleration,* 31–33.

31. See Gregory, *Salvation at Stake,* 260–61.

32. For the full account of Lambert's ordeal, see *AM* (1583), 1101–29.

33. See Patrick Collinson, *The Elizabethan Puritan Movement* (London, 1967).

34. See Ralph Houlbrooke, *Church Courts and the People during the English Reformation, 1520–1570* (Oxford, 1979), and Martin Ingram, *Church Courts, Sex and Marriage in England, 1570–1640* (Cambridge, 1989).

35. For more on Browne, see *EM*, 2(2): 509, and 3(1): 51; *Narratives*, 212–37.

36. For a sample of Rich, see Richard Watson Dixon, *History of the Church of England, from the Abolition of the Roman Jurisdiction* (Oxford, 1891–1902), 3:212.

37. *PP*, 364–65. Once in prison, the prisoner bore his own expenses. See chap. 3.

38. *LP*, 12(1): 258.

39. Elizabeth would discover this when she made a progress through East Anglia. See *SP*, 12/45/16 [?1578].

40. See, for example, Aylmer's crackdown on the university press at Cambridge, *SP*, Dom., Eliz. I, vol. clxi, no. 1.

41. *SP*, 12/133/11 [?1579]. Not all justices refused to conform, however; in Norwich and Suffolk, for example, the justices under question—William Gibbon, James Hubbard, and Philip Awdley—conformed. See William Raleigh Trimble, *The Catholic Laity in Elizabethan England, 1558–1603* (Cambridge, Mass., 1964), 93–94.

42. See the letter from John Bradford to Hopkins: "O happy day that you were made sheriff! By the which as God in this world would promote you to a more honorable degree, so by suffering in this room he hath exalted you in heaven, and in the sight of his church and children, to a much more excellent glory. When was it read that a sheriff of a city hath suffered for the Lord's sake? Where read we of any sheriff, that hath been cast in prison for conscience to Godwards?" See John Bradford, *The Writings of John Bradford* (Cambridge, 1848–53), 2:246.

43. See David Loades, *Tudor Government: Structures of Authority in the Sixteenth Century* (London, 1997), 167–200.

44. *AM* (1583), 1036. See also John Frith, *A boke made by John Frith, . . .* (Antwerp, 1533), A3v–L3; Robert E. Fulup, "John Frith (1503–1533) and his Relation to the Origin of the Reformation in England" (Ph.D. diss., University of Edinburgh, 1956).

45. See Diarmaid MacCulloch, *Tudor Church Militant: Edward VI and the Protestant Reformation* (London, 1999), 29–31, 132–34. In the case of the Anabaptist Joan Bocher, for example, bishops repeatedly took her into their homes and attempted to persuade her to recant, but in the end it was Cranmer who played a role in convincing a reluctant Edward VI to sign the warrant for her execution. For a discussion of Cranmer and Bocher, see Diarmaid MacCulloch,

Thomas Cranmer: A Life (New Haven, 1996), 475–76; John Davis, "Joan of Kent, Lollardy and the English Reformation," *JEH* 33 (1982): 232–33; G. H. Williams, *The Radical Reformation* (London, 1962), 779.

46. For the way Bale in particular shaped his accounts, see also John N. King, *English Reformation Literature: The Tudor Origins of the Protestant Tradition* (Princeton, 1982); Leslie P. Fairchild, "John Bale and Protestant Hagiography in England," *JEH* (1973): 145–60; and *John Bale: Mythmaker for the English Reformation* (West Lafayette, Ind., 1976). G. R. Elton, for example, tends to place Bonner in the loathsome functionary category, though he states that Mary and Cardinal Pole were the ultimate instigators of the persecution policies. Lacey Baldwin Smith, on the other hand, emphasizes Bonner's concern for order in the realm, while the most recent study by Gina Alexander regards Bonner as a greedy, ambitious time-server. The most sympathetic treatment, which attributes Bonner's actions to a genuine concern for heresy and the Catholic Church, is Merrill F. Sherr's unpublished dissertation. See G. R. Elton, *England under the Tudors* (London, 1955), 220; Alexander, "Bonner and the Marian Persecutions"; and Merrill F. Sherr, "Bishop Bonner: Bulwark against Heresy" (Ph.D. diss., New York University, 1969).

47. *AM* (1583), 1984.

48. For a good example of the contingent and ever-changing nature of religious life in the sixteenth century, see Eamon Duffy, *The Voices of Morebath: Reformation and Rebellion in an English Village* (New Haven, 2001).

49. See Susan Brigden, *New Worlds, Lost Worlds: The Reign of the Tudors* (London, 2000), esp. 165–71. See also Brigden's definitive *London and the Reformation* (Oxford, 1989), and Cynthia B. Herrup, *The Common Peace: Participation and the Criminal Law in Seventeenth-Century England* (Cambridge, 1997).

50. See Susan Wabuda, "Henry Bull, Miles Coverdale and the Making of Foxe's Book of Martyrs," in *Martyrs and Martyrologies,* ed. Diana Wood, Studies in Church History 30 (Oxford, 1993), 245–58; John N. King, "Fiction and Fact in Foxe's 'Book of Martyrs,'" in *John Foxe and the English Reformation,* ed. David Loades (Aldershot, U.K., 1997), 12–35; and the work of Thomas Freeman, primarily "Fate, Faction, and Fiction in Foxe's Book of Martyrs," *Historical Journal* 43 (2000): 601–23; "Text, Lies, and Microfilm: Reading and Misreading Foxe's Book of Martyrs," *Sixteenth Century Journal* 38 (1995); and— especially pertinent to this study—"The Importance of Dying Earnestly: The Metamorphosis of the Account of James Bainham in Foxe's 'Book of Martyrs,'" in *The Church Retrospective,* ed. R. N. Swanson (Suffolk, U.K., 1997), 267–88. See also the seminal article by Patrick Collinson, "Truth and Legend: The Veracity of John Foxe's Book of Martyrs," in A. C. Duke and C. A. Tamse, eds., *Clio's Mirror: Historiography in Britain and the Netherlands* (Zutphen, Holland, 1985), 31–54.

51. Lake and Questier, "Agency, Appropriation and Rhetoric," 64–73.

52. For martyrs in general, see Gregory, *Salvation at Stake*. For the ways in which individuals shaped and manipulated the persecutory process toward their own martyrdom, see John Knott, *Discourses of Martyrdom in English Literature, 1563–1694* (Cambridge, 1993). See also the essays in *Martyrs and Martyrologies*, ed. Wood, and Lacey Baldwin Smith, *Fools, Martyrs, Traitors* (New York, 1997), esp. chaps. 1, 7, 8.

Notes to Chapter Two

1. *AM* (1583), 1709.

2. *AM* (1583), 2022.

3. See Patrick Collinson, "The English Conventicle," in *Voluntary Religion*, ed. W. J. Sheils and Diana Wood, Studies in Church History 23 (Cambridge, 1986). It is not clear how many conventicles actually eluded the authorities in the century, but those that were unveiled constituted the most well-known groups and were almost always revealed by some kind of tip-off from within or outside their ranks.

4. For an agricultural apprehension, see *AM* (1583), 2048, and the case of Gouch and Alice Driver, who in 1558 were found in a haystack after authorities had poked around with a pitchfork.

5. The most extensive study of informers, though limited to the Cromwell years, remains Elton's *Policy and Police* [*PP*]; see esp. 327–82. See also Ian W. Archer, *The Pursuit of Stability: Social Relations in Elizabethan London* (Cambridge, 1991), esp. his discussion on the household and apprentice structures of stability (and surveillance). See also Cynthia B. Herrup, *The Common Peace: Participation and the Criminal Law in Seventeenth-Century England* (Cambridge, 1997), chap. 5; and, for the French perspective, Raymond A. Mentzer, Jr., *Heresy Proceedings in Languedoc, 1500–1560* (Philadelphia, 1984), chap. 6.

6. Guilds and other corporations were expected to fulfill self-supervisory functions that oversaw the actions of apprentices, for example, who undertook questionable activities or placed themselves in possibly disruptive environments. Such was the case with the Mercers' Company, which ordered its householders in 1548 to "look to his apprentices or other servants that they do not run to Paul's [Cross] a gazing or gaping as they have been wont to do heretofore, for because there shall be no sermons there yet a while." Mercers' Company, Acts of Court, fol. 224r, cited in Susan Brigden, *London and the Reformation* (Oxford, 1989), 344–45, 444.

7. An earlier directive came from 1530, for example, when Thomas More commanded all men, down to the lowliest village constable, to help in the fight

against heretics, which meant that sheriffs, for instance, were to assist bishops if necessary. See Peter Ackroyd, *The Life of Thomas More* (New York, 1998), 276–86.

8. For a good example of this resistance, see David Loades, "Essex Inquisitions of 1556," *BIHR* 35 (1962): 87–97.

9. *AM* (1583), 1536.

10. *AM* (1583), 2012.

11. See Archer, *The Pursuit of Stability*, 221–24; J. Kent, *The English Village Constable* (Oxford, 1986). See also John Stow, *Abridgement or Summarie of the English Chronicles* (1607), 502, B.L. Landsdowne MS 114/4.

12. Gina Alexander, "Bonner and the Marian Persecutions," in *The English Reformation Revised,* ed. Christopher Haigh (Cambridge, 1992), 162. The practice of appointing royal commissioners continued through all the Tudor reigns, including Mary's. Indeed, as David Loades has pointed out, Mary saw no irony in renouncing the royal supremacy, but retaining, for her own purposes, a key instrument in its enforcement. See David Loades, *The Reign of Mary Tudor: Politics, Government, and Religion in England, 1553–1558* (London, 1979), 331–55.

13. For an example of this, see John Craig, "Cooperation and Initiatives: Elizabethan Churchwardens and the Parish Accounts of Mildenhall," *Social History* 18 (1993).

14. *CPR,* 3:81.

15. Alexander, "Bonner and the Marian Persecutions," 162. One of the more zealous commissioners was Dr. John Story, who impatiently told Bonner, at John Philpot's trial, to be done with it already and "rid this heretic away."

16. Eric Carlson, "The Origin, Function and Status of the Office of Churchwarden, with Particular Reference to the Diocese of Ely," in *The World of Rural Dissenters,* ed. Margaret Spufford (Cambridge, 1995).

17. *Before the Bawdy Court: Selections from Church Court and Other Records Relating to the Correction of Moral Offences in England, Scotland, and New England, 1300–1800,* ed. P. E. H. Hair (New York, 1972), 107.

18. Martin Ingram, *Church Courts, Sex and Marriage in England 1570–1640* (Cambridge, 1987), 327–28.

19. John Coffey, *Persecution and Toleration in Protestant England, 1558–1689* (London, 2000), 100.

20. *EM,* 3(1): 470–71. Another function of these government presences was, in Gina Alexander's words, to "ensure that burnings took place without risk of riot or disturbance" and also to be "on the alert to see that the bishops carried out their responsibilities properly." See Alexander, "Bonner and the Marian Persecutions," 161.

21. According to John Bellamy, the querelae was meant to encourage the king's subjects to come forward through a channel different from the usual

bills presented to twelve men of the grand jury. See *The Tudor Law of Treason* (Toronto, 1979), chap. 3.

22. See, for example, M. Lindsay Kaplan, *The Culture of Slander in Early Modern England* (Cambridge, 1997); Ralph Houlbrooke, *Church Courts and the People during the English Reformation, 1520–1570* (Oxford, 1979), 82–83, 87, 276–77; Martin Ingram, *Church Courts, Sex and Marriage in England,* esp. 299; Christopher Haigh, "Slander and the Church Courts in the Sixteenth Century," *Transactions of the Lancashire and Cheshire Antiquarian Society* 78 (1975): 2; and J. H. Baker, "'Such Disagreement betwyx Neighbours': Litigation and Human Relations in Early Modern England," in *Disputes and Settlements: Law and Human Relations in the West,* ed. John Bossy (Cambridge, 1983), 170–71.

23. Quoted in Herrup, *The Common Peace,* 93–95.

24. Ibid., 95–98.

25. M. W. Beresford, "The Common Informer, the Penal Statutes and Economic Regulation," *Economic History Review* 2 (1927): 157. See also Joseph A. Limprecht, "Common Informers and Law Enforcement in England, 1603–1640" (Ph.D. diss., University of California, Berkeley, 1968).

26. See especially the case of George Whelpay, an early informer working relatively unprofitably in the years 1538–43, in G. R. Elton, "Informing for Profit," *Cambridge Historical Journal* 11 (1954): 149–67.

27. Bellamy, *Tudor Law of Treason,* 92.

28. Alan Harding, *A Social History of English Law* (Baltimore, 1966), 76–77.

29. See W. S. Holdsworth, *History of English Law* (London, 1903), 9:238–41. For the case of Thomas More—and his accuser, Richard Rich—see J. Duncan Derrett, "The Trial of Thomas More," *EHR* 79 (1964): 449–77. See also E. E. Reynolds, *The Trial of St. Thomas More* (London, 1964), 107–17.

30. G. R. Elton, ed., *The Tudor Constitution: Documents and Commentary,* 2nd ed. (Cambridge, 1982), 61–67.

31. *EHD,* no. 125.

32. See Houlbrooke, *Church Courts and the People,* 216–22.

33. See *LP,* 5:1067, in which a rector in Suffolk, Richard Croukar, got in trouble on concealment charges for preaching that "the priest is bound to conceal treason revealed to him in confession."

34. To his credit, Marshall also "laments to hear how poor people be indicted for small matters of pretended heresy, as by the bishop of Lincoln in his diocese, while the proud and stubborn against the word of God go unpunished." *LP,* 11:325.

35. *The Lisle Letters,* ed. Muriel St. Cate Byrne (Chicago, 1981), 2:257–63. See also Diarmaid MacCulloch, *Thomas Cranmer: A Life* (New Haven, 1996), 142, 280.

36. A good and balanced (if dated) account of Walsingham's cultivation of informers is Conyers Read, *Mr. Secretary Walsingham and the Policy of Queen*

Elizabeth (Oxford, 1925), 2:317–39. See also the portrait of Walsingham in John Bossy, *Giordano Bruno and the Embassy Affair* (New Haven, 1991).

37. See Robert Persons, *Memoirs*, ed. J. H. Pollen (Catholic Record Society Misc., 2, 1906), 181.

38. For more on the increased activity, and the Catholic priests' evasion of it, see Alan Dures, *English Catholicism, 1558–1642* (Harlow, U.K., 1983); Michael L. Carrafiello, "English Catholicism and the Jesuit Mission of 1580–1581," *Historical Journal* 37 (1994): 761–74; Carrafiello, *Robert Persons and English Catholicism, 1580–1610* (Selinsgrove, Pa., 1998); and Thomas M. McCoog, *The Society of Jesus in Ireland, Scotland, and England, 1541–1588: "Our Way of Proceeding?"* (Leiden, 1996), 129–264.

39. *SP,* Dom., Eliz. I, vol. cli, no. 23.

40. Ibid., no. 63.

41. *SP,* Dom., vols. clxxxvii, no. 81, clxxxix, no. 22, and cxc, no. 62.

42. Ibid., cxcv, no. 21.

43. For more on the life of Berden, see Read, *Mr. Secretary Walsingham,* 2:330–34.

44. Cromwell, for example, received the following note from what was certainly one of his agents, placed in the household of the earl of Derby: though the master was properly submissive to the king's policies, "I hear light words among his servants," though "at my coming to London I shall show your lordship more." See *PP,* 328.

45. *PP,* 124–26. While others of his community had rejected the merciful pardons of the king, Fordam continued, he himself would strive toward diligence "for the love and favor of God and his brethren." He was "therefore the more bound to search out such words as dan Richard Clyve did speak unnaturally, 'which I willed my kinsman, the abbot of Winchcumbe's servant, to deliver you.'"

46. *LP,* 11:859; David Knowles, *The Religious Orders in England* (Cambridge, 1959), 3:207.

47. See E. Margaret Thompson, *The Carthusian Order in England* (London, 1930), 404–5.

48. *LP,* 10:311, 119.

49. *SP,* Dom., vol. clxviii, nos. 29, 30.

50. Ibid., no. 51. Moreover, Williams insisted his conscience was clean, since "he never toucheth [any] maid but from the knee upward."

51. Apparently, the devoted friend and messenger Austin Bernher raised concerns about Grimbald during a visit to the prison, for Ridley later acknowledged to Bernher that "at your last being here you cast cold water upon mine affection towards Grimbald." See *EM,* 3(1): 223–28.

52. Ridley continued to praise Grimbald for, among other things, translating into English the works of Lorenzo Valla, Aeneus Sylvius, and other

humanists who could benefit the "Church of Christ in England"—or at least make it so that "the papists would glory but a little to see such books go forth in English."

53. The betrayer was not Grimbald, Ridley wrote in a letter to Cranmer and Latimer, but "one which my brother trusted to carry [the writings] . . . *unto* Grimbald." Nicholas Ridley, *The Works of Nicholas Ridley,* ed. Henry Christmas, Parker Society 39 (Cambridge, 1841), 337, 391.

54. Quoted from L. R. Merrill, *The Life and Poems of Nicholas Grimald* (New Haven, 1925), 37.

55. Ibid., 41–43; see appendix 1. Grimbald finally ended the letter by writing in terms of the civic and other forms of duty he was fulfilling: "Why . . . O kindest and best of men, should I hesitate in matters of this sort to give you my opinion boldly and freely? Where then can I speak, who can I implore, into whose bosom shall I pour the public complaint if not into his who has authority, and who especially favors 'pure religion and undefiled?'"

56. The consequence of Grimbald's actions is difficult to assess; certainly he was behind the wretched imprisonment of George Shipside, but his role in the persecution of Ridley and others seems to have been to buttress a case already taking its course. Though he thus provided the authorities with damaging information, the most that perhaps could be said for him, in the end, is that he expedited an inevitable process. Ridley, of course, was martyred; as for Grimbald, he began his new career as a Roman Catholic by translating a few works, including Cicero's *De Officiis* (dedicated to a Roman Catholic bishop), and overseeing the publication of Thomas More's works. His fate is not clear after Mary's reign ended, and he slides away from the record, though he probably died before 1562.

57. See also *Select Cases in Star Chamber,* ed. I. S. Leadam (Selden Society 15; 1910), 220.

58. See *AM* (1583), 1036, 1032.

59. See also MacCulloch, *Thomas Cranmer: A Life,* 280–81. For a full story of Benger and his tribulations, see *PP,* 317–21.

60. *Unpub. Docs.,* 1:363–64.

61. H. Ellis, *Original Letters Illustrative of English History,* 3d ser. (London, 1824–46), 1(2): 85–89. See also *PP,* 342.

62. Fol. 25a, Lichfield Episcopal Archives, MS B.C. 13. Translation modernized by author. See also John Fines, "Heresy Trials in the Diocese of Coventry and Lichfield, 1511–12," *JEH* 14 (1963): 160–74.

63. See especially the letter from Salter to Cromwell in Thompson, *The Carthusian Order in England,* 387–90.

64. *AM* (1583), 1100–1101. For the correspondence of Lyst, see *LP,* 6:116, 334, 1264. For the fate of the Observants, see Knowles, *Religious Orders,* 3:208–11.

See also Peter Marshall, "Papist as Heretic: The Burning of John Forest, 1538," *The Historical Journal* 41 (1998): 351–74. Lyst himself went on to study for the priesthood at Oxford, and when he was offered the chance to return to the cloister, wisely declined the offer.

65. *Unpub. Docs.*, 1:362. Bellamy went on to bear Topcliffe a child, and was forced to marry Topcliffe's servant, Nicholas Jones. See also Henry Foley, *Records of the English Province of the Society of Jesus: Historic Facts Illustrative of the Labours and Sufferings of Its Members in the Sixteenth and Seventeenth Centuries* (London, 1877), 1:350.

66. For accounts of Crome's preaching, see for example *LP,* 14(2): 1539. For Crome in general, see Susan Wabuda, "Equivocation and Recantation during the English Reformation: The 'Subtle Shadows' of Dr Edward Crome," *JEH* 44 (1993): 224–42; R. H. Brodie, "The Case of Dr Crome," *Transactions of the Royal Historical Society,* n.s., 9 (1905): 295–304; *DNB,* 5:138–40.

67. *LP,* 1(2): 842–48; *APC,* 1:414. Crome, in his sermon, denied the real presence and, more damagingly, claimed, using Henry's own statements, that there was no purgatory. The latter was a particularly unwise remark, since Henry, through the settlement, had since rescinded his previous doctrine and would not have liked to have had his own words thrown back at him.

68. "[W]riggling before [its] questions," as Hughes put it. See Philip Hughes, *The Reformation in England,* 5th ed. (New York, 1963), 2:64–68. Crome promised, on his knees, to repudiate his sermon at a new sermon at Paul's Cross. As he stood on the pulpit, however, with reformist allies and royal chaplains before him, Crome suddenly declared that he "came not hither to recant," and proceeded to reaffirm what he had boldly stated before. After the sermon he was returned once more to the council. See also *LP,* 1(2): 842–48; *APC,* 1:414.

69. *APC,* 1:414; *Wrioth. Chron.,* 1:166–70; *Grey Friars,* 50–51.

70. See Wabuda, "Equivocation and Recantation," 236; *LP,* 1(2): 484–89.

71. Hugh Latimer, *Sermons by Hugh Latimer,* ed. George Elwes Corrie, Parker Society 27 (Cambridge, 1844), 1:279.

72. *SP,* 10/14/16–17; *C* 66/847, m. 33d.

73. *AM* (1965), 7:718–19.

74. Herrup, *The Common Peace,* 85–92. See also Archer, *The Pursuit of Stability,* 1–17.

75. Indeed, some early forms of informing could be seen in the "hue and cry," in which a person witnessing a felony was required to sound a general alarm, calling, "Out! Out!", which then brought on fellow townspeople who, under threat of fines and imprisonment, had to chase down the offender with bows, arrows, knives, and other weapons. See James Stephen, *A History of Criminal Law of England* (London, 1883), 1:190.

76. For the traditional account of the history of information in England, see Holdsworth, *History of English Law,* 9:236–41. See also A. Harding, "Plaints and Bills in the History of English Law," in *Legal History Studies* (Cardiff, U.K., 1975).

77. See Christopher Haigh, *English Reformations* (Oxford, 1984), chap. 11. Not all regions underwent persecution in the same manner, however; whereas London experienced much activity, in Norwich, for example, "there was not a single charge from a citizen or arrest by the magistrates made resulting from the Six Articles." See Muriel C. McClendon, "Religious Toleration and the Reformation: Norwich Magistrates in the Sixteenth Century," in *England's Long Reformation, 1500–1800,* ed. Nicholas Tyacke (London, 1998), 93. See also Brigden, *London and the Reformation* (Oxford, 1989), 325–77.

78. A particularly good account of witchcraft accusations and their background can be found in Malcolm Gaskill, "Witchcraft in Early Modern Kent: Stereotypes and the Background to Accusations," in *Witchcraft in Early Modern Europe: Studies in Culture and Belief,* ed. Jonathan Barry et al. (Cambridge, 1996), 257–87. See also Brian Levack, *The Witch-Hunt in Early Modern Europe* (London, 1987), esp. 116–42.

79. See Robin Clifton, "Fear of Popery," in *The Origins of the English Civil War,* ed. Conrad Russell (London, 1973), 144–67.

80. A good overview of this idea in practice is McClendon, "Religious Toleration and the Reformation," 87–108.

81. See *AM* (1583), 2028–29. Strangers, especially a foreign conventicle of thirty, were especially vulnerable to being informed upon, not only because of their outsider status, but also because the informer would not have enough personal or vested interest to provoke pangs of conscience.

82. *Narratives,* 62–65, 157–60.

83. *Camden Miscellany* (Camden Society 39), 54–55.

84. *Original Letters Relative to the English Reformation* (Cambridge, 1846–47), 1:230.

85. *AM* (1965), 5:33, 4:585.

86. *AM* (1583), 1212–13. Testwood met his martyrdom bravely, and his imperatives at Windsor had been undoubtedly religious, but he was also a prankster who intentionally persisted with his provocative behavior. As his case illustrates, in some ways, individuals such as he tended to bring trouble upon themselves through obnoxious actions; indeed, it is almost as if the qualities that characterized martyrs—single-mindedness, hardheadedness, self-righteousness, indifference toward others' opinions, perhaps a grating sanctimoniousness—could also make those same individuals very unwanted members of the community. People could come to love or hate individuals such as Testwood for the same

reason they could come to love or hate martyrs; that is, they could either be admiring of their forthright and godly boldness or despising of their unbending and offensive bluntness.

87. *AM* (1583), 1536.

88. For Palmer, see *AM* (1583), 1934–40.

89. *Narratives,* 60–65.

90. See, for example, the case of Edward Underhill, who described how the high constable placed in charge of apprehending him was actually his neighbor and "my very friend." As Underhill writes, the sympathetic constable "desired the Sheriff and his company to stay without, for [fear of] frightening of my wife, being newly laid. And he would go [himself] and fetch me unto [the sheriff]." *Narratives,* 135–36.

91. 27 Elizabeth, c.13, in *Statutes of the Realm,* ed. A. Luders et al. (London, 1810–28), 4(1): 720. See also Holdsworth, *History of English Law,* 4:521–22.

92. Article 39 states: "No freeman shall be taken or imprisoned or disseised or outlawed or exiled or in any way destroyed, nor will we go upon him nor send upon him, except by the lawful judgment of his peers or by the law of the land." As Nelson B. Lasson writes, "the provision's general and comprehensive phraseology was aimed at certain definite abuses of power by King John, consisting in the main of his practice of taking the law into his own hands and, without legal judgment of any kind or respect for any form of legal procedure whatever, proceeding with or sending an armed force to punish by imprisonment of seizure of property or worse, some person who displeased or disobeyed him. The object of the provision was to prevent in the future all such extra-legal procedure, to affirm the validity of feudal law and custom against arbitrary caprice and the indiscriminate use of force, and to prohibit constituted authority from placing execution before judgment." See Nelson B. Lasson, *The History and Development of the Fourth Amendment to the United States Constitution* (Baltimore, 1937), 20.

93. William John Cuddihy, "Search and Seizure in Great Britain and the American Colonies, from 1000 to 1791" (M.A. thesis, California State University, Fullerton, 1974), 8–16.

94. 39 Elizabeth, c.13 (1597), in *Statutes of the Realm,* 4(2): 913–14.

95. See Holdsworth, *History of English Law,* 4:137–42. See also Thomas Skyrme, *History of the Justices of the Peace,* vol. 1 (Chichester, U.K., 1991).

96. *AM* (1583), 1690–91.

97. See I. D. Thornley, "The Destruction of Sanctuary," in *Tudor Studies . . . Presented to A. F. Pollard,* ed. R. W. Seton Watson (London, 1924), 182–207.

98. *AM* (1583), 1937.

99. *LP,* 9:691.

100. Eagles earned the nickname "Trudge-over-the-world," "because of his continual travels from place to place, exhorting and confirming the brethren." See *AM* (1583), 2009–10; *APC*, 5:310–12; 6:129, 131, 142.

101. For more on the English mission, see Carrafiello, "English Catholicism and the Jesuit Mission," 761–74; see also Carrafiello, *Robert Persons and English Catholicism*, 11–21. See, for example, the case of William Bishop, who was immediately captured in 1581 upon landing in Rye; though he stated that he was a merchant, his claim quickly fell apart under questioning. Eventually, he was banished. Adrian Morey, *The Catholic Subjects of Elizabeth I* (Totowa, N.J., 1978), 177–78. See also Dures, *English Catholicism, 1558–1642*, and McCoog, *The Society of Jesus*, 129–264.

102. *AM* (1583), 2083.

103. *AM* (1583), 1940–41.

104. *AM* (1583), 1194–95.

105. John Gerard, *The Autobiography of a Hunted Priest*, trans. Philip Caraman (New York, 1965), 65.

106. *AM* (1583), 1703. Samuel "meekly yielded himself into their clutches of his own accord."

107. 27 Elizabeth, c.2, in *Statutes of the Realm*, 4(1): 706–8. See also Elton, *Tudor Constitution: Documents and Commentary*, 424–26.

108. Quoted in C. Devlin, *The Life of Robert Southwell* (London, 1956), 181. See also Morey, *The Catholic Subjects*, 181, and Michael A. Mullett, *Catholics in Britain and Ireland, 1558–1829* (New York, 1998), 1–26.

109. James Chambers, *The English House* (New York, 1985), 71–72.

110. Jeffrey L. Singman, *Daily Life in Elizabethan England* (Westport, Conn., 1995), 73–80.

111. Owen spent twenty-five years in this task, even though he would be twice captured—the second time when he was starved out of his own hiding place in Hindlip and taken to the Tower, where he died under torture. See David Mathew, *Catholicism in England, 1535–1935* (London, 1986), 47.

112. As John Guy writes, it was a 1381 statute that prevented anyone from leaving or entering the realm without a license, unless he was a fisherman or a merchant. See John Guy, *Tudor England* (Oxford, 1988), 314.

113. Checke's sister, for example, married William Cecil, while Checke himself became the son-in-law of Sir John Mason. See C. H. Garret, *The Marian Exiles: A Study in the Origins of Elizabethan Puritanism* (Cambridge, 1938), 114–15. See also John Strype, *The Life of the Learned John Checke . . .* (Oxford, 1821), 94–97.

114. *AM* (1583), 2077.

115. See *Tudor Royal Proclamations (The Later Tudors, 1553–1587)*, ed. Paul L. Hughes and James F. Larkin (New Haven, 1964–69), 57–60.

116. *APC,* 5:180.

117. See 13 Elizabeth, c.5, in *Statutes of the Realm,* 4(1): 537–38. See also Loades, "The Essex Inquisitions of 1556."

118. William Raleigh Trimble, *The Catholic Laity in Elizabethan England, 1558–1603* (Cambridge, Mass., 1964), 247–48.

119. See Garret, *The Marian Exiles,* 1–20. Garret is vehemently of the opinion that the Protestant Marian exiles, especially as they were coordinated by William Cecil and funded by English merchants, were skillful manipulators, directing themselves "to the fulfillment of a clearly conceived purpose," to develop themselves into a coherent political opposition with every intention of returning to England one day.

120. Mowntayne was subsequently committed to Cambridge Castle and charged with treason; released on bail, he ended up escaping to the continent. See the Mowntayne account in *Narratives,* 177–212.

121. *Span. Cal.,* 10:217.

122. The words were written by Nicholas Ridley, who chose to stay in England, where he eventually was condemned and burned under Mary. See Ridley, *Works,* 419. The figure of 800 is Foxe's; Philip Hughes corroborates the number by coming up with a total of 788 Protestant émigrés. See Hughes, *The Reformation in England,* 2:197–200.

123. Ridley, *Works,* 62. See also the letter to Mrs. Wilkinson: "Remember that Christ, when his hour was not yet come, departed out of the country into Samaria, to avoid the malice of the scribes and Pharisees; and commanded his apostles, that if they were pursued in one place, they should fly to another."

124. *AM* (1583), 2080–81.

125. For a list of Hall's corpus of printed works, see the bibliography in Charles Martin, *Les Protestants anglais réfugiés à Genève au temps de Calvin 1555–1560* (Geneva, 1915), 297–330. See also John N. King, "'The Light of Printing': William Tyndale, John Foxe, John Day, and Early Modern Print Culture," *Renaissance Quarterly* 54 (2001): 52–83.

126. See John Bossy, "The Character of Elizabethan Catholicism," *Past and Present* 21 (1962): 47, 50. See also Bossy, *The English Catholic Community, 1570–1850* (Oxford, 1976), 11–15.

127. See Christopher Haigh, "The Continuity of Catholicism in the English Reformation," *Past and Present* 93 (1981): 37–69. Haigh's thesis has been challenged in recent years, however, by Peter Lake, Michael Questier, and others.

128. Leo F. Solt, *Church and State in Early Modern England, 1509–1640* (Oxford, 1990), 102–10.

129. Holdsworth, *History of English Law,* 5:25–29, 49.

130. *LP,* 4(2): 4511.

131. Knox's pamphlet of 1555, issued from Frankfurt, could in fact have been responsible for increased persecution in England. According to Whitehead in a letter to Calvin, "Before the publication of that book, not one of our brethren had suffered death: but as soon as it came forth, we doubt not but that you are well aware of the number of excellent men who have perished in the flames." *Orig. Lett.*, 2:761.

132. The defense was acceptable, for not only was Hales off the hook, but so did he manage to have the messenger, John Brett, arrested. See Brett's "Narrative," in I. S. Leadam, ed., "A Narrative of the Pursuit of English Refugees in Germany under Queen Mary," *Transactions of the Royal Historical Society*, n.s., 11 (London, 1897), 113–231; and J. E. Oxley, *The Reformation in Essex to the Death of Mary* (Manchester, U.K., 1965), 198–99.

133. For an account of Knox's Frankfurt sojourn, see his own narrative in Knox, *The Works of John Knox*, ed. David Laing (Edinburgh, 1846–64), 4:41–49.

134. *LP*, 16:104–5, n. 240. See also Bellamy, *Tudor Law of Treason*, 90. Despite Henry's attempts to divide Europe and stave off a possible Catholic crusade from the continent by dangling various marriage unions that would unite him either with France or with Charles V, by 1539 Charles and Francis I had come to some agreements through treaties and truces, leaving England alone and in a panic that an invasion from all sides was at hand. The year 1540— the year of Blanche Rose (but also the year of the Anne of Cleves disaster)— witnessed a lessening of the panic as diplomatic efforts increased, but relations with France remained raw. For more on the tensions of this time, see J. J. Scarisbrick, *Henry VIII* (Berkeley, 1968), 360–71.

135. This would not be the last time that Charles would adhere to the treaty. See, for example, the case of Ronald Brancetour, Gerald Fitzgerald, and others in 1540, whom Charles refused to send back to England, in a decision based not simply on national antagonisms, but also on the emperor's adherence to treaty over common law. See Bellamy, *Tudor Law of Treason*, 88.

136. *LP*, 5:164–65.

137. *AM* (1583), 1077–78; see in general 1075–80. See also David Daniell, *William Tyndale: A Biography* (New Haven, 1994), 363–65.

138. Strype, *Life of the Learned John Checke*, 94–107.

139. Bede Camm, *Lives of the English Martyrs*, 1st ser. (London, 1905), 2:14–110.

140. *SP*, Dom., vol. lxxviii, no. 51.

141. Quoted in A. O. Meyer, *England and the Catholic Church under Queen Elizabeth*, trans. J. R. McKee (New York, 1967), 170. See also the report from the Jesuit Richard Holtby to Henry Garnet, in *Church History of England*, ed. M. A. Tierney (London, 1839–43), 3:77–78: "If we converse openly, if we buy or sell, if we traffic in our necessary affairs, or take care of our own commodities,

if we laugh, recreate ourself, or carry any indifferent countenance, then are we either too wealthy, or else too well, to live: such prosperous fortune is not tolerable in men of our profession. . . . If we live in secret and delight ourself to be solitary, if we cut off all access of our neighbours, or refuse to keep company with such as love us not, then do we busy our heads, in their conceit, to devise against them secret conspiracies."

142. *AM* (1583), 1709, 1711–13.

143. Eventually, Underhill persuaded the sheriff—who was charged with bringing him to Newgate—to have bailiffs, rather than guards, escort him to the prison, "for order's sake." The sheriff granted the request, and Underhill walked through Cheapside with the sheriff's men trailing at a distance behind, "so that it was not well perceived that I was apprehended, but by the great company that followed." *Narratives,* 132–74.

144. See W. H. C. Frend, *Martyrdom and Persecution in the Early Church* (New York, 1967), 307.

145. *AM* (1583), 1505. Hooper was self-consciously placing his fate on scriptural terms, echoing, among others, Peter the Apostle's decision not to flee Rome, but to face his martyrdom.

146. *AM* (1583), 1740.

147. Matt. 26:49–55.

148. *AM* (1583), 1984–86.

Notes to Chapter Three

1. *Select Cases before the King's Council in the Star Chamber, Commonly Called the Court of Star Chamber, 1477–1544* (London, 1903–11), 2:15–16.

2. Conyers Read, *Mr. Secretary Walsingham and the Policy of Queen Elizabeth* (Oxford, 1925), 2:237–30, esp. 327 n. 3.

3. Seán McConville, *A History of English Prison Administration,* vol. 1 (London, 1981), 5. See also Ralph B. Pugh, *Imprisonment in Medieval England* (Cambridge, 1968), 192–207; Christopher Harding, Richard Ireland, and Philip Rawlings, *Imprisonment in England and Wales* (London, 1985), 55, 107.

4. Pugh, *Imprisonment,* 26–47.

5. Benefit of clergy—the exemption of individuals from the jurisdiction of secular or criminal courts—was not abolished completely until 1827, but its usage underwent increasing limitations in the sixteenth century. See Stephen, *History of Criminal Law,* 1:viii; F. Pollock and F. W. Maitland, *The History of English Law* (Cambridge, 1923), vol. 1, s.v. "benefit of clergy."

6. Joyce Youings, *The Dissolution of the Monasteries* (London, 1971), 78–81, 117–31; A. L. Beier, "Vagrants and the Social Order in Elizabethan England," *Past and Present* 64 (1974): 3.

7. See Stow, 2:19.

8. Pugh, *Imprisonment*, 347–48.

9. *AM* (1583), 2005. For Colchester Castle, see Laquita M. Higgs, *Godliness and Governance in Tudor Colchester* (Ann Arbor, Mich., 1998), esp. 165–81.

10. *EM*, 3 (1): 554.

11. Women at York Castle included Elizabeth Dyneley, wife of York's lord mayor; Margaret Clitherow, a butcher's wife; and Isabell Porter, who "sayeth that she cometh not to the church, because there is not a priest as there ought to be, and also that there is not the Sacrament of the Altar" (*SP,* Dom., vol. cxvii, no. 23).

12. Wisbech Castle housed the more important Catholics, including, in 1580, bishops Watson, Young, Windham, Oxenbridge, and Abbot Feckenham. See *SP,* 12/143/17. For recusants confined in the castle of Framlingham, Suffolk, which covered recusants in Suffolk and Norfolk, see *APC,* 12:82–83, 124.

13. For an account of Wisbech and the "Wisbech Stirs," see Arnold Pritchard, *Catholic Loyalism in Elizabethan England* (Chapel Hill, N.C., 1979), 78–101.

14. For a more detailed description of the Poultry Street compter, see Frederick J. Froom, *A Site in Poultry* (London, 1950), 15–27. Originally established in the early fifteenth century in what was once a mansion owned by the Blount family, the compter was like other prisons in that it contained desegregated areas which varied in their conditions according to who could pay fees to rapacious wardens. In the sixteenth century, the compter was home not only to disruptive drunkards or criminals, but to religious dissidents such as the Separatists, six of whom died in the prison in the later part of the century.

15. Stow, 1:350.

16. Nicholas Ridley, *The Works of Nicholas Ridley,* ed. Henry Christmas, Parker Society 30 (Cambridge, 1841), 359.

17. For an example of Catholics in the Fleet, including John Finch, see *Unpub. Docs.,* 1:32. Finch, however, was "not able to pay the great charge of the Fleet, [and was] removed not long after into a miserable and loathsome prison, which was made for the poorer sort of Catholickes, the which is termed by the heretikes the Howse of Roges or of Correction." For general information on the Fleet, see M. Bassett, "The Fleet Prison in the Middle Ages," in *University of Toronto Law Journal,* no. 2 (1944). See also A. Jessop, ed., *The Economy of the Fleet* (Camden Society, 1879).

18. Catholic Record Society 2 (1942), lists xvii, xviii, xxii–l, xxxix, 228–31, 234–38, 251–53, 282–84.

19. Cranmer's Register, fols. 67v, 70. See also Diarmaid MacCulloch, *Thomas Cranmer: A Life* (New Haven, 1996), 260–61.

20. Pugh, *Imprisonment*, 278–79, 286–94.

21. *Narratives*, 143–44. Spelling modernized by author.

22. *SP*, 12/141/29; see also Philip Hughes, *The Reformation in England,* 5th ed. (New York, 1963), 3:428–40.

23. *AM* (1583), 1604.

24. Interestingly, Hales's first attempt on his own life occurred shortly after he received a letter from John Bradford. See John Bradford, *The Writings of John Bradford,* ed. A. Townsend (Cambridge, 1848–53), 2:85. Hales's suicide attempt also gave ammunition to Gardiner, who described Protestantism as the "doctrine of despair." See *AM* (1965), 6:395, 688, 710–17; Bradford, *Writings,* 2:85–86; Ridley, *Works,* 363; *EM,* 3(1): 274. See also J. A. Muller, *Stephen Gardiner and the Tudor Reaction* (New York, 1926), 228–30.

25. See also John Gerard, *The Autobiography of a Hunted Priest,* trans. Philip Caraman (New York, 1965), 77–80.

26. John Coffey, *Persecution and Toleration in Protestant England, 1558–1689* (London, 2000), 97–98.

27. Latimer, *Works,* 258–59; *AM* (1965), 8:593. See also David Loades, *The Oxford Martyrs* (New York, 1970), 168–69; MacCulloch, *Thomas Cranmer: A Life,* 560–62.

28. John Strype, *Memorials of . . . Thomas Cranmer,* ed. P. E. Barnes (London, 1853), 1:630–32; David Selwyn, "Cranmer's Library: Its Potential for Reformation Studies," in *Thomas Cranmer: Churchman and Scholar,* ed. Paul Ayris and David Selwyn (Woodbridge, U.K., 1993), 45–51.

29. *AM* (1583), 1711.

30. *Narratives,* 147–49.

31. See Verstegan's letter to Baines in September of 1592 (Stoneyhurst MS *Anglia I,* fol. 12); and Juan Yepez, *Historia particular de la persecution de Inglaterre* (Madrid, 1599), 643.

32. *AM* (1583), 1703–4.

33. *AM* (1583), 1984–86. Indeed, the vivid description given by Miles Coverdale, while fitted to his propaganda purposes, was not untrue of prison conditions. Prisoners such as Woodman and Samuel, Coverdale wrote, languished "in fetters and chains, and loaded with so many irons that they could scarcely stir: some tied in the stocks, with their heels upwards; some having their legs in the stocks, and their necks chained to the wall with gorgets of iron, some with both hands and legs in the stocks at once; sometimes both hands in, and both legs out; sometimes the right hand with the left leg, or the left hand with the right leg, fastened in the stocks with manacles and fetters, having neither stool or stone to sit on, to ease their woeful bodies: some standing in Skevington's gives, which were most painful engines of iron, with their bodies doubled." See Miles Coverdale, *Remains,* ed. George Pearson, Parker Society 14 (Cambridge, 1846).

34. Gerard, *A Hunted Priest,* 77.

35. *PP,* 366–68.

36. *APC* (1556), 5:316.

37. Little Ease was also the destination of Edmund Campion, who languished there for four days. See Thomas M. McCoog, ed., *The Reckoned Expense: Edmund Campion and the Early English Jesuits* (Rochester, N.Y., 1996); see also Evelyn Waugh, *Edmund Campion* (Oxford, 1980), 170.

38. Pugh, *Imprisonment,* 226, 236–37.

39. *AM* (1583), 2089; see in general 2087–89.

40. *Unpub. Docs.,* 1:351.

41. *AM* (1965), 8:251–53.

42. William Roper, "The Life of Sir Thomas More," in *Two Early Tudor Lives,* ed. Richard Sylvester and Davis P. Harding (New Haven, 1962), 239–44.

43. Quoted in Gamini Salgado, *The Elizabethan Underworld* (Totowa, N.J., 1977), 169.

44. *Letters and Papers, Foreign and Domestic, of the Reign of Henry VIII,* ed. J. S. Brewer, J. Gairdner, and R. S. Brodie (London, 1862–1932), 5:67 ff.

45. Gerard, *A Hunted Priest,* 68.

46. *Narratives,* 150.

47. John Hooper, *Later Writings of Bishop Hooper* (Cambridge, 1852), 619–21.

48. *A Collection of Seventy-Nine Black Letter Ballads and Broadsides* (London, 1867), 16–17.

49. Salgado, *Elizabethan Underworld,* 172.

50. The words are Thomas Dekker's.

51. According to Foxe, Samuel claimed he was never hungry or thirsty again, which fortified him for his eventual martyrdom. See *AM* (1583), 1703–4.

52. *AM* (1583), 1136.

53. *AM* (1583), 1494.

54. *EHD,* 5:660–69.

55. *Privy Council Registers Preserved in the Public Record Office, Reproduced in Facsimile . . . ,* 34 vols. (London, 1967), 10: fol. 504.

56. Nicholas Harpsfield, *Life and Death of Sr Thomas More, Knight, Sometymes Lord High Chancellor of England,* ed. Elsie Vaughan Hitchcock and R. W. Chambers, Early English Text Society (London, 1932), 175. For another description of More's illnesses, see the account written by his daughter Margaret Roper, excerpted in E. E. Reynolds, *The Trial of St. Thomas More* (London, 1964), 320.

57. *AM* (1583), 1033–35. Later, Foxe writes, three others, "eating nothing but salt fish from February to the midst of August, died all three together within the compass of one week."

58. *AM* (1583), 1796.

59. Ridley, *Works,* 377.

60. *Narratives,* 153–54.

61. *APC* (1579), 11:174–75.

62. *APC* (1579), 11:253–54.

63. A. Peel, "Congregational Martyrs at Bury St Edmunds: How Many?" *Transactions of the Congregational History Society* 15 (1945–48): 64–67.

64. *AM* (1583), 1920–21.

65. Another case of bribes being sought by jailers to release iron fetters occurred with John Gerard in the 1590s. At the Poultry Counter, Henry Garnet wrote, "the gaoler put very heavy irons on his legs [but took them off when Gerard] gave him some money. The following day the gaoler, thinking that if he took off the irons, he would doubtless give him more, took them off but got nothing. After some days he came to put them on again and received a reward; and then taking them off did not get a farthing. They went on playing thus with one another several times, but at least the gaoler, seeing that he did not give him anything for taking off his irons, left him for a long time in confinement, so that the great toe of one foot was for almost two years in great danger of mortification." MSS. *Anglia A*, ii, no. 27. See also Gerard, *A Hunted Priest*, 71.

66. For a keeper's own account, see the pocket diaries of one of the officers at the Tower, in *Chronicle of Queen Jane and of two years of Queen Mary*, ed. J. G. Nichols, Camden Society 48 (London, 1850), 49–50.

67. Gerard, *A Hunted Priest*, 100.

68. John Hooper, *Works*, Parker Society (Cambridge, 1851), 319.

69. See *AM* (1583), 1493; *Narratives*, 147–49; Roper, "The Life of Sir Thomas More," 240.

70. *Narratives*, 147–49.

71. See also the case of the (Protestant) jailer Thomas Philips, whose duty was to oversee the Marchioness of Exeter at the Tower in Henry's reign, and his letter to the lieutenant, appealing that she be given more comfort. Quoted in M. H. and R. Dodds, *The Pilgrimage of Grace and the Exeter Conspiracy* (Cambridge, 1915), 2:324–25.

72. Gerard, *A Hunted Priest*, 111–12, 114.

73. *AM* (1583), 1228.

74. Indeed, Bradford had a few chances to escape, according to Foxe, especially when he was given privileges to roam the back of King's Bench prison and confer with Laurence Saunders, who was in turn allowed to loiter behind the adjoining Marshalsea prison.

75. Ridley, *Works*, 370. Cf. "Mistress Irish, mine hostess, told me that Master Hooper is hanged, drawn, and quartered for treason, but I did not believe [her]." Indeed, "it is not the first tale that mine hostess has told me of Mr Hooper." Ridley, *Works*, 373. See also Loades, *The Oxford Martyrs*, 180. Mrs. Irish's husband was also not above stirring rumors: at one point he reported to Ridley that John Bradford was "in great faith" with Gardiner.

76. *AM* (1583), 1894–95.

77. *AM* (1583), 1622–23.

78. *EM*, 3 (1): 221–29, for example.

79. *AM* (1583), 1604–6.

80. PRO, London, State Papers 14/61/91, 99. See also G. Anstruther, *Vaux of Harrowden* (Newport, R.I., 1953), 412.

81. Topcliffe's own account of his methods were explained in a letter to Elizabeth: "To stande against the walle, His feett standinge upon the ground, and his hands but as high as he can reatche ageinst the walle . . . will inforce him to tell all." Quoted from Pierre Janelle, *Robert Southwell, the Writer: A Study in Religious Inspiration* (New York, 1935), 65.

82. *AM* (1583), 1561, 1562.

83. Ridley, *Works*, 363.

84. Roper, "The Life of Sir Thomas More," 239.

85. Quoted in P. McGrath and J. Rowe, "The Imprisonment of Catholics for Religion under Elizabeth I," *Recusant History* 20 (1991): 423. See also Peter Lake and Michael Questier, "Prisons, Priests and People," in *England's Long Reformation 1500–1800*, ed. Nicholas Tyacke (London, 1998), 202.

86. *Letters and Memorials of Father Robert Persons, S.J.*, ed. L. Hicks, vol. 1, Catholic Record Society 39 (London, 1942), 179.

87. See, for example, the aforementioned Catholic sympathizer Simon Houghton, keeper of Newgate, who coordinated visits between his prisoners and Catholics in London. Lake and Questier, "Prisons, Priests and People," 203.

88. Gerard, *A Hunted Priest*, 120–21.

89. For more on Epaphroditus and his rhetorical significance in Paul, see Craig S. Wansink, *Chained in Christ: The Experience and Rhetoric of Paul's Imprisonment* (Sheffield, U.K., 1996), 126–29.

90. Matt. 25:18.

91. *AM* (1583), 1927–28.

92. David Knowles, *The Religious Orders in England* (Cambridge, 1959), 3:235–36.

93. According to Strype, Elizabeth Vane seems to have been the wife of Sir Ralph Vane, who was beheaded with the Duke of Somerset during Edward's reign. She herself lived on through Mary, and died in 1568 in Holborn, London. See also *EM*, 3(1): 226–27.

94. Thomas Freeman, "'The good ministrye of godlye and vertuouse women': The Elizabethan Martyrologists and the Female Supporters of the Marian Martyrs," *Journal of British Studies* 39 (2000): 8–33.

95. Bradford, *Writings*, 2:127; *AM* (1965), 7:250. See also Bradford, *A godlye Medytacyon composed by the faithfull and constant seruant of God. J.B. Precher*

who latlye was burnte in Smythfelde for the testimonie of Jesus Christ . . . (London, 1559), sigs. B4 [C5].

96. Freeman, "'The good ministrye of godlye and vertuose women,'" 15.

97. *AM* (1583), 1506.

98. *AM* (1583), 1496–97.

99. See Bradford, *Writings,* 2:34, 186.

100. *AM* (1583), 1216.

101. *AM* (1583), 1496–97.

102. Roper, "The Life of Sir Thomas More," 84.

103. See Harpsfield, *Life and Death of Sr Thomas More,* 95–96. Roper also recounts the story.

104. Margaret did not bring up the issue immediately afterwards, though she did continue trying to influence him. See Reynolds, *The Trial of St. Thomas More,* 318–19, 322–24.

105. *AM* (1583), 1604.

106. See Lake and Questier, "Prisons, Priests and People," 210–11, and the case of the minister named Mell.

107. BL, Lansdowne MS 56, fol. 14r. See also Lake and Questier, "Prisons, Priests and People," 218.

108. See John Clement's "Confession and Protestation of the Christian Faith," in *EM,* 3(2): 446–47. According to Strype, Clement was a wheelwright imprisoned along with John Careless in the King's Bench; set to be burned, Careless died instead in prison, and was "buried in the backside of the King's Bench in a dunghill." See *EM,* 3(2): 587. Strype also writes: in prison some "denied the godhead of Christ; some denied his manhood; others denied the godhead of the Holy Ghost, original sin, the doctrine of predestination and free election, the descent of Christ into hell . . . the baptism of infants."

109. *EM,* 3(1). Strype only supposes the author is Hart; he is mistaken, however, that Hart was in prison himself. As Martin and others point out, there is little evidence for this. See J. W. Martin, "English Protestant Separatism at its Beginnings: Henry Hart and the Free-Will Men," *Sixteenth Century Journal* 7 (1976): 55–74.

110. John Philpot, *The Examinations and Writings of John Philpot,* ed. Robert Eden (Cambridge, 1842), 271, 314.

111. Godfrey Anstruther, *Seminary Priests* (Woodchester, U.K., 1966), 1:328; Lake and Questier, "Prisons, Priests and People," 205.

112. See, for example, the case of James Bowland, who was compelled by fear to recant.

113. Lake and Questier, "Prisons, Priests and People," 225. Lake and Questier, in this article and others, have disputed one of the premises of Christopher Haigh, who has argued that Elizabethan Catholics, cloistered in the aristocratic

homes of patrons, were not only alienated from average people but failed to convey their message attractively to the land. See the following articles by Christopher Haigh: "The Continuity of Catholicism in the English Reformation," *Past and Present* 93 (1981): 37–69; "From Monopoly to Minority: Catholicism in Early Modern England," *Transactions of the Royal Historical Society*, 5th ser., 31 (1981): 129–47; "The Church of England, the Catholics, and the People," in *The Reign of Elizabeth I*, ed. C. Haigh (London, 1984), 195–219.

114. *LP*, 13:1024.

115. See R. W. Dale, *History of English Congregationalism* (London, 1907).

116. *LP*, 5:67ff.

117. See Pritchard, *Catholic Loyalism*, 78; see also T. G. Law, *The Archpriest Controversy* (Camden Society, 1896).

118. Gerard, *A Hunted Priest*, 104.

119. Garnet, Italian letter (fol. 117Ab), quoted in Janelle, *Robert Southwell*, 69–70.

120. Philpot, *Examinations and Writings*, 231.

121. Ridley, *Works*, 363.

122. Bradford, *Writings*, 2:41, 72, 74.

123. Ibid.

124. Cresacre More, *The Life of Sir Thomas More* (1726), 335. See also Harpsfield, *Life and Death of Sr Thomas More*, 134.

125. As Gerard wrote, orange juice—"which cannot be read with water"— "cannot be delivered without the recipient knowing whether or not it has been read. If it has been read and contains something that compromises him, he can disown it." Lemon juice, on the other hand, came through in multiple moistenings, thus allowing for multiple readers. See Gerard, *A Hunted Priest*, 119.

126. Allerton, for example, wrote out an account of his examinations in his own blood. See *AM* (1583), 2014.

127. Cf. Ridley, *Works*, 381.

128. See the case of Nicholas Ridley in Loades, *The Oxford Martyrs*, 177–78. When his writings were seized by the authorities, Ridley became more apprehensive about seeing any of his tracts appear in print, at least while he was still alive. "It was not in my mind that anything should have come abroad in my name until our bodies had been laid at rest," he wrote. Ridley, *Works*, 361.

129. The entirety of the petition is reprinted in J. A. Froude, *History of England from the Fall of Wolsey to the Death of Elizabeth* (London, 1856–70), 2:79–82.

130. Roper, "The Life of Sir Thomas More," 244.

131. See ibid., 91; Harpsfield, *Life and Death of Sr Thomas More*, 182. The fact that Thomas More was forced to rely on biblical quotations from memory attests to his own dearth of reading material, despite periodic successes in having books smuggled to him in a sack.

132. For the consolatory writings of More's fellow sufferer, John Fisher, see *A spirituall consolation, written by Iohn Fyssher Bishoppe of Rochester, to hys sister Elizabeth, at suche tyme as hee was prisoner in the Tower of London. . . .* (London, 1578), sig. [D8].

133. Quoted in *AM* (1583), 1834–35.

134. See Phil. 1:28; 2:1–4, 14; 4:2–3.

135. See also Frith, *A boke made by John Frith prisoner in the tower of London . . .* (Antwerp, 1533).

136. Gardiner's pen name was Marcus Antonius. See Loades, *The Oxford Martyrs*, 184. For other examples of theological clarification, see the letter from prison of John Lascelles, in *AM* (1583), 1241.

137. Philpot, *Examinations and Writings*, 249–50. Hartipole was once an ally of Anne Askew, harboring her in her home.

138. Bradford, *Writings*, 2:50.

139. See, for example, Thomas More, *Dialogue of Comfort against Tribulation*, ed. Frank Manley (New Haven, 1977).

140. Philpot, *Examinations and Writings*, 261.

141. *AM* (1583), 1511.

142. Bradford, *Writings*, 2:47.

143. Ibid., 43.

144. *The Writings of Cyprian, Bishop of Carthage*, trans. Robert E. Wallis (London, 1868–69), epistle 33.

145. Cyprian, for example, was especially important for the advice he gave: flight was preferable to falling into the sin of spiritual pride. See *The Writings of Cyprian*, epistles 56–57. See also Joseph A. Fichter, *Saint Cecil Cyprian, Early Defender of the Faith* (1942), and W. H. C. Frend, *Martyrdom and Persecution in the Early Church* (New York, 1967), 308–13.

146. See also the letters of Nicholas Sheterden to his mother, brother, and wife, *AM* (1583), 1676–78; and the letter of John Noye to his wife, *AM* (1583), 2022–23.

147. Ridley, *Works*, 384.

148. Bradford, *Writings*, 2:41.

149. Ibid.

Notes to Chapter Four

1. Until recently, examination records have tended to be neglected by historians, even though interrogations served as means by which the accused were able to declare themselves on a public stage, take control of the theological debate, and place themselves within a tradition of Christian persecution. Those

writers who have explored the subject have tended, on the other hand, to come from the fields of literature and drama. For the most recent work on the subject, see Sarah Covington, "The Heresy Examinations of John Philpot: Defiance, Bold Speaking, and the Making of a Martyr," *Reformation* 7 (2002): 79–133, and John Knott, *Discourses of Martyrdom in English Literature, 1563–1694* (Cambridge, 1993). See also Ritchie D. Kendall, *The Drama of Dissent: The Radical Poetics of Nonconformity, 1380–1590* (Chapel Hill, 1986). For a valuable dissection of one examination—that of Anne Askew—see the work of Elaine Beilin, especially her introduction, in *The Examinations of Anne Askew* (Oxford, 1996).

2. See chap. 1, n. 30.

3. Knott, *Discourses of Martyrdom*, 23, points out the way in which Foxe deleted John Rogers's mention of the bishop of Ely's speaking to him "very gentlye, trulye."

4. See Beilin, *Examinations of Anne Askew*, introduction. The Protestant John Rogers left his own interrogation transcriptions in a corner of the prison after his death; the documents were later printed out, in amended form, by John Foxe. See Joseph L. Chester, *John Rogers* (London, 1861), and the transcription of Rogers's account. See also *AM* (1583), 1484–92, and Knott, *Discourses of Martyrdom*, 7, 22–23, 60–61.

5. Ruth H. Blackburn, *Biblical Dramas under the Tudors* (The Hague, 1971), 13–28.

6. See Kendall, *Drama of Dissent*. For an overview of the dialogue tradition, see David Marsh, *The Quattrocento Dialogue: Classical Tradition and Humanist Innovation* (Cambridge, Mass., 1980); Elaine V. Beilin, "A Challenge to Authority: Anne Askew," in *Redeeming Eve: Women Writers of the English Reformation* (Princeton, 1987); and John N. King, *English Reformation Literature: The Tudor Origins of the Protestant Tradition* (Princeton, 1982).

7. Gina Alexander, "Bonner and the Marian Persecutions," in *The English Reformation Revised*, ed. Christopher Haigh (Cambridge, 1987), 172–73.

8. *AM* (1583), 1984–86. During the same period, Thomas Haukes was subjected to at least eight lengthy examinations, where—like the others—a variety of tactics were used, including attempts by the authorities to persuade him by rational argument, threaten him with imprisonment in Newgate, and bring in former coreligionists who had recanted and now urged Haukes to do the same. Haukes (along with Philpot and Woodman) remained firm in his Protestantism, however—"Jesu! Jesu! What stubbornness and arrogentness is this!" the bishop of London, Edmund Bonner, railed at one point—which culminated in a hasty formal trial and his final condemnation.

9. After Nicholas Shaxton recanted his Protestantism in 1546, for example, he used the opportunity of his old friend Anne Askew's burning to preach a

sermon explaining why he had been wrong, which had the result, according to Crowley, that "certain honest men informed me of the great number of them that through [Shaxton's] recantation" were once again conformed to the crown's religious policy. If Shaxton, on the other hand, had held firm to his faith, Crowley continued, then Henry "might through your constancy have been moved to search the scriptures for the truth of your opinions." See Robert Crowley, *The Confutation of xiii Articles whereunto Nicolas Shaxton, late byshop of Salisburye subscribed and caused be set forthe . . .* (London, 1548), sig. [B8v].

    10. John H. Langbein, *Torture and the Law of Proof: Europe and England in the Ancien Regime* (Chicago, 1977), 3, 73–74. Torture extended beyond the pre-liminary stage of questioning, however, and was also employed after the inter-rogations had ended and an indictment had been handed down, as was the case with the practice known as *peine forte et dure,* used against those who refused to make a plea upon indictment. Since refusal could at that time prevent a trial from going forward, the practice of "pressing"—of gradually laying weights upon the defendants—was used until they either made a plea or were crushed to death. Such was the ordeal of Margaret Clitherow, whose refusal to make a plea on her indictment of harboring priests in 1586 led to her being laid on her back with her arms outstretched and tied to posts "so that her body and her arms made a perfect cross" as the weight was lowered onto her, eventually crushing her to death. See John Mush, "A True Report of the Life and Mar-tyrdom of Mrs Margaret Clitherow," in *The Troubles of Our Catholic Forefathers, Related by Themselves,* ed. John Morris, 3rd ser. (London, 1877), 1:397, 432. See also Claire Cross, "An Elizabethan Martyrologist and His Martyr: John Mush and Margaret Clitherow," in *Martyrs and Martyrologies,* ed. Diana Wood, Studies in Church History 30 (Oxford, 1993), 275–81.

    11. *A declaration of the favourable dealing of her Majestie's commissioners, appointed for the examination of certayne traytors, and of tortures unjustly reported to be done upon them for matters of religion* (1583), repr. Somers Tracts, I (2nd ed., 1809), 209–12. See also A. O. Meyer, *England and the Catholic Church under Elizabeth* (New York, 1967), 179–81.

    12. See John F. Davis, *Heresy and Reformation in the South-East of England, 1520–1559* (London, 1983), 7. See also John A. Thomson, *The Later Lollards, 1414–1520* (Oxford, 1965). The more peripatetic court of audience was also fre-quently used in putting heretics on trial, though more so during the earlier time of the Lollards.

    13. This mix of secular and ecclesiastical authority was in accordance with the statute *De haeretico comburendo.* For a general discussion of consistory courts, *De haeretico comburendo,* and the issue of religious conformity, see Ralph Houl-brooke, *Church Courts and the People during the English Reformation, 1520–1570* (Oxford, 1979), esp. 214–60.

14. Jurors were expected to possess a minimum requirement of wealth, since the idea was to make them immune to bribes; as Bellamy points out, however, by the sixteenth century the crown "sought to empanel those whose rank and wealth was equivalent to that of the accused"—as was the case with the trial of the earl of Surrey in 1546, when jurors consisted of the knights and squires of Norfolk. Most jurors fulfilled their duty, though some resisted, as was the case in the trial of Edmund Campion, when, in William Allen's words, "three of the first of that impanel being Squiers belike fearing God and doubting that justice should have no free course that day" refused to show up. See John Bellamy, *The Tudor Law of Treason* (Toronto, 1979), 166–68.

15. *PP,* 388–93.

16. The break with Rome in 1533 instigated some important changes regarding the heresy charge, requiring previous articles to be scratched out while others were added. In the period from 1520 through 1533, for example, bishops were compelled to update their formularies in order to condemn the new reformist ideas as well as earlier heresies such as Lollardy. When Lutheran elements became incorporated into policies of the 1530s, however, articles defining heresy as the refusal to recognize pilgrimages, for example, were erased, though others—especially those upholding the validity of transubstantiation—remained unaltered. With the passage of the Act of Six Articles in 1538, a swing back toward conservatism then required additional adjustments, though some articles—primarily against the sacramentarian heresy—remained constant. See *The Works of Archbishop Cranmer,* ed. J. E. Cox (Cambridge, 1843), 2:448; John Strype, *Memorials of . . . Thomas Cranmer,* ed. P. E. Barnes (London, 1853), 2:744, 870. See also Diarmaid MacCulloch, *Thomas Cranmer: A Life* (New Haven, 1996), 579.

17. In the time of Edward's reign, when traditional heresy trials were repealed, the trials that did exist, against Anabaptists, for example, were conducted through the lay courts, with bishops present, after an indictment had been handed down by the least three justices of the peace. See 1 Edw. VI, c.1, in *Statutes of the Realm,* 4(1). See also Jennifer Loach, *Edward VI* (New Haven, 1999), 124–25. With Mary, parliamentary statutes brought about a restoration of medieval heresy laws that theoretically reinstituted the church's sole power over the trial process, though that process would again continue to be impelled, according to the fifteenth-century statute *De haeretico comburendo,* by officials such as sheriffs, as well as justices and councilors, who took on as active a role as they had under the Supremacy. See David Loades, *The Oxford Martyrs* (New York, 1970), 165. The trials of Nicholas Ridley, Hugh Latimer, and Cranmer may have originated in Rome and been mandated by its Inquisitor-General, who delegated authority to the bishop of Gloucester, James Brooks, and ordered that a papal delegate—as well as proctors of the crown—be present among the questioners. See MacCulloch, *Thomas Cranmer,* 573–74. Brooks was

aided by the dean of Windsor, Dr. Weston, a "mercenary man," in Strype's words. See *EM,* 3(2): 65–66. This was the exception, however, as even Mary hung on to the prerogative of the Supremacy when it suited her, which meant creating royal commissions for religious matters, and using the privy council to set the terms of persecution and give orders to bishops such as Edmund Bonner. See Alexander, "Marian Persecutions," 162.

18. *AM* (1583), 1679.

19. *AM* (1583), 1197–200.

20. Defendants, by contrast, are imbued with apostolic simplicity; see, for example, the description by Foxe of Hugh Latimer, who is presented as "plain speaking" in accordance with his beliefs. Knott, *Discourses of Martyrdom,* 74.

21. Similarly, Edmund Bonner, the bishop of London, is depicted as a blood-curdling monster, who at one point screams, "They call me bloody Bonner. A vengeance on you all! I would fain be rid of you, but you have a delight in burning. But if I might have my will, I would sew your mouths, and put you in sacks and drown you." Bonner, however, seems to have also been defensive—or at least prickly—about his status; at one point, Foxe gives an example of his particular coarse humor when he reports the bishop "sitting at the board with his claret wine . . . [and saying] that where he hath been noted to be a blood-sucker, he never sucked any other blood, but that only in the goblet." *AM* (1965), 8:452. See also John Gerard on his examiner/persecutor Young, who "died for his sins, and died as he lived—miserably." According to Gerard, after Young went out searching houses for Catholics "one rainy night, at two or three o'clock," he "became ill, contracted consumption and died." John Gerard, *The Autobiography of an Elizabethan* (London, 1963), 92. Writers here were also borrowing from the tradition of the tyrant play, first set out in the New Testament with Caiaphas, seen "rending his robes" in Matthew and Mark. See Kendall, *Drama of Dissent,* 57–58.

22. J. H. Baker writes of the Inns of Court that "they helped in a broader way to form the character of English society. They were, already by 1450, the third university of England, a university which may have had more influence on the gentry than Oxford or Cambridge. Here the future statesmen, members of parliament, sheriffs, country magistrates, and official classes, joined together in work and play. . . . Erasmus was a poor judge of the qualities of the common law, but he perceived that those who succeeded in it were highly regarded: 'there is no better way to eminence [in England], for the nobility are mostly recruited from the law.'" See J. H. Baker, "The English Legal Profession," in *The Legal Profession and the Common Law* (London, 1986), 98; see also his "Inns of Court and Chancery as Voluntary Associations," in ibid., 45–47.

23. For background on Cromwell's legal past, see G. R. Elton, *The Tudor Revolution in Government* (Cambridge, 1953); "King or Minister? The Man

behind the Henrician Reformation," *History* 39 (1954); "The Political Creed of Thomas Cromwell," *Transactions of the Royal Historical* Society, 5th ser., 6 (1956).

24. Story held Catholic tendencies under Henry, only to recant his views at the beginning of Edward's reign; eventually, however, he came into trouble when, as a sitting M.P., he declared, "Woe unto the land whose king is a child!" For this he was reprimanded by parliament and imprisoned in the Tower. Henry Hallam, *Constitutional History* (London, 1846), 1:271.

25. See Baker, "English Legal Profession," 78–79.

26. Ibid., 78–80. The law was not necessarily aligned with the establishment or authorities, however. As will be seen, defendants could also have a background in the law and thus present excellent legal challenges from the other side; moreover, institutions such as the Inns of Court were notorious places for both recusants and Puritans later on in the century, even though supposedly reformed judges exerted control over them. The freedom enjoyed by the Inns of Court was due in part to the fact that the lawyers were given almost unlimited powers of exemption, including exemption from the crime of recusancy, and could therefore enjoy privileges of belief; while later measures were also enacted to exclude papists from the Inns, this did not reverse a deep association of some Catholics with the law—as was the case with the Thomas More—related Roper family, which continued to hold its clerkship at the Court of King's Bench. See Geoffrey de C. Parmiter, *Elizabethan Popish Recusancy in the Inns of Court* (London, 1976). See also C. W. Brooks, *Pettyfoggers and Vipers of the Commonwealth: The 'Lower Branch' of the Legal Profession in Early Modern England* (Cambridge, 1986), 270, and Elliot Rose, *Cases of Conscience: Alternatives open to Recusants and Puritans under Elizabeth I and James I* (Cambridge, 1975), 65.

27. Good lawyers, for example, knew how to shape—or, one could say, distort—evidence toward their own favor. During the interrogations of Marian Protestants, for example, examiners were known to manipulate scripture or the writings of defendants in order to bring on a confession, leading Foxe to compare them to "God's enemies from the beginning," who "falsify, wrest, and deprave all things, whatsoever maketh not to their faction and affection, be it ever so true and just."

28. *AM* (1965), 5:803–4.

29. Davis, *Heresy and Reformation*, 11; A. G. Dickens, *The English Reformation*, 2nd ed. (London, 1989), 80. Bilney was allowed to abjure without acknowledging the beliefs ascribed to him—a turn of events that inspired More to rail against the stretching of the law. See also Greg Walker, "Saint or Schemer? The 1527 Heresy Trial of Thomas Bilney Reconsidered," *JEH* 40 (1989): 219–20.

30. E. E. Reynolds, *The Trial of St. Thomas More* (London, 1964), 339.

31. J. H. Baker, "Learning Exercises in the Medieval Inns of Court and Chancery," in *The Legal Profession and the Common Law: Historical Essays* (London, 1986), 7–23.

32. More was an alumnus of Lincoln's Inn, one of the four colleges that comprised the Inns of Court. See Baker, "Learning Exercises," 93.

33. *AM* (1965), 8:58–59.

34. MacCulloch, *Thomas Cranmer,* 578.

35. It should be pointed out that handwriting was also very important in presenting evidence as incriminating. In 1543, for example, Stephen Gardiner accused John Marbeck of disobeying the Act of Six Articles by presenting him with evidence of his writings and scribbled marginalia—which could be matched to a piece of writing from an earlier written statement that had been intended as a confession, but instead came out as a reassertion of belief. Marbeck, however, remained obstinate in his claim of innocence, and refused to budge from this position throughout his ordeal. See *AM* (1965), 5:166. During his own preliminary examination thirty years later, the Jesuit John Gerard offered to reply to the charges against him in writing, which Topcliffe was "delighted to do," "hoping to trip me up in what I wrote, or at least to get a sample of my handwriting"; in this way, he could "prove that certain papers found in the search of the houses [where he had been hidden] belonged to me." But Gerard "saw the trap" and wrote false words in a "feigned hand." See John Gerard, *Autobiography of an Elizabethan* (London, 1965), 69–70.

36. *The Troubles of Our Catholic Forefathers,* 1:73–77.

37. Friendliness was, in fact, a common method that interrogators used, especially at the beginning of the examination process. Bonner, for example, kissed John Philpot's hand early on in the examination and said, perhaps with some feigned innocence, "I am right sorry for your trouble, and I promise you before it was within these two hours, I knew not of your being here. I pray you tell me what was the cause of your sending hither; for I promise you I know nothing thereof as yet, neither would I you should think, that I was the cause thereof. And I marvel that other men will trouble me with their matters; but I must be obedient to my betters." Later in the examination, when Philpot still proved obstinate, Bonner nevertheless ordered that Philpot be brought "to the cellar, and let him drink a cup of wine," in a gesture of sympathy that would unravel over the course of later examinations. See also the case of Tyms, who seems to have been well-liked by his persecutors, though they were also using friendliness as a tactic: "Ah, good fellow!" they said to him, "thou art bold, and thou hast a good fresh spirit; we would thou hadst learning to thy spirit." "I thank you," Tyms replied, adding, "and both you be learned, and I would you had a good spirit to your learning." See *AM* (1583), 1896–97. Another tactic in the interrogator's bag of tricks was the bluff, which like the other tactics was

not altogether successful. During one of his examinations in 1594, for example, the priest John Gerard was told by his examiner, Young, "How much more sensible Father Southwell is. Like yourself he was obstinate from the beginning. Now, he is ready to conform, and wanted to talk with some learned man." Southwell, of course, never conformed, nor was he about to, even though Young—according to Gerard—swore on a Bible that Southwell "has offered to treat with a view to accepting our religion." But Gerard remained unmoved, saying, "I don't believe for a moment that Father Southwell wishes to treat with anyone, I mean from any faltering on his part or from any wish to learn from a heretic what he should believe." Gerard, *Autobiography,* 74, 75.

38. *AM* (1583), 1920. Still, Martin remained pleasant: "By my troth," he said before leaving, "thou art a pleasant fellow as ever I talked with of all the Protestants."

39. Sherwin Bailey, "Robert Wisdom under Persecution, 1541–43," *JEH* 2 (1951): 180–81.

40. Quoted from E. E. Reynolds, *The Field is Won* (New York, 1978), 335.

41. Gerard, *Autobiography,* 69.

42. Instigated at the urging at Bishop Cuthbert Tunstall, the work consisted of a long, ongoing dialogue between a character named "More" and "the Messenger," a tutor to the children of one of More's friends, who had lately drunk in the heretical, Lutheran views circulating in the 1520s. Geoffrey Elton, by the way, tends to portray More as a singularly violent and zealous persecutor, overlooking the *Dialogue Concerning Heresies,* and focusing instead on works such as the Tyndale Confutation. See Elton, "Persecution and Toleration in the English Reformation," in *Persecution and Toleration,* ed. W. J. Sheils, Studies in Christian History 21 (Cambridge, 1984), 164–71.

43. See the letter of More to Colet, which described his having been "stirred" at the powerful preachings of the Lutheran Thomas Bilney, in *The Correspondence of Sir Thomas More,* ed. Elizabeth F. Rogers (Princeton, 1947), 6. The most famous trial which More attended was that of Thomas Bilney, who underwent examination by Cuthbert Tunstall, John Fisher, and others. More was also present at the trial of John Tewkesbury, a Protestant preacher, in 1531. See Thomas More, *Dialogue Concerning Heresies,* vol. 6, pt. 1 of *The Complete Works of St. Thomas More,* ed. Thomas M. C. Lawler, Richard C. Marius, et al. (New Haven, 1981), 410. For background on the writing of the *Dialogue,* see Peter Ackroyd, *The Life of Thomas More* (New York, 1998), 279–83.

44. The treatise's dialogue took place over the course of weeks, however, in a series of private sessions conducted in a leisurely, unhurried manner. While the treatise certainly gained a wide readership, realities of heresy trials often made it impossible for authorities to follow through such a plan as More laid out, thus rendering his treatise, for the most part, theoretical.

45. *AM* (1583), 2030. For another example of a heated interrogation, see the case of Elizabeth Young, whose examiner, Sir Roger Cholmley, seems to have become incensed when she refused to swear on oath. "Twenty pounds, it is a man in a woman's clothes!" he shrieked, "twenty pounds it is a man!" Bonner replied, "Think you so, my lord?" and assented with others to have her swear that she was a woman, which Young refused to do. The matter was dropped when she then suggested that she be examined by other women as to her sex, leaving Cholmley to mumble, "Thou art an ill-favored whore." See *AM* (1583), 2067.

46. *AM* (1583), 1553–54.

47. *AM* (1583), 1668–69.

48. MacCulloch, *Thomas Cranmer*, 573–74, 578–79. In the exchange between the two men, Cranmer pointed out that Brooks had once taken the oath of supremacy, too; Brooks replied, however, that "I knew not then what an oath did mean, and yet to say the truth, I did it compulsed, compulsed I say by you, master Cranmer; and here you were the author and cause of my perjury." Quoted from MacCulloch, *Thomas Cranmer*, 578.

49. More answered, "Then in good faith there is no difference between your grace and me, but that I shall die today, and you tomorrow." William Roper, "The Life of Sir Thomas More," in *Two Early Tudor Lives*, ed. Richard Sylvester and Davis P. Harding (New Haven, 1962), 71.

50. See Philip Hughes, appendix 3, "The Heretical Past of Judges in the Marian Persecution," in *The Reformation in England* (New York, 1954), 2:349–52.

51. For Bonner's deprivation see *Wrioth. Chron.*, 2:33–34. See also Loach, *Edward VI*, 119. Among the problems witnessed by Bonner, and which caused him to rebel against Protestantism, was the influx of Anabaptists and other heretical sects into the realm, as well as difficulties such as the bitter vestments controversy, when the radical John Hooper, upon his nomination as bishop of Gloucester in 1550, denounced the "shameful" oath he would have to take and the vestments—namely, the surplice—he would be made to wear. Upon Mary's accession to the throne, Bonner was subsequently returned to power as bishop of London, where he fulfilled his functions as an active persecutor until Elizabeth came to power and he was sent back to the Marshalsea.

52. *AM* (1583), 1897.

53. Gardiner enjoyed the king's favor for much of the 1540s, though he became opposed to Somerset and Cranmer under Edward's reign and returned to Catholicism, resulting in his imprisonment. Gardiner, it should be said, was certainly Machiavellian in his way—Henry believed there was a "colored doubleness" to him—yet his imprisonment over the course of five years under Edward for refusing to relent on his belief in transubstantiation, and his writing of a sharp treatise upholding the real presence, does attest to some theo-

logical constancy on his part. See, in general, Glyn Redworth, *In Defence of the Church Catholic: The Life of Stephen Gardiner* (Oxford, 1990).

54. Gardiner was correct; there was no such phrase by St. Paul as the "scales falling from my eyes" in his treatise.

55. *AM* (1583), 1485.

56. Thomas Cranmer, as mentioned, also labeled his interrogator, James Brooks, bishop of Gloucester, a perjurer—"You, my lord, are perjured"—for having taken the oath forsaking the pope. See *AM* (1583), 52–53.

57. *AM* (1583), 1693.

58. *AM* (1583), 1896.

59. *AM* (1583), 1589.

60. For Draicot, see A. G. Dickens, *The Marian Reaction in the Diocese of York* (London, 1957), 7.

61. See S. T. Bindoff, *History of Parliament 1509–1558* (London, 1982), 2:578–79.

62. Quoted in Christopher Haigh, "The Continuity of Catholicism in the English Reformation," *Past and Present* 93 (1981): 37. See also H. Clifford, *Life of Jane Dormer, Duchess of Feria* (London, 1887), 38–39.

63. Walker, "Saint or Schemer?" 223. Eventually, Bilney in fact did recant, in a way, when he formally acknowledged being defamed for heretical opinions—which was not to say that he admitted to actually holding those heretical opinions.

64. *Unpub. Docs.*, 1:178–79.

65. *Unpub. Docs.*, 1:184.

66. See Alexandra Walsham, *Church Papists: Catholicism, Conformity and Confessional Polemic in Early Modern England* (London, 1993).

67. Bishop John Fisher, for example, argued, among other things, that the real presence was the true doctrine, since it was unanimously accepted by Catholics, whereas Protestants such as Luther and Oecolampadius were in strong disagreement over it. See Edward J. Sturtz, *The Works and Days of John Fisher* (Cambridge, Mass., 1967), 341.

68. *AM* (1583), 1920.

69. *AM* (1583), 1896.

70. When he returned, Knight was pleased when Marbeck told him that he had written on the paper, but when Knight read the words, "he cast it [away] in a great fume, swearing by our Lord's body that he would not for twenty pounds carry it to his lord and master," and that Marbeck would find himself "utterly undone." See also John Careless's refusal to name names, *AM* (1583), 1214–15.

71. In the formal trial phase, see, for example, John Fines, "Heresy Trials in the Diocese of Coventry and Lichfield, 1511–12," *JEH* 14 (1963): 169–70.

72. *AM* (1583), 825. See in general *AM* (1583), 821–36, for Longland's persecutions. See also Margaret Bowker, *The Henrician Reformation* (Cambridge, 1981), 57–64, and Knott, *Discourses of Martyrdom*, 62.

73. See Beilin, "A Challenge to Authority," 29–35. See also Mendelson and Crawford, who write that Askew's silence and fortitude represented women's ability to work around the stricture of "God and nature" of women's inferiority, since "Duty to God, to her conscience, might be [considered] heroic." Thus did "[p]atriarchy's very resilience [create] contradictions which made resistance and subversions possible." Sara Mendelson and Patricia Crawford, *Women in Early Modern England, 1550–1720* (Oxford, 1998), 17.

74. J. W. Martin, "The Protestant Underground Congregations of Mary's Reign," in *Religious Radicals in Tudor England* (London, 1989), 129.

75. See J. W. Martin, "Elizabethan Familists and English Separatism," in ibid., 179–201.

76. Gerard refused to divulge any information, even under torture. See Gerard, *Autobiography*, 107–13.

77. Ibid., 66–67.

78. Hooper was a committed Zwinglian from early on, who wrote of the sacraments that they "doth derogate the mercy of God, as though His holy Spirit could not be carried by faith into the sorrowful and penitent conscience except it ride always in a chariot and external sacrament." See *The Early Writings of John Hooper*, ed. Samuel Carr, Parker Society 20 (Cambridge, 1843), 131. For a concise explanation of Hooper's eucharistic doctrine, see Horton Davies, *Worship and Theology in England* (Princeton, 1970), 100–102.

79. For an explanation of grace and transubstantiation, see Frith, *A boke made by John Frith*, sigs. A3v–L3. See also Brad Gregory, *Salvation at Stake: Christian Martyrdom in Modern Europe* (Cambridge, Mass., 1999), 102, 126.

80. Cranmer's views on the real presence shifted over the course of his archbishopric, from a total belief in transubstantiation, to a more Lutheran notion, held after 1538, and finally, after 1546, a radical belief in a Calvinist doctrine, which he came to embrace under the influence of Ridley. See, for example, MacCulloch, *Thomas Cranmer*, 399–408.

81. *AM* (1583), 1589–90.

82. *AM* (1583), 1982.

83. *AM* (1583), 1675. During her examination, Elizabeth Young also asked, "Did [Jesus] give the cup the name of his blood, or else the wine that was in the cup?" See *AM* (1583), 2065–70.

84. *AM* (1583), 1686–87. Newman even wrote it out: "They which eat the flesh, and drink the blood of Christ, dwell in him, and he in them. The wicked dwell not in Christ, nor he in them: Ergo, The wicked eat not the flesh, nor drink the blood of Christ."

85. *AM* (1583), 2048–49.

86. *AM* (1583), 1665.

87. See John Fisher, *De Veritate Corporis*, sigs. 6–6v.

88. Cranmer was foreshadowing the writings of John Jewel, and specifically the Apology, which stated that "we [the English church] are come, as near as we possibly could, to the church of the apostles and of the old catholic bishops and fathers, which church we know hath hitherto been sound and perfect and, Tertullian termeth it, a pure virgin, spotted as yet with no idolatry nor with any foul or shameful fault; and have directed according to their customs and ordinances not only our doctrine but also the sacraments and the form of common prayer." See Jewel, "Apology," in John Jewel, *Works* (Cambridge, 1848), 3:77.

89. *AM* (1583), 2039–41.

90. *AM* (1583), 1562. See also the trial of Robert Smith, who stated, "I believe there is one catholic church, or faithful congregation, which, as the apostle saith, is builded upon the prophets and apostles, Christ Jesus being head corner-stone." *AM* (1583), 1692–94.

91. *AM* (1583), 1982.

92. *AM* (1583), 1982–83.

93. *AM* (1583), 2067.

94. *AM* (1583), 1591, 2024–25.

95. *AM* (1583), 1591.

96. To this, Tyms replied that "The Old Testament beareth witness of those things which are written in the New, for there is nothing taught in the New Testament, but it was foreshadowed in the law and prophets." *AM* (1583), 1897.

97. William Allen, *A True, sincere and modest defence of English Catholiques* (1584), 7.

98. These ideas would become especially articulated with John Jewel, in his *Apologie of the Church of England*, ed. John E. Booty (London, 1963), 130–31.

99. *Unpub. Docs.*, 1:77.

100. *State Trials*, 1:104–70.

101. *Unpub. Docs.*, 1:85–86.

102. Gerard, *Autobiography*, 98–99.

103. *Unpub. Docs.*, 1:171.

104. Gerard, *Autobiography*, 99.

105. Allen, *A True, sincere and modest defence*, 44–45.

106. *AM* (1583), 2014–15.

107. For the full proceedings, see *AM* (1583), 1101–29.

108. Hughes, *The Reformation in England*, 3:291–92. According to John Tedeschi, in the Roman Inquisition "various safeguards for the rights of the

accused were part of the trial procedure"; this meant, for instance, that the accused were allowed legal defense if they requested it, even if they had already made a confession. The reasons for this, Tedeschi continues, were, "First, the right to a defense was sanctioned by natural law . . . and should be denied no one. But second, from a practical point of view, the due observance of the provisions for defense . . . would silence later cries and appeals that the trial had not been allowed to run its regular course." This was lacking in England. See John Tedeschi, "The Organization and Procedures of the Roman Inquisition: A Sketch," in *The Prosecution of Heresy: Collected Studies on the Inquisition in Early Modern Italy* (New York, 1991), 135–36.

109. Bellamy, *Tudor Law of Treason*, 142.

110. John Fisher also raised the point during his final arraignment as to "whether a single testimony of one man may be admitted as sufficient to prove me guilty of Treason for speaking these words or no? And whether my answer, negatively, may not be accepted against his affirmative to my avail and benefit or no?" *State Trials*, 1:401.

111. See, for example, *PP*, 295; Bellamy, *Tudor Law of Treason*, 166–70.

112. *State Trials*, 1:401.

113 MacCulloch, *Thomas Cranmer*, 575. *AM* (1965), 7:527–30. See also Loades, *The Oxford Martyrs*, 213–15; Alan Chester, *Hugh Latimer* (Philadelphia, 1954), 211–15.

114. *AM* (1583), 1769. See also Loades, *The Oxford Martyrs*, 213–15; Alan Chester, *Hugh Latimer* (Philadelphia, 1954), 211–15.

115. Chester, *Latimer*, 212.

116. Gerard, *Autobiography*, 94.

117. Beilin, *Examinations of Anne Askew*, xv–xlii.

118. *AM* (1583), 1938.

119. For a discussion of Latimer's and other Protestants' simple rhetorical style, see Knott, *Discourses of Martyrdom*, 69–78.

120. Roper, "The Life of Sir Thomas More," 89.

121. See J. Duncan Derrett, "The Trial of Thomas More," *EHR* 79 (1964): 467, 477.

122. *AM* (1583), 1666–67, 1670.

123. MacCulloch, *Thomas Cranmer*, 575–76.

124. Like John Bland, Philpot also protested the law under which he was being tried. "You know that our faith is not grounded upon the civil law," he said to Bonner; "therefore it is not material to me whatsoever the law saith." When Bonner then asked by what law Philpot should be judged—for example, the common law—Philpot replied that "our faith dependenth not upon the laws of man" but on God, or the word of God through scripture. See Covington, "The Heresy Examinations," 85–86, 100–101, and *AM* (1583), 1817.

125. *SP,* Dom., Eliz. I, vol. lx, no. 47 (December, 1569).

126. *State Trials,* 1:1090–94.

127. *Unpub. Docs.,* 1:183–85. See also the case of the priest William Freeman, who in 1595 missed a legal opportunity to overturn his indictment, which had incorrectly listed his name as "Robert Freeman." Freeman, however, did use conscience and attack a witness against him as "a minister's sonne, himself a Puritane, & therefore no frend to Catholickes, & committed for murder." Ibid., 353–55.

128. See Thomas M. McCoog, "'Playing the Champion': The Role of Disputation in the Jesuit Mission," in *The Reckoned Expense: Edmund Campion and the Early English Jesuits,* ed. Thomas M. McCoog (London, 1996), 119–29. See also John O'Malley, *The First Jesuits* (Cambridge, Mass., 1993).

129. McCoog, "'Playing the Champion': The Role of Disputation," 135.

130. Smith continues: "But, my lord, to put you out of doubt because I am weary, I will strain courtesy with you: I perceive you will not, with your doctors, come unto me, and I am determined not to come unto you, by God's grace; for I have hardened my face against you as hard as brass." Smith was eventually burned.

131. *AM* (1583), 1589.

132. "It would be enough to raise an army against the Queen," Topcliffe added. Gerard, *Autobiography,* 95.

133. Brad Gregory discusses at some length the issue of Nicodemism and Protestantism; Gregory, *Salvation at Stake,* 150–62. Peter Holmes has also done significant work on the subject, especially in its political connotations. See Peter Holmes, *Resistance and Compromise: The Political Thought of the Elizabethan Catholics* (Cambridge, 1982), and *Elizabethan Casuistry,* ed. Peter J. Holmes (London, 1981). See also Rose, *Cases of Conscience.* A good recent work on the subject of the choices faced by Elizabethan Catholics is Walsham, *Church Papists,* chap. 4.

134. *AM* (1965), 7:668. For triumph felt by provincial magistrates when a Christian recanted in the years of the early church, see Tertullian, *Apologeticus* ii:13–17; Origen, *Contra Celsum* viii:44; Lactantius, *Div. Inst.* v:11.15.

135. *Wrioth. Chron.,* 1:142–43. See also Susan Wabuda, "Equivocation and Recantation during the English Reformation: The 'Subtle Shadows' of Dr Edward Crome," *JEH* 44 (1993): 228.

136. E. Margaret Thompson, *The Carthusian Order in England* (London, 1930), 395. See also David Knowles, *The Religious Orders in England* (Cambridge, 1959), 3:229–35, and Dom Lawrence Hendriks, *The London Charterhouse* (London, 1889), 139–48.

137. *EM,* 3(2): 61–63.

138. See Loades, *The Oxford Martyrs,* 194–95.

139. *AM* (1583), 1876–77.

140. For other interpretations of Bilney's recantation and behavior afterwards, see Walker, "Saint or Schemer?" 232–34. For Bilney in general, see *AM* (1583), 999–1013.

141. Dickens, *Marian Reaction,* 7; *AM* (1965), 8:225. For others who recanted their recantations, see the cases of Elizabeth Cooper and Cicley Ormes in *AM* (1965), 8:380–81, 427–29.

142. The best recent examination of recantation strategies is Wabuda, "Equivocation and Recantation." See also *AM* (1965), 5:696, and Bailey, "Robert Wisdom," 180–81. Though not all commentators agreed on the acceptability of recanting, others continued to defend the practice, or at least the practitioners, as was the case with John Foxe, who wrote that Edward Crome, Alexander Seton, and others may have recanted in Henry's time, "and yet [they remained] good soldiers after in the church of Christ."

143. Wabuda does describe, however, the way in which Foxe changed his view of Crome over the various editions of his *Acts and Monuments*: in the first edition, Crome was treated favorably, though more pointed criticisms began to emerge in the subsequent editions. See Wabuda, "Equivocation and Recantation," 238–39. For Crome as recounted by Foxe, see *AM* (1583), 1234–35.

144. Among the bishops were Edmund Guest, the bishop of Rochester; Edmund Scambler, the bishop of Chester; and William Alley, the bishop of Exeter. See Andrew Pettegree, "Nicodemism and the English Reformation," in *Marian Protestantism: Six Studies* (Scolar Press, 1996).

145. Calvin wrote, referring to Luke, "that if we are ashamed of [Christ] before other people, he likewise will be ashamed of us when he appears in his majesty with the angels of God." See John Calvin, *Petit traicté monstrant que c'est que doint faire un homme fidele . . .* (Geneva, 1543). For other anti-Nicodemite treatises see John Ponet, *A short treatise of politike power* (1556). See also the following treatises, smuggled into England from the continent in Mary's reign: Wolfgang Musculus, *The Temporysour,* trans. Robert Pownal (Wesel, 1555), sig. Aiiii, and Peter Martyr Vermigli, *Treaties of the Cohabitacyon of the Faithfull with the Unfaithfull.* For a good overview of Calvin's position, see Gregory, *Salvation at Stake,* 155–57.

146. As mentioned in chapter 2, Nicholas Ridley, for example, advised Protestants to "fly out of the realm" rather than compromise in any way with the enemy. Ridley, *The Works of Nicholas Ridley,* ed. Henry Christmas, Parker Society 39 (Cambridge, 1843), 419. See also Perez Zagorin, *Ways of Lying: Dissumulation, Persecution, and Conformity in Early Modern Europe* (Cambridge, Mass., 199), 141.

147. George Joye, *Present Consolation for the Sufferers of Persecution for Righteousness* (1544), D2, D4, D4v [D8v]. See also Charles C. Butterworth and

Allan G. Chester, *George Joye, 1493?–1553: A Chapter in the History of the English Bible and the English Reformation* (Philadelphia, 1962).

148. Zagorin, *Ways of Lying,* 223. Indeed, Ridley may have condemned the practice, but it did not prevent him from later praising Edward Crome, the notorious recanter, as showing "the most godly and fatherly constancy in confessing the truth of the gospel." See Coverdale, *Certain most godly, fruitful and comfortable letters* (London, 1564), 60–62. For other Protestant strategies of survival during Mary's reign, see also Brett Usher, "Backing Protestantism: The Godly, the Exchequer, and the Foxe Circle," in *John Foxe: An Historical Perspective,* ed. David Loades (Aldershot, U.K., 1999), 233–51.

149. *AM* (1583), 2067.

150. *AM* (1583), 1067–68.

151. See the following treatise by an anonymous Elizabethan author: *A displayinge of an horrible secte of grosse and wicked heretiques naming themselves the Familie of Love* (London, 1578).

152. For more on the Familists and their association with dissimulation, see Zagorin, *Ways of Lying,* 128–30.

153. *A displayinge of an horrible secte,* N1r.

154. Martin, "Elizabethan Familists and English Separatism," 197.

155. Peter Marshall, "Papist as Heretic: The Burning of John Forest, 1538," *Historical Journal* 41 (1998): 363–66.

156. Christopher Bagshaw, for example, very much opposed equivocation. See Holmes, *Resistance and Compromise,* 122.

157. Rose, *Cases of Conscience,* 88.

158. Persons, *A Brief Discours contayning certyne reasons why catholiques refuse to goe to Church,* reprinted in Catholic Record Society 2:178f. See also Holmes, *Resistance and Compromise,* 100–108, and Zagorin, *Ways of Lying,* 141–45.

159. J. W. Allen, *A History of Political Thought in the Sixteenth Century* (London, 1960), 360–66.

160. Knowles, *Religious Orders,* 3:229–31.

161. See Rose, *Cases of Conscience,* 90.

162. *Unpub. Docs.,* 1:350.

163. Robert Devlin, *Robert Southwell* (London, 1956), 311ff.

164. Pliny, *Ep.* 10.96. See also Marcus Aurelius's description of Christians as people deserving death for their "obstinate opposition," *Meditations* 11.3, and Craig S. Wansink, *Chained in Christ: The Experience and Rhetoric of Paul's Imprisonment* (Sheffield, U.K., 1996), 123.

165. Arthur J. Droge and James D. Tabor, *A Noble Death: Suicide and Martyrdom among Christians and Jews in Antiquity* (San Francisco, 1992), 132.

166. *AM* (1583), 1553–54.

167. More was thus content to spend the rest of his days in prison, but the government knew this would not do, given More's prominence in influencing others, and Henry's desire to make a statement to Rome for presuming to give John Fisher the cardinal's hat. See *PP,* 404–6. Elton vehemently makes the case for the government's—or Cromwell's—desire to exert moderation, legalism, and patience when it came to More; only after Rome had impudently intervened in England's affairs by making Fisher a cardinal did a furious Henry decide to go all out. Elton, however, needs to argue such a case in order for his larger thesis—of a Cromwell effectively and legally enforcing Reformation policy, with the help of lower-level officials—to work; in any case, Elton states, More was the glaring exception to the way Henry's government before 1540 went about its policies toward heretics, traitors, or deniers of the supremacy.

168. *State Trials,* 1:1070–72.

169. *Acts of English Martyrs Hitherto Unpublished,* ed. J. H. Pollen (London, 1891), 91–94. See also Holmes, *Resistance and Compromise,* 60–61.

170. *AM* (1583), 2024–25.

171. *AM* (1583), 1934.

172. *AM* (1583), 1205, esp. 1206.

173. *AM* (1583), 1035–36.

174. *AM* (1583), 1566.

175. "There is no disputing with a heretic."

176. *AM* (1583), 1566.

177. *AM* (1583), 1596.

178. *AM* (1583), 1592.

179. See *AM* (1583), 1801–2, 1816, 1821, 1827. Still, this outburst did not prevent the bishop of Bath from pulling Bonner by the sleeve as the reading continued and urging him to ask one more time "whether he will recant or no"; Bonner, however, replied, "O let [Philpot] alone," and finished reading the sentence.

180. *Unpub. Docs.,* 1:184,

181. Holinshed, 4:578.

182. *State Trials,* 1:1070–72.

183. *State Trials,* 1:402.

184. *Unpub. Docs.,* 1:87.

185. *Acts of English Martyrs,* 108–9.

Notes to Chapter Five

1. For heresy executions in general, see William Monter, "Heresy Executions in Reformation Europe," in *Tolerance and Intolerance in the European*

Reformation, ed. Ole Peter Grell and Bob Scribner (Cambridge, 1996), 48–65. See also Pieter Spierenberg, *The Spectacle of Suffering: Executions and the Evolution of Repression: From a Preindustrial Metropolis to the European Experience* (Cambridge, 1984).

2. V. A. C. Gatrell, *The Hanging Tree: Execution and the English People, 1770–1868* (Oxford, 1996).

3. Peter Lake and Michael Questier, "Agency, Appropriation and Rhetoric under the Gallows: Puritans, Romanists and the State in Early Modern England," *Past and Present* 153 (1996): 65.

4. See Elaine Scarry, *The Body in Pain: The Making and Unmaking of the World* (Oxford, 1985), 55–59; for a critique of the above, see Janel M. Mueller, "Pain, Persecution and the Construction of Selfhood in Foxe's *Acts and Monuments,*" in *Religion and Culture in Renaissance England,* ed. Claire McEachern and Debora Shuger (Cambridge, 1997), 161–87. See also Brent D. Shaw, "Body/Power/Identity: Passions of the Martyrs," *Journal of Early Christian Studies* 4 (1996): 269–93, and Esther Cohen, "The Animated Pain of the Body," *American Historical Review* 105 (2000): 36–68.

5. *AM* (1583), 1704.

6. For Catholic uses of execution narratives, see A. G. Dickens and John Tonkin, "Weapons of Propaganda: The Martyrologies," in *The Reformation in Historical Thought* (Cambridge, Mass., 1985), 39–57.

7. Raymond A. Mentzer, Jr., *Heresy Proceedings in Languedoc, 1500–1560* (Philadelphia, 1984), 122, 127.

8. Philip Jenkin, "From Gallows to Prison: The Execution Rate in Early Modern England," *Criminal Justice History* 7 (1986): 52–53; *Albion's Fatal Tree,* ed. Douglas Hay et al. (London, 1975), 22. See also Cynthia B. Herrup, "Law and Morality in Seventeenth-Century England," *Past and Present* 106 (1985): 102–23.

9. Sixteenth-century accounts tend to put the number high, at two thousand, while the nineteenth-century historian James Fitzjames Stephens gave an estimate of eight hundred a year under Henry. The most comprehensive, albeit flawed, attempt to factor in execution rates before the nineteenth century was done by Leon Radzinowicz, in *A History of the English Criminal Law and its Administration,* 5 vols. (London, 1948–86).

10. Jenkins, "From Gallows to Prison," 62.

11. See J. G. Bellamy, *The Criminal Trial in Later Medieval England* (Toronto, 1998), 155.

12. Jenkin, "From Gallows to Prison," 57. See also Geoffrey F. Nuttall, "The English Martyrs 1535–1680: A Statistical Review," *JEH* 22 (1971): 191–97.

13. Burning was also the punishment extracted on arsonists or—according to Bracton—individuals convicted of plotting against a lord's life. See F. Pollock and F. W. Maitland, *The History of English Law* (Cambridge, 1923), 2:492, 511.

14. F. Donald Logan, *Excommunication and the Secular Arm in Medieval England* (Toronto, 1968), 69. Logan writes, "Before 1382 no specific procedure existed in England for invoking the secular arm against heretics. Unless ad hoc arrangements were made—and this seems to have happened in the thirteenth century—the bishop would have recourse to the machinery available against obdurate excommunicates. This state of affairs could continue only as long as heresy cases were rare. The old methods were found inadequate to deal with the Lollards, and, as a result, the bishops of Canterbury province in 1382 . . . requested the king for a specific procedure for dealing with heretics." This would lead to the bishops being commissioned to demand secular aid, and eventually the passage of the statute *De haeretico comburendo,* which made heresy a secular offense.

15. John Laurence, *A History of Capital Punishment* (London, 1960), 11.

16. *AM* (1583), 1944. Catholics—most notably Robert Persons—immediately attacked the veracity of the Guernsey story, stating, among other things, that the three women were themselves thieves and strumpets, and that Perotine, the pregnant woman, murdered her (illegitimate) child by not revealing she was pregnant, which would have spared her the execution. According to Mozley, however, none of Foxe's attackers could back up their claims with evidence, whereas Foxe named eyewitnesses and quoted documents; "wherever we can test him," Mozley writes, "he is justified." See J. F. Mozley, *John Foxe and His Book* (New York, 1970), 223–41.

17. Latimer, *Sermons by Hugh Latimer,* ed. George Elwes Corrie, Parker Society 27 (Cambridge, 1844), 525.

18. Elias Canetti, *Crowds and Power* (New York, 1962), 50, 75–80. See also George Rudé, *The Crowd in History: A Study of Popular Disturbances in France and England, 1730–1848* (London, 1995).

19. For a general discussion of mutilation, see Stephen Greenblatt in *The Body in Parts: Fantasies of Corporeality in Early Modern Europe,* ed. David Hillman and Carla Mazzeo (New York, 1997), 221–41.

20. Jer. 19:7.

21. Coke, quoted in *State Trials,* 2:184. The biblical quote is from Jer. 8:2. The same intention was also behind the practice of hanging a dead body in chains. One might also mention that quartering and disembowelment constituted an act of desecration; while Natalie Zemon Davis has argued that mutilation of bodies and corpses in sixteenth-century France was the province of Catholics—who may have viewed the dead body as more charged than Protestants did, subject as it was to purgatory and prayers for the dead—Protestants in Elizabeth's time were as zealous as anyone in ensuring not only the death of a traitor or criminal, but the posthumous humiliation of that individual. See Natalie Davis, *Society and Culture in Early Modern France* (Stanford, 1975), 82, 83.

22. Another innovation was boiling alive, which was put into effect in 1531, and was inspired by the case of one Richard Roose, a cook who had been accused of poisoning the household of the bishop of Rochester. Roose was subsequently boiled to death in a large cauldron suspended over a fire. The act was repealed under Edward, in 1547. See Laurence, *A History of Capital Punishment*, 8–9.

23. Nuttall, "English Martyrs 1535–1680," 191–97. See also Brad S. Gregory, *Salvation at Stake: Christian Martyrdom in Early Modern Europe* (Cambridge, Mass., 1999), 280, for a discussion of these numbers, and of women, such as Margaret Clitherow, who desired martyrdom along with the priests they had harbored.

24. John Coffey, *Persecution and Toleration in Protestant England, 1558–1689* (London, 2000), 100–101.

25. See John F. Davis, *Heresy and Reformation in the South-East of England, 1520–1559* (London, 1983); Oliver, "Sir John Oldcastle: Legend or Literature?" *The Library*, 5th ser., 1946–47.

26. For the emerging doctrine of non-resistance in England, see J.W. Allen, *A History of Political Thought in the Sixteenth Century* (London, 1957), 125–33; see also Peter Holmes, *Resistance and Compromise: The Political Thought of Elizabethan Catholics* (Cambridge, 1982).

27. See E. Margaret Thompson, *The Carthusian Order in England* (London, 1930), 380.

28. See A. G. Dickens, *The English Reformation*, 2nd ed. (London, 1989), 293–301; Philip Hughes, *The Reformation in England* (New York, 1963), 2:254–304.

29. Catholic Record Society 5:200.

30. The two other women, Margaret Ward and Anne Line, were executed by hanging in 1588 and 1601, respectively, for the crime of aiding and sheltering priests. For an account of Margaret Clitherow's life, see John Mush, "A True Report of the Life and Martyrdom of Mrs Margaret Clitherow," in *The Troubles of Our Catholic Forefathers Related by Themselves*, ed. John Morris, 3rd ser. (London, 1877), 397–98, 432. See also Claire Cross, "An Elizabethan Martyrologist and His Martyr," in *Martyrs and Martyrologies*, ed. Diana Wood, Studies in Church History 30 (Oxford, 1993), 275–81.

31. Monter, "Heresy Executions in Reformation Europe," 48–64.

32. The figure of 7 percent is arrived at by calculating a rough number of 400 executed between Henry and Mary (less than a handful were killed under Edward) against Monter's 3,000. While this does not account for Elizabeth's reign, the issue is somewhat moot anyway, since executions of Catholics did not really begin until later in her reign, and especially in the late 1580s.

33. See Thomas M. McCoog, "The Flower of Oxford: The Role of Edmund Campion in Early Recusant Polemics," *Sixteenth Century Journal* 24 (1993): 899–913.

34. *Calendar of State Papers relating to Scotland and Mary, Queen of Scots, 1547–1603* (London, 1858), vol. 2, no. 328.

35. *AM* (1583), 2047. See also the case of Rawlins White: according to Foxe, "the head officers of the town, that had the charge of his execution, were determined to burn him, because they would sooner [be] rid of him; having not indeed a writ of execution awarded, as by the law they should have. Whereupon one Henry Lewis, the recorder of the town that then was, seeing that they went about to burn him without any warrant by writ, came to them and told them, that if they did burn him before they had the writ, 'De haereticis comburendis,' the wife of the said Rawlins would, upon just cause, by law, call their duties into question. Immediately upon this advertisement, they sent to London for the writ above-named." *AM* (1583), 1556–58.

36. *AM* (1583), 2047. In addition, some individuals were burned even though they had recanted—an act which was technically illegal, though later in her reign, Mary banned stakeside recantations, taking them to be insincere.

37. See, for example, the directive to the sheriffs by Elizabethan authorities, in Hughes, *Reformation in England,* app. 3, 3:412–13.

38. In 1533, for example, one document from Canterbury reported that "14s. 8d." was paid to cover the expense "of bringing a heretic from London," along with additional fees paid out for loads of wood (for burning), gunpowder, and a stake.

39. At the execution of the Catholic John Felton in 1570, for example, the sheriff read a proclamation which stated that "The queen, our sovereign lady, Elizabeth, by the grace of God, queen of England, France, and Ireland, defender of the true, ancient, and catholic faith, straightly chargeth and commandeth by us her said officers, all, and every [of] her loving subjects, on pain that shall fall thereof, that all, and every of them, whosoever, not appointed to the execution of John Felton, late attainted of High Treason, and thereof found guilty, by the Oath of 12 honest and discreet men, according to her highness's Laws, to depart the place; that is to say, twenty foot from this place, where the said John Felton must receive execution for his High treason, according to his Judgment; which said John Felton is here ready to receive Execution, according to the Judgment to him appointed. Thus willing all and every one, to depart . . . that each officer, according to his office, in this manner appointed, may do his, or their office, without let or disturbance in this behalf. And thus God save the queen." *State Trials,* 1:1087.

40. *AM* (1583), 1538.

41. The sheriff allowed Barnes to continue, which led to another exhortation, this time on saints, after which the sheriff then said, "Have you any thing more to say?" Barnes did, and requested that he make five requests of the king, the first being that "whereas his grace hath received into his hands all the goods

and substance of the abbeys—"; suddenly, the sheriff interrupted with a "stop there," though he allowed Barnes to continue with his requests and confession. *AM* (1583), 1200. For a justification of Barnes's execution, see John Standish, *A Lytle treatyse . . . againste the protestacion of Robert Barnes at ye time of his deth* (London, 1540), sig. A2v.

42. *AM* (1583), 1624.

43. *AM* (1583), 1567. Sheriffs could also cut short the attempts of the condemned to pray. See the case of Alexander Gouch in *AM* (1965), 8:496.

44. See Joseph Gillow, *A literary and biographical history; or, Bibliographical dictionary of the English Catholics, from the breach with Rome, in 1534, to the present time* (New York, 1968), 1:173, and Diego de Yepez, *Historia particular de la persecucion de Inglatera . . .* (Madrid, 1599).

45. *Unpub. Docs.*, 1:327. See also Bellamy, *Tudor Law of Treason*, 191.

46. Bellamy, *Tudor Law of Treason*, 359.

47. See *The Rambler*, n.s., 3 (1860): 380; Morris, *The Troubles of our Catholic Forefathers*, 1:99.

48. *AM* (1583), 1567.

49. *APC* (1554–56), 3:153. In addition, Rich was himself ordered to be present at various executions, and to seek out the assistance of the earl of Oxford and Sir John Raynesforth, together with their servants and officers—all of which Rich seems to have done with diligence. *APC*, 5:141, 148, 153. See also J. E. Oxley, *The Reformation in Essex to the Death of Mary* (Manchester, U.K., 1965).

50. *LP*, 8:250–54, n. 666. Henry desired to be in attendance as well; according to Chapuys, he could, in fact, have been present, in disguise.

51. *AM* (1583), 1100–1101. See also Judith Makens, "Hugh Latimer and John Forest: Rituals of Martyrdom," *Reformation* 6 (2002): 29–48.

52. *AM* (1583), 1240–41.

53. For a discussion of the contexts and places of sermons, see J. W. Blench, *Preaching in England in the Late Fifteenth and Sixteenth Centuries* (Oxford, 1964), and Susan Wabuda, *Preaching during the English Reformation* (Cambridge, 2002), esp. 40–63.

54. According to Foxe, Draicot then "went to his inn, for great sorrow of her death, and there laid [himself] down, and slept, during all the time of her execution." *AM* (1583), 1951.

55. *AM* (1583), 1690–91.

56. *AM* (1583), 1537.

57. *Unpub. Docs.*, 1:87. Some evidence exists of a preacher succeeding in his role, however. In 1538, for example, Rowland Taylor was said to have been so eloquent that the ten men and women about to be executed thanked "the King and his officers for their just execution." *LP*, 13(1): n. 1509.

58. *AM* (1583), 1240.

59. David Loades, *The Oxford Martyrs* (New York, 1970), 218–19.

60. Laurence, *A History of Capital Punishment*, 86; *Unpub. Docs.*, 1:186.

61. *LP*, 10:374, 401.

62. *Unpub. Docs.*, 1:288.

63. *AM* (1583), 2010.

64. *AM* (1583), 1036.

65. *AM* (1583), 1567.

66. *AM* (1583), 1770.

67. See, for example, the executioner who kneeled before the Carthusian John Houghton and asked his forgiveness. Thompson, *Carthusian Order in England*, 399.

68. *Unpub. Docs.*, 1:359.

69. Bellamy, *Tudor Law of Treason*, 202. See also Bede Camm, *Lives of the English Martyrs*, 1st ser. (London, 1905), 2:557.

70. *Unpub. Docs.*, 1:207, 359. Lake and Questier point out that Richard Sheldon did not view the muttering as a miracle, but rather as evidence, in its invocation of Gregory, of "the inveterate superstition of the papists." See Lake and Questier, "Agency, Appropriation and Rhetoric," 81.

71. David Knowles, *The Religious Orders in England* (Cambridge, 1959), 3:232.

72. Nicholas Harpsfield, *The Life and Death of Sr Thomas More, Knight, Sometymes Lord High Chancellor of England*, ed. Elsie Vaughan Hitchcock and R. W. Chambers, Early English Text Society (London, 1932), 204.

73. Edmund Bonner, *Homilies Sette Forth by the Righte Reverende Father in God, Edmund, Byshop of London* (London, 1555), fol. 26v.

74. Thomas More, *Dialogue Concerning Heresies*, vol. 6, pt. 1 of *The Complete Works of St. Thomas More*, ed. Thomas M. C. Lawler, Richard C. Marius, et al. (New Haven, 1981), 408.

75. The sheriff continued, "Speak to thy God, that he may deliver thee now; or else to strike me down, to the example of this people." *AM* (1583), 1680.

76. *AM* (1583), 2005.

77. *APC*, 5:135.

78. *Unpub. Docs.*, 1:288, 293.

79. See, for example, Foxe's letter to Elizabeth (summer 1575) in Thomas Fuller, *Church History of Britain* (London, 1837), 2:576–77.

80. Rogers would live on to endure the flames himself, in the time of Mary. See *AM* (1583), 1484–93.

81. *APC* (1550), 3:19. For criticism of this story, see, for example, R. W. Dixon, *History of the Church of England from the Abolition of the Roman Jurisdiction* (London, 1884–1910), 3:238 n.

82. See R. H. Pogson, "Reginald Pole and the Priorities of Government in Mary Tudor's Church," *History Journal* 18 (1975).

83. See Renard's letter to Philip II describing the execution of John Rogers, and the sympathy of the crowds, in *Span. Cal.*, 13:138–39, n. 149.

84. Bonner to Pole, July 1558, Petyt MS 538, xlviii, fol. 3.

85. Conyers Read, *Mr. Secretary Walsingham and the Policy of Elizabeth I* (Cambridge, 1925), 2:266–80.

86. For a good description and analysis of execution crowds, especially after the seventeenth century, see V. A. C. Gatrell, *The Hanging Tree: Execution and the English People, 1770–1868* (New York, 1996).

87. David Nicholls, "The Theater of Martyrdom in the French Reformation," *Past and Present* 121 (1988): 49.

88. Peter Burke, *Popular Culture in Early Modern Europe* (London, 1978), 198.

89. See Lake and Questier, "Agency, Appropriation and Rhetoric," 97–99.

90. Morris, *The Troubles of our Catholic Forefathers*, 1:99. See also Bellamy, *Tudor Law of Treason*, 203.

91. Strype quotes "Dorman, an Oxford man (who wrote certain books for Popery)" as writing: "A kind of practice among Christian martyrs never, I trow, heard of, the sooner to despatch themselves, as with my own eyes I saw Ridley and Latimer burned"; moreover, Dorman wrote in the margin, "This agreeth not with the martyrdom of Polycarpus." *EM*, 3 (1): 387. Protestants in Elizabeth's reign could also claim that Catholics had died very un-martyrlike deaths; according to Anthony Munday's apocryphal telling, "Campion . . . looked dead in the face, so soone as he sawe the place of execution, and remained quaking and trembling unto the death." See Anthony Munday, *A Breefe and True Reporte* (London, 1582), sigs. B1r–3v.

92. For a good analysis of the baiting crowd, see Canetti, *Crowds and Power;* Rudé, *The Crowd in History*.

93. Bellamy, *Tudor Law of Treason*, 198.

94. *State Trials*, 1:1088.

95. *State Trials*, 1:1091–92. For a discussion of the role of ballads and broadsides in general, see Tessa Watt, *Cheap Print and Popular Piety, 1550–1640* (Cambridge, 1991). See also Alexandra Halasz, *Marketplace of Print: Pamphlets and the Public Sphere in Early Modern England* (Cambridge, 1997).

96. *AM* (1583), 2041–42.

97. *AM* (1583), 1682.

98. Robert Whiting, *Local Responses to the English Reformation* (New York, 1998), 124.

99. *AM* (1583), 1567.

100. See the case of the hardened prisoner who converted at Nutter's execution, in Lake and Questier, "Agency, Appropriation and Rhetoric," 84.

101. *Unpub. Docs.*, 1:359–60.

102. *Unpub. Docs.*, 327. See also Bellamy, *Tudor Law of Treason*, 208.

103. See *Douai Diaries*, ed. R. Knox (London, 1878), 327–38, no. 23. See also Catholic Record Society 58:50–51. For the fate of the Catholic relics, see Gregory, *Salvation at Stake*, 298–303.

104. *Acts of English Martyrs Hitherto Unpublished*, ed. J. H. Pollen (London, 1891), 343 and 325–26.

105. Miles Huggarde, *The Displaying of the Protestantes, and sondry [of] their practises, with a description of diuers their abuses of late frequented . . .* (London, 1556), fol. 44.

106. Thomas Freeman, "The Importance of Dying Earnestly: The Metamorphosis of the Account of James Bainham in Foxe's *Book of Martyrs*," in *The Church Retrospective*, ed. R. N. Swanson, Studies in Church History 33 (London, 1997), 267–88.

107. The notes were sent on to the publisher, Richard Verstegan. See Gregory, *Salvation at Stake*, 289–90.

108. Thomas Alfield, *A True Reporte of the Death and Martyrdome of M. Campion*, sigs. [A4r–v].

109. See Catholic Record Society 5:227–30.

110. *LP*, 8:250–54, n. 666. Quoted from Lawrence Hendriks, *The London Charterhouse: Its Monks and Its Martyrs* (London, 1889), 155–57.

111. According to John Scarisbrick, the death of John Fisher, "a prince of the Holy Roman Church," rang louder overseas, especially in Rome, than did More's death. See J. J. Scarisbrick, *Henry VIII* (Berkeley, 1968), 334.

112. Brad Gregory makes an excellent case against historians who attempt to fit early modern martyrs into various sociological, psychological, or anthropological categories; see Gregory, *Salvation at Stake*, 99–105. Two of the foremost practitioners of the sociological approach are Donald Weinstein and Rudolph Bell, in *Saints and Society: The Two Worlds of Western Christendom, 1000–1700* (Chicago, 1982). Gregory, however, tends to overlook some of the very valid conclusions and statistics brought forward by Weinstein and Bell concerning the role of age, gender, place, and time of the martyr-saints in early modern Europe.

113. Matt. 24:9, 13.

114. For a good account of the degrading ceremony undergone by Latimer, Cranmer, and Ridley, see Loades, *Oxford Martyrs*, 218; see also Nicholls, "Theater of Martyrdom," 55.

115. Thomas More, *Dialogue of Comfort against Tribulation,* ed. Leland Miles (Bloomington, Ind., 1966), for example 105–11, 118–26. See Paul D. Green, "Suicide, Martyrdom, and Thomas More," in *Studies in the Renaissance* 19 (1972): 135–55. For a general discussion of the meanings suicide held for early modern English people, see Michael MacDonald, *Sleepless Souls: Suicide in Early Modern England* (Oxford, 1990).

116. Letter to Margaret Roper from the Tower, in *The Correspondence of Sir Thomas More,* ed. Elizabeth F. Rogers (Princeton, 1947), 253.

117. *AM* (1583), 1703–4.

118. *AM* (1583), 1623–24.

119. [?Harpsfield, N.], *Bishop Cranmer's Recantacyons,* ed. Lord Houghton, Philobiblon Society Miscellanies 15 (1877–84), 79–82.

120. *AM* (1583), 1714.

121. *Calendar of State Papers relating to Scotland and Mary, Queen of Scots, 1547–1603,* vol. 2, no. 328. See also *State Trials,* 1:404.

122. *AM* (1583), 1124.

123. *AM* (1583), 1769.

124. *AM* (1583), 1690.

125. *Unpub. Docs.,* 1:78. Bell's fellow Catholic, John Finch, also spent his last night in prison exhorting prisoners to repentance. See *Unpub. Docs.,* 1:87.

126. *AM* (1583), 1596.

127. *APC,* 14:57–58.

128. According to a royal order released in 1371, "[T]he King has learned by credible witness, that the air upon Tower Hill is so tainted . . . as to strike the men swelling all about and the passer by with disgust and loathing, and that great danger is acknowledged to arise therefrom, to the nuisance of the said men and others there having their conversation or passing by and to the manifest peril of their life: and the King will no longer endure these grievous and intolerable faults." *Calendar of the Close Rolls* (London, 1911), 13:365, 402.

129. Stow, 2:72–73, 262.

130. Loades, *Oxford Martyrs,* 218.

131. Thomas Stapleton, *The Life and Illustrious Martyrdom of Sir Thomas More* (1588), 279.

132. Bellamy, *Tudor Law of Treason,* 187–88.

133. *AM* (1583), 1538.

134. *AM* (1583), 1492–93.

135. See, for example, George Eagles, who in 1557 rode on a hurdle carrying a book of Psalms, "the which he read very devoutly all the way with a loud voice, till he came [to the gallows]." *AM* (1583), 2010.

136. *AM* (1583), 1558–59.

137. *AM* (1583), 1623–24.

138. More did so, "alter[ing] his apparel," though he did send the executioner some gold, in imitation of his hero, St. Cyprian. Harpsfield, *Life and Death of Sr Thomas More,* 203.

139. Hendriks points out that "[had] the monks been indeed guilty of high treason, they should have been degraded, and then executed in secular clothing; but ecclesiastical law had no more force, for the King of England had become a pope." Hendriks, *London Charterhouse,* 151–52. See also Knowles, *Religious Orders,* 3:232.

140. *AM* (1583), 1567.

141. *AM* (1583), 1623–24.

142. *Unpub. Docs.,* 1:357.

143. *Unpub. Docs.,* 1:357–58.

144. *AM* (1583), 2002.

145. *AM* (1583), 1944–45.

146. *AM* (1583), 2010.

147. *AM* (1583), 1195.

148. *Unpub. Docs.,* 1:359.

149. See Mervyn James, *English Politics and the Concept of Honour* (Oxford, 1978), 55. Not everyone was allowed to speak, however; see, for example, the 1555 case of George Marsh, who at his execution site "began to speak to the people, showing the cause of his death, and would have exhorted them to stick unto Christ." The sheriff, as mentioned earlier, shut him up, however, though Marsh was allowed to pray. See *AM* (1965), 7:53.

150. J. A. Sharpe, "'Last Dying Speeches': Religion, Ideology and Public Execution in Seventeenth-Century England," *Past and Present* 107 (1985): 144–67.

151. For a discussion of these issues, see Lacey Baldwin Smith, "English Treason Trials and Confessions in the Sixteenth Century," *Journal of the History of Ideas* 15 (1954): 483–87. See also Bellamy, *Tudor Law of Treason,* 200–201.

152. *State Trials,* 1:1091–92.

153. Quoted in Hendriks, *London Charterhouse,* 151–53.

154. *State Trials,* 1:1050–72. See also Richard Simpson, *Edmund Campion* (London, 1867), 319, 321.

155. *Unpub. Docs.,* 1:186.

156. See Mary Catherine O'Connor, *The Art of Dying Well: The Development of the Ars Moriendi* (New York, 1942); Roger Chartier, "Texts and Images: The Arts of Dying, 1450–1600," in *The Cultural Uses of Print in Early Modern France* (Princeton, 1987); Gregory, *Salvation at Stake,* 50–62.

157. *Here begynneth a lityll treatise shorte and abredged spekynge of the arte and crafte to well know to dye,* trans. William Caxton (London, 1490), sigs. A1v, A2.

158. Quoted in Gregory, *Salvation at Stake,* 53. See also Thomas à Kempis, *The Imitation of Christ,* trans. Leo Sherley-Price (London, 1952), 57–60.

159. *AM* (1583), 1213–14.

160. *AM* (1583), 1194–97.

161. *AM* (1583), 1623–24.

162. Huggarde wrote, "Where is their modestie, their pacience, their charities, their love, that is required of a martyr?" Stephen and Paul, he wrote, did not display such taunting pride, after all. See *Displaying of the Protestantes,* fols. 46v–47v.

163. *AM* (1583), 1680.

164. *AM* (1583), 1596. Later on, during the reign of Elizabeth, the deranged Puritan William Hacket was put to death not only unrepentant, but still under the delusion that he was king of Europe; when the hangman began to go about his business, he was met with the words, "Thou bastard, wilt thou hang Hacket thy king?" See William Camden, *Annals or the History of the most renowned and victorious princess Elizabeth, late Queen of England* (London, 1635), 403.

165. For the circumstances surrounding Forest, see Peter Marshall, "Papist as Heretic: The Burning of John Forest, 1538," *The Historical Journal* 41 (1998): 351–74.

166. *State Trials,* 1:1095.

167. *Unpub. Docs.,* 1:336.

168. *State Trials,* 1:1087–88.

169. *State Trials,* 1:1091–92.

170. Arthur J. Droge and James D. Tabor, *A Noble Death: Suicide and Martyrdom among Christians and Jews in Antiquity* (San Francisco, 1990), 119.

171. John Fisher, *A spirituall consolation, written by Iohn Fyssher Bishoppe of Rochester* [London, 1578], sigs. F5v–[F6].

172. See Patrick Collinson, "The English Conventicle," in *Voluntary Religion,* ed. W. J. Sheils and Diana Wood, Studies in Church History 23 (Cambridge, 1986), 42–50.

173. Diarmaid MacCulloch, *Thomas Cranmer: A Life* (New Haven, 1996), 582. See also Harpsfield, *Cranmer's Recantacyons,* 48–50.

174. Hall, *Chronicles,* 623; *SP,* Dom., Eliz. I, vol. ccxvii, no. 1 (in *SP,* 2:549).

175. *Unpub. Docs.,* 1:78.

176. More, *Dialogue of Comfort against Tribulation,* ed. Miles, 312. For a discussion of the depiction of pain in general, see Lionello Puppi, *Torment in Art: Pain, Violence, and Martyrdom* (New York, 1991), 11–69.

177. Helen White, *Tudor Books of Saints and Martyrs* (Madison, 1963), 161–62.

178. *AM* (1583), 1505–11.

179. *AM* (1583), 1131.

180. Shaw, "Body/Power/Identity," 289–90.

181. Quoted in ibid., 290.

182. *AM* (1583), 1596.

183. See John Philpot, *The Examinations and Writings of John Philpot* (Cambridge, 1842), 161.

184. *AM* (1583), 1592–93.

185. See also Christopher Haigh, *English Reformations: Religion, Politics and Society under the Tudors* (Oxford, 1993).

186. Huggarde, *Displaying of the Protestantes*, fol. 64r–v.

187. See Lake and Questier, "Agency, Appropriation and Rhetoric," 79–80.

188. This was especially the case with Jesuits and Puritans—the "busy controllers"—who, in Lake and Questier's words, "could and did adopt and exploit popular forms and assumptions as part of a wider strategy of proselytization and, for Catholics in Elizabethan and early Stuart England at least, of openly subversive ideological resistance." Ibid., 95.

189. Lacey Baldwin Smith, *Fools, Martyrs, Traitors: The Story of Martyrdom in the Western World* (New York, 1997), 206–7.

190. Penry Willliams, *The Tudor Regime* (Oxford, 1979), 289–92.

191. Quoted in Richard Challoner, *Memoirs of Missionary Priests* (London, 1924), 176–77.

SELECT BIBLIOGRAPHY

The following is a list of the most important sources utilized throughout this book, rather than a complete list of references cited.

Manuscript Sources

Bodleian Library, Oxford
  Brasenose College Manuscripts
  Tanner Manuscripts

British Library, London
  Papers of John Foxe in the Harleian Collection, specifically fols. 92–103 of MS 421
  Harleian Manuscripts 283, 286, 417, 421, 425, 444
  Lansdowne Manuscripts
  Cotton Manuscripts

Emmanuel College Library, Cambridge
  MSS 260, 261, 262

Greater London Record Office
  DL/C [Act books of the London consistory court]

Guildhall Library
  MS 9531/10, Register of Bishop Cuthbert Tunstall
  MS 9531/12, pt. 1, Register of Bishop Edmund Bonner

Lambeth Palace Library
  Archiepiscopal registers of Thomas Cranmer and Reginald Pole

Public Record Office, London
    State Papers 12 and 15

Primary Printed Sources

Acts of English Martyrs Hitherto Unpublished. Ed. J. H. Pollen. London,
    1891.
Acts of the Privy Council of England. Ed. J. Dasent. London, 1890–1907.
All the submyssyons and recantations of T. Cranmer. London, 1556.
Archdeacon Harpsfield's Visitation, 1557. Ed. L. E. Whatmore. Catholic
    Record Society 23–24. London, 1942–46.
Aubrey, John. *Brief Lives.* Ed. O. L. Dick. London, 1950.
Bale, John. *A Declaration of Edmund Bonner's Articles.* London, 1554.
————. *Select Works.* Ed. Henry Christmas. London, 1849.
*Before the Bawdy Court: Selections from Church Court and Other Records
    Relating to the Correction of Moral Offences in England, Scotland, and
    New England, 1300–1800.* Ed. P. E. H. Hair. New York, 1972.
*Blood and Knavery: A Collection of English Renaissance Pamphlets and Bal-
    lads of Crime and Sin.* Ed. Joseph H. Marshburn and Alan R. Velie.
    Rutherford, N.J., 1973.
Bonner, Edmund. *Homilies Sette Forth by the Right Reverende Father in God,
    Edmunde, Byshop of London.* London, 1555.
————. *An Honest and Godlye Instruction and Information for the Tradynge
    and Bringinge vp of Children.* London, 1555.
————. *A profitable and necessarye doctryne.* London, 1555.
Bradford, John. *The Writings of John Bradford.* Ed. A. Townshend. 2 vols.
    Cambridge, 1848–53.
Burnet, G. *The History of the Reformation of the Church of England.* Ed.
    Nicholas Pocock. Vols. 4–7. Oxford, 1865.
*Calendar of Letters, Despatches, and State Papers relating to the Negotiations
    between England and Spain. . . .* 13 vols. London, 1862–1954.
Calendar of Patent Rolls, Philip and Mary. 4 vols. London, 1936–39.
*Calendar of State Papers, Domestic series, of the reigns of Edward VI, Mary,
    Elizabeth and James I. 1547–[1625] preserved in the State paper depart-
    ment of Her Majesty's Public Record Office.* 12 vols. London, 1856–72.
*Calendar of State Papers relating to Scotland and Mary, Queen of Scots,
    1547–1603.* 2 vols. London, 1858.
Camden, William. *Annales rerum anglicarum et hibernicarum regnante
    Elizabetha.* Ed. T. Hearne. London, 1717.

Campion, Edmund. *Ten Reasons proposed to his Adversaries in the Name of the Faith and presented to the Illustrious Members of Our Universities.* London, 1914.

The Canons of 1571 in English and Latin. With notes by William Edward Collins. Church Historical Society. London, 1899.

Cardwell, Edward, ed. *Documentary Annals of the Reformed Church of England.* 2 vols. Oxford, 1839.

Cecil, William. *The Execution of Justice in England.* Folger Documents of Tudor and Stuart Civilization. Ithaca, N.Y., 1965.

Christopherson, John. *An exhortation to alle menne to take hede and beware of rebellion.* London, 1554.

Chronicle of the Grey Friars of London. Ed. J. G. Nichols. Camden Society 53. London, 1852.

Chronicle of Queen Jane, and of two years of Queen Mary. Ed. J. G. Nichols. Camden Society 48. London, 1850.

Clarke, Samuel. *A Collection of the Lives of Ten Eminent Divines . . . and of Some Other Eminent Christians.* London, 1662.

A Collection of Original Letters from the Bishops to the Privy Council, 1564. Ed. M. Bateson. Camden Society, n.s., 53. London, 1895.

Coverdale, Miles. *Remains.* Ed. George Pearson. Parker Society 14. Cambridge, 1846.

Coverdale, Miles, [and Henry Bull], eds. *Certain most godly and comfortable letters of such true Saintes and holy martyrs of God.* London, 1564.

Cranmer, Thomas. *Miscellaneous Writings and Letters of Thomas Cranmer.* Ed. John Cox. Cambridge, 1846.

Darlington, Ida, ed. *London Consistory Court Wills 1492–1547.* London Record Society 3. London, 1967.

Depositions and other Ecclesiastical Proceedings from the Courts of Durham Extending from 1311 to the Reign of Elizabeth. Publications of the Surtees Society, 1845. London, 1846.

Dickens, A. G. "Robert Parkyn's Narrative of the Reformation." *English Historical Review* 62 (1947): 58–83.

Dowling, M., and Rose Hickman. "Religion and Politics in Mid-Tudor England Through the Eyes of an English Protestant Woman." *Bulletin of the Institute of Historical Research* 55 (1982): 94–102.

Durham Quarter Sessions Rolls, 1471–1625. Ed. C. M. Fraser. Newcastle-upon-Tyne, U.K., 1991.

Edward VI. *The Chronicle and Political Papers of King Edward VI.* Ed. W. K. Jordan. London, 1966.

Ellis, H. *Original Letters Illustrative of English History.* 3d series. 11 vols. London, 1824–46.

English Historical Documents. Vol. 5, 1485–1558. Ed. C. H. Williams. London, 1967.

Foxe, John. *Actes and Monuments of these latter and perillous dayes.* London, 1563.

————. *Acts and Monuments.* London, 1570.

————. *Acts and Monuments of matters most speciall and memorable* . . . London, 1583.

————. *The Acts and Monuments of John Foxe.* Ed. George Townsend. 8 vols. New York, 1965.

Frere, W. H., and W. M. Kennedy. *Visitation Articles and Injunctions.* 3 vols. Alcuin Club Collection, xiv, xv, xvi, 1910. London, 1910.

Gardiner, Stephen. *De Vera Obedientia.* Trans. John Bale. Hamburg, 1553.

————. *The Letters of Stephen Gardiner.* Ed. J. A. Mueller. Cambridge, 1933.

Gee, H., and W. J. Hardy, eds. *Documents Illustrative of English Church History.* London, 1896.

Gerard, John. *The Autobiography of a Hunted Priest.* Trans. Philip Caraman. New York, 1965.

Godwin, F. A. *A Catalogue of the Bishops of England.* London, 1601.

Grafton, Richard. *A Chronicle at large* . . . London, 1568.

Hale, W. H., ed. *A Series of Precedents and Proceedings in Criminal Causes, 1475–1640, extracted from act books of ecclesiastical courts in the diocese of London.* London, 1847.

Hall, Edward. *The Union of the two Noble and Illustre Famelies of Lancastre and Yorke.* Ed. H. Ellis. London, 1809.

Hampshire Churchwardens' Accounts. Ed. J. F. Williams. London, 1913.

Harpsfield, Nicholas. *Dialogi sex.* Antwerp, 1566.

————. *Life and Death of Sr Thomas More, knight, sometymes Lord high Chancellor of England.* Ed. Elsie Vaughn Hitchcock and R. W. Chambers. Early English Text Society. London, 1932.

Holinshed, Raphael. *Chronicles.* Ed. H. Ellis. 6 vols. 1807–8.

Hooper, John. *Later Writings of Bishop Hooper.* Ed. Charles Nevison. Cambridge, 1852.

Hughes, Paul L., and James F. Larkin, eds. *Tudor Royal Proclamations (The Later Tudors, 1553–1587).* New Haven, 1964–69.

Knell, Thomas. *An Epitaph or Rather a Short Discourse Made Upon the Life and Death of D. Bonner.* London, 1569.

Lambeth Churchwardens' Accounts, I. Ed. C. Drew. Surrey Record Society 18. London, 1941.

Latimer, Hugh. *Sermons by Hugh Latimer*. Ed. George Elwes Corrie. Parker Society 27. Cambridge, 1844.

Letters and Papers, Foreign and Domestic, of the Reign of Henry VIII. Ed. J. S. Brewer, J. Gairdner, and R. S. Brodie. 21 vols. London, 1862–1932.

Machyn, Henry. *The Diary of Henry Machyn, Citizen and Merchant Taylor of London, 1550–1563*. Ed. J. G. Nichols. Camden Society 42. London, 1848.

Major, Kathleen. *A Handlist of the Records of the Bishop of Lincoln and of the Archdeacons of Lincoln and Stow*. Lincoln, 1953.

Marbecke, John. *The Lyves of Holy Sainctes, Prophetes, Patriarches, and Others, Contayned in Holye Scripture*. London, 1574.

More, Thomas. *The Correspondence of Sir Thomas More*. Ed. Elizabeth F. Rogers. Princeton, 1947.

———. *A Dialogue of Comfort against Tribulation*. Ed. Frank Manley. New Haven, 1977.

Myre, John. *Instructions for Parish Priests*. Ed. E. Peacock. Early English Text Series, o.s., 31. London, 1868.

Narratives of the Days of the Reformation, Chiefly from the Manuscripts of John Foxe the Martyrologist. Ed. J. G. Nichols. Camden Society 77. London, 1859.

Original Letters Relative to the English Reformation, 1531–58. Ed. H. Robinson. 2 vols. Parker Society. Cambridge, 1846–47.

Philpot, John. *The Examinations and Writings of John Philpot*. Ed. Robert Eden. Cambridge, 1842.

Pocock, Nicholas, ed. *Records of the Reformation*. 2 vols. Oxford, 1870.

Pollard, A. F. *Tudor Tracts 1532–1588*. New York, 1964.

Pollen, John Hungerford, ed. *Unpublished Documents relating to the English Martyrs*. London, 1908.

Proceedings and Ordinances of the Privy Council of England, 1386–1542. Ed. N. H. Nicolas. 7 vols. 1834–37.

Purvis, J. S. *Tudor Parish Documents of the Diocese of York*. Cambridge, 1948.

Registers of Cuthbert Tunstall, Bishop of Durham 1530–59 and James Pilkington, Bishop of Durham 1561–76. Ed. Gladys Hinde. Surtees Society. London, 1952.

Ridley, Nicholas. *The Works of Nicholas Ridley*. Ed. Henry Christmas. Parker Society 39. Cambridge, 1841.

Roper, William. *The Life of Sir Thomas More*. London, 1567.

Sanders, N. "Report to Cardinal Moroni on the Change of Religion in 1558–1559." Ed. F. A. Gasquet. Catholic Record Society 1. London, 1904–5.

Stapleton, Thomas. *The Life and Illustrious Martyrdom of Sir Thomas More.* London, 1558.

State Papers . . . King Henry VIII. 2 vols. London, 1831–52.

State Trials. Ed. William Cobbett et al. 33 vols. London, 1809–26.

Statutes of the Realm. Ed. A. Luders et al. 11 vols. London, 1810–28.

Stow, John. *A Survey of London.* Ed. C. L. Kingsford. 2 vols. Oxford, 1908.

Strype, J. *Ecclesiastical Memorials, relating chiefly to religion, and the Reformation of it . . . under King Henry VIII, King Edward VI, and Queen Mary I.* 3 vols. Oxford, 1822.

———. *Annals of the Reformation and Establishment of Religion in the Church of England.* Oxford, 1824.

Thurston, Herbert S., ed. *The Lives of the Saints by Alban Butler.* Vols. 1–12. London, 1926.

Vergil, Polydore. *The Anglica Historia of Polydore Vergil, 1485–1537.* Ed. D. Hay. Camden Society, 3rd ser., 74. London, 1950.

Visitations in the Diocese of Lincoln 1517–1531. Ed. A. Hamilton-Thompson. Lincoln Record Society. Hereford, 1940–47.

Wriothesley, Charles. *A Chronicle of England During the Reigns of the Tudors, 1485–1559.* Ed. W. D. Hamilton. 2 vols. Camden Society, n.s., 11 and 20. London, 1875–77.

Selected Secondary Sources

Alexander, Gina. "Bonner and the Marian Persecutions." In *The English Reformation Revised,* ed. C. Haigh, 117–75. Cambridge, 1987.

Aston, Margaret. *Faith and Fire: Popular and Unpopular Religion, 1350–1600.* London, 1988.

Baker, Derek, ed. *Reform and Reformation: England and the Continent c.1500–c.1750.* Oxford, 1979.

Beilin, Elaine V. "A Challenge to Authority: Anne Askew." In *Redeeming Eve: Women Writers of the English Reformation.* Princeton, 1987.

Bellamy, John. *The Tudor Law of Treason.* Toronto, 1979.

Betteridge, Thomas. *Tudor Histories of the English Reformation, 1520–1583.* Aldershot, U.K., 1999.

Bossy, J. A. "The Character of Elizabethan Catholicism." *Past and Present* 21 (1962): 39–59.

———. *The English Catholic Community, 1570–1850.* London, 1975.

Bowker, Margaret. "Lincolnshire 1536: Heresy, Schism or Religious Discontent?" In *Schism, Heresy and Religious Protest,* ed. Derek Baker, 195–212. Studies in Church History 9. Cambridge, 1972.

Brigden, Susan. "The Early Reformation in London, 1520–1547: The Conflict in the Parishes." Ph.D. diss., University of Cambridge, 1979.

———. *London and the Reformation*. Oxford, 1989.

———. *New Worlds. Lost Worlds: The Rule of the Tudors*. New York, 2000.

Coffey, John. *Persecution and Toleration in Protestant England, 1558–1689*. London, 2000.

Collinson, Patrick. *The Elizabethan Puritan Movement*. London, 1967.

———. *The Religion of Protestants: The Church in English Society 1559–1625*. Oxford, 1982.

———. "The English Conventicle." In *Voluntary Religion*, ed. W. J. Sheils and Diana Wood Studies in Church History 23. Cambridge, 1986.

———. "Truth and Legend: The Veracity of John Foxe's Book of Martyrs." In *Elizabethan Essays*, 151–77. London, 1994.

Covington, Sarah. "The Heresy Examinations of John Philpot: Defiance, Bold Speaking and the Making of a Martyr." *Reformation* 7 (2002): 81–133.

Craig, John. "Cooperation and Initiatives: Elizabethan Churchwardens and the Parish Accounts of Mildenhall." *Social History* 18 (1993).

Crawford, F. "The Rule of Law? The Laity, English Archdeacons' Courts and the Reformation to 1558." *Paregon* 4 (1986).

Cross, Claire. *Church and People 1450–1660: The Triumph of the Laity in the English Church*. Glasgow, 1976.

Davies, C. S. L. "Popular Religion and the Pilgrimage of Grace." In *Order and Disorder in Early Modern England*, ed. A. Fletcher and J. Stevenson. Cambridge, 1985.

Davis, J. F. "Joan of Kent, Lollardy and the English Reformation." *Journal of Ecclesiastical History* 33 (1982): 225–33.

———. *Heresy and Reformation in the South-East of England, 1520–1559*. London, 1983.

Davis, Kenneth R. "No Discipline, No Church: An Anabaptist Contribution to the Reformed Tradition." *Sixteenth Century Journal* 12 (1982): 43–58.

Dickens, A. G. *The English Reformation*. 2nd ed. London, 1989.

Duffy, Eamon. *The Stripping of the Altars: Traditional Religion in England, 1400–1580*. New Haven, 1982.

———. *The Voices of Morebath: Reformation and Rebellion in an English Village*. New Haven, 2001.

Dures, Alan. *English Catholicism, 1558–1642*. Harlow, U.K., 1983.

Elton, G. R. *Policy and Police: The Enforcement of the Reformation in the Age of Thomas Cromwell*. Cambridge, 1972.

———. *Reform and Reformation: England 1509–58*. Cambridge, Mass., 1977.

Fines, J. "Heresy Trials in the Diocese of Coventry and Lichfield, 1511–1512." *Journal of English History* 14 (1963): 160–74.

Fletcher, Anthony, and Peter Roberts, eds. *Religion, Culture and Society in Early Modern England: Essays in Honour of Patrick Collinson*. Cambridge, 1994.

Freeman, Thomas. "Notes on a Source for John Foxe's Account of the Marian Persecution in Kent and Sussex." *Historical Research* 67 (1994): 203–11.

———. "The Importance of Dying Earnestly: The Metamorphosis of the Account of James Bainham in Foxe's Book of Martyrs." In *The Church Retrospective*, ed. R. N. Swanson. Studies in Church History 33. London, 1997.

———. "Fate, Fact and Fiction in Foxe's Book of Martyrs."*Historical Journal* 43 (2000): 601–23.

———. "'The good ministrye of godlye and vertuouse women': The Elizabethan Martyrologists and the Female Supporters of the Marian Martyrs." *Journal of British Studies* 39 (2000): 8–33.

Gaskill, Malcolm. "Witchcraft in Early Modern Kent: Stereotypes and the Background to Accusations." In *Witchcraft in Early Modern Europe: Studies in Culture and Belief*, ed. Jonathan Barry et al. Cambridge, 1996.

Gregory, Brad S. *Salvation at Stake: Christian Martyrdom in Early Modern Europe*. Cambridge, Mass., 1999.

Grell, Ole Peter, and Bob Scribner, eds. *Tolerance and Intolerance in the European Reformation*. Cambridge, 1996.

Haigh, Christopher. "The Continuity of Catholicism in the English Reformation." *Past and Present* 93 (1981): 37–69.

———. "Anticlericalism and the English Reformation." *History* 68 (1983): 391–407.

———. *The Reign of Elizabeth I*. London, 1984.

———. *Reformation and Resistance in Tudor Lancashire*. Cambridge, 1987.

———. *English Reformations: Religion, Politics and Society under the Tudors*. Oxford, 1993.

Haigh, C., ed. *The English Reformation Revised*. Cambridge, 1987.

Heal, F., and R. O'Day, eds. *Church and Society in England: Henry VIII to James I*. London, 1977.

Herrup, Cynthia. *The Common Peace: Participation and the Criminal Law in Seventeenth-Century England*. Cambridge, 1997.

Hill, Christopher. "From Lollards to Levellers." In *Rebels and Their Causes*, ed. M. Cornforth. London, 1978.

Holmes, Peter. *Resistance and Compromise: The Political Thought of the Elizabethan Catholics*. Cambridge, 1982.

Horst, Irvin. *The Radical Brethren: Anabaptism and the English Reformation*. Nieuwkoop, Holland, 1972.

Houlbrooke, Ralph. "Persecution of Heresy and Protestantism in the Diocese of Norwich under Henry VIII." *Norfolk Archaeology* 35 (1973): 308–26.

———. *Church Courts and the People during the English Reformation, 1520–1570*. Oxford, 1979.

Hughes, Philip. *The Reformation in England*. 5th ed. New York, 1963.

Hutton, Ronald. "The Local Impact of the Tudor Reformations." In *The English Reformation Revised*, ed. C. Haigh, 114–38. Cambridge, 1987.

Ingram, Martin. *Church Courts, Sex and Marriage in England, 1570–1640*. Cambridge, 1987.

James, M. E. "Obedience and Dissent in Henrician England." *Past and Present* 48 (1970): 3–78.

Jordan, W. K. *The Development of Religious Toleration in England*. 4 vols. London, 1932–40.

King, John N. *English Reformation Literature: The Tudor Origins of the Protestant Tradition*. Princeton, 1982.

———. "'The Light of Printing': William Tyndale, John Foxe, John Day, and Early Modern Print Culture." *Renaissance Quarterly* 54 (2001): 52–85.

Knott, John. *Discourses of Martyrdom in English Literature, 1563–1694*. Cambridge, 1993.

Kumin, Beat. *The Shaping of a Community: The Rise and Reformation of the English Parish, c. 1400–1560*. Aldershot, U.K., 1996.

Lake, Peter. "The Significance of the Elizabethan Identification of the Pope as Antichrist." *Journal of Ecclesiastical History* 31 (1980): 161–78.

Lake, Peter, and Michael Questier. "Prisons, Priests and People." In *England's Long Reformation 1500–1800*, ed. Nicholas Tyacke, 195–233. London, 1988.

———. "Agency, Appropriation and Rhetoric under the Gallows: Puritans, Romanists, and the State in Early Modern England." *Past and Present* 153 (1996): 64–107.

Lander, S. "Church Courts and the Reformation in the Diocese of Chichester, 1500–58." In *The English Reformation Revised*, ed. C. Haigh, 34–55. Cambridge, 1987.

Laursen, John Christian, and Cary J. Nederman, eds. *Beyond the Persecuting Society: Religious Toleration before the Enlightenment*. Philadelphia, 1998.

Litzenberger, Caroline. *English Reformation and the Laity: Gloucestershire 1540–80*. Cambridge, 1997.

Loades, D. M. "The Essex Inquisitions of 1556." *Bulletin of the Institute of Historical Research* 35 (1962): 87–97.

———. "The Enforcement of Reaction, 1553–1558." *Journal of Ecclesiastical History* 16 (1965): 59–66.

———. *The Oxford Martyrs*. London, 1970.

———. *The Reign of Mary Tudor*. London, 1979.

———. *Tudor Government: Structures of Authority in the Sixteenth Century*. London, 1997.

MacCulloch, Diarmaid. *Suffolk and the Tudors: Politics and Religion in an English County 1500–1600*. Oxford, 1970.

———. *Thomas Cranmer: A Life*. New Haven, 1996.

Marsh, Christopher. *Popular Religion in Sixteenth-Century England: Holding Their Peace*. New York, 1998.

Marshall, Peter. *The Catholic Priesthood and the English Reformation*. Oxford, 1994.

———. "Papist as Heretic: The Burning of John Forest, 1538." *Historical Journal* 41 (1998).

Martin, J. W. *Religious Radicals in Tudor England*. London, 1989.

Mayer, Thomas F. *Reginald Pole: Prince and Prophet*. Cambridge, 2000.

McClendon, Muriel. "Religious Toleration and the Reformation: Norwich Magistrates in the Sixteenth Century." In *England's Long Reformation, 1500–1800*, ed. Nicholas Tyacke, 87–116. London, 1998.

———. "Reconsidering the Marian Persecution: The Urban Context." In *Protestant Identities: Religion, Society, and Self-Fashioning in Post-Reformation England*, ed. Muriel McClendon, Joseph P. Ward, and Michael MacDonald, 195–233. Stanford, 1999.

———. *Quiet Reformation: Magistrates and the Emergence of Protestantism in Tudor Norwich*. Stanford, 1999.

McCoog, Thomas M. *The Society of Jesus in Ireland, Scotland, and England, 1541–1588*. New York, 1996.

———, ed. *The Reckoned Expense: Edmund Campion and the Early English Jesuits*. New York, 1996.

McGrath, Patrick. "Elizabethan Catholicism: A Reconsideration." *Journal of Ecclesiastical History* 35 (1984): 414–28.

Moreau, J.-P. *Rome ou l'Angleterre? Les Réactions politiques des catholiques anglais au moment du schisme (1529–1553)*. Paris, 1984.

Mueller, Janel M. "Pain, Persecution and the Construction of Selfhood in Foxe's *Acts and Monuments*." In *Religion and Culture in Renaissance England*, ed. Claire McEachern and Debora Shuger, 161–87. Cambridge, 1997.

Pettegree, Andrew. *Foreign Protestant Communities in Sixteenth-Century London.* Oxford, 1986.

————. "Nicodemism and the English Reformation." In *Marian Protestantism: Six Studies,* 86–117. Scolar Press, 1996.

Pogson, R. H. "The Legacy of the Schism: Confusion, Continuity, and Change in the Marian Clergy." In *The Mid-Tudor Polity, c. 1540–60,* ed. J. Loach and R. Tittler. Totowa, N.J., 1980.

Prall, Stuart E. *Church and State in Tudor and Stuart England.* Arlington Heights, Ill., 1993.

Redworth, G. *In Defence of the Church Catholic: The Life of Stephen Gardiner.* Oxford, 1990.

Scarisbrick, J. J. *Henry VIII.* Berkeley, 1968.

Sharpe, J. A. "Last Dying Speeches': Religion, Ideology and Public Execution in Seventeenth-Century England." *Past and Present* 107 (1985): 144–67.

————. *Instruments of Darkness: Witchcraft in England, 1550–1750.* London, 1996.

Smith, Lacey Baldwin. *Fools, Martyrs, Traitors: The Story of Martyrdom in the Western World.* New York, 1997.

Spierenberg, Pieter. *The Spectacle of Suffering: Executions and the Evolution of Repression: From a Preindustrial Metropolis to the European Experience.* Cambridge, 1984.

Spufford, Margaret. *The World of Rural Dissenters.* Cambridge, 1995.

Strauss, Paul. "In Hope of Heaven: English Recusant Prison Writings of the Sixteenth Century." Ph.D. diss., University of Nevada, 1997.

Trimble, William Raleigh. *The Catholic Laity in Elizabethan England, 1558–1603.* Cambridge, Mass., 1964.

Usher, Brett. "Backing Protestantism: The London Godly, the Exchequer and the Foxe Circle." In *John Foxe: An Historical Perspective,* ed. David Loades, 105–34. Aldershot, U.K., 1999.

Wabuda, Susan. "Equivocation and Recantation during the English Reformation: The 'Subtle Shadows' of Dr Edward Crome." *Journal of Ecclesiastical History* 44 (1993): 224–42.

————. "Henry Bull, Miles Coverdale and the Making of Foxe's Book of Martyrs." In *Martyrs and Martyrologies,* ed. Diana Wood, 245–58. London, 1993.

————. *Preaching during the English Reformation.* Cambridge, 2002.

Watt, Tessa. *Cheap Print and Popular Piety, 1550–1640.* Cambridge, 1991.

Whiting, Robert. "Abominable Idols: Images and Image-breaking under Henry VIII." *Journal of Ecclesiastical History* 33 (1982): 30–47.

————. *The Blind Devotion of the People: Popular Religion and the English Reformation.* Cambridge, 1989.

Willison, George F. *Saints and Strangers.* London, 1946.

Wood, Diana, ed. *Martyrs and Martyrologies.* Studies in Church History 30. Oxford, 1993.

INDEX

SARAH COVINGTON

is assistant professor of history at Elizabethtown College.